LESTER NUBY, JR.

FIRST

BREAKING GENERATIONAL POVERTY

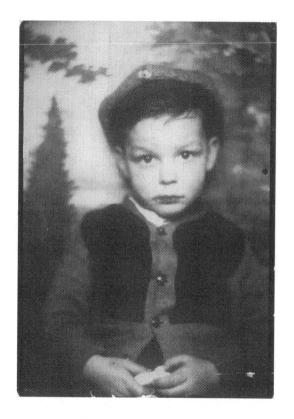

Contributor: Dr. Jacqueline F. Nuby

Editors: Martha Sue Sanford and Kimberly Reynolds

iUniverse, Inc.
Bloomington

First
Breaking Generational Poverty

iUniverse books may be ordered through booksellers or by contacting:

iUniverse
1663 Liberty Drive
Bloomington, IN 47403
www.iuniverse.com
1-800-Authors (1-800-288-4677)

ISBN: 978-1-4759-2925-6 (sc)
ISBN: 978-1-4759-2924-9 (e)
ISBN: 978-1-4759-2926-3 (hc)

Library of Congress Control Number: 2012909461

Printed in the United States of America

iUniverse rev. date: 7/26/2012

Contents

To My Granddaughter

Sarah Kirstin Witcher, who was born December 17, 1997, filled a void in my life. The happiness she has brought my wife Jackie and me over the past fourteen years is indescribable.

<u>DEGRADATION:</u>

CONTINUED POVERTY OF THE

MAJORITY OF THE PLANET'S INHABITANTS

AND THE EXCESSIVE CONSUMPTION

BY THE WELL-OFF MINORITY

Dr. Klaus Topfer

United Nations—September 1999

<u>DANGER!</u>

THE UNITED STATES GOVERNMENT HAS REACHED
THE STAGE OF KLEPTOCRACY.

THIS IS A FORM OF POLITICAL AND GOVERNMENT
CORRUPTION

WHERE THE GOVERNMENT EXISTS TO INCREASE THE

PERSONAL WEALTH AND POLITICAL POWER OF ITS

OFFICIALS AND RULING CLASS AT THE EXPENSE

OF THE WIDER POPULATION.

PREFACE

BREAKING GENERATIONAL POVERTY

Many people living in poverty are products of generational poverty. Generational poverty is handed down from one generation to another. The cycle is rarely broken. When entire families are struggling to meet their basic needs, a "culture of poverty" begins to be formed. Generational poverty is thought to be one of the most difficult obstacles in becoming what this world looks at as "successful." I know about this phenomenon because I was born into generational poverty. It is my hope that this book will have a positive effect on those in poverty and those on the edge of slipping into the abyss. I am qualified to write about the subject of poverty because I lived it.

The core of this book is about my life as far back as I remember, perhaps from the age of three and half. I was born on April 30, 1938, in rural north Alabama. This was a turbulent time The Great Depression was lingering, World War II was on the horizon, and my family was in abject poverty. My biological father was murdered five months prior to my birth, leaving an uneducated wife who had to live with her immediate family along with me in order to survive. Life was already very difficult, and the death of my father placed a mental and physical trauma on my mama that had to be overwhelming.

We lived adjacent to a railroad station where trains stopped to take on passengers and let passengers off, as well as to fill the locomotive with coal and water. Sometimes trains stopped to unload caskets of soldiers that were returning from war to be buried in their communities.

My grandpa was a sharecropper, barely one step above slavery. He was a very proud man who refused to take governmental commodities, even though they were available within two miles from where we lived. Having food, clothing, and shelter was a continuing battle for our family.

When I was almost four years old, my mother married James Edward Alvis, who became my stepfather. His plight in life was not much better than the rest of us. His mother had died at birth and he was abandoned by his father. He was also an uneducated man, but with a heart of gold, one of the kindness men I have ever known. He treated me like his own son. In less than a year, he was drafted into the army and sent to the raging war in Europe. It was difficult for me to understand.

As a small boy, I knew that I did not want to spend the rest of my life in such a depraved state. I began to look for a way out of the chains of poverty. I started by observing people around me. I watched my family, friends, farm workers, visitors, neighbors, and hoboes. I watched and paid close attention to those people who displayed intelligence, motivation, passion, vision, and the willingness to work hard. I started noticing that those in poverty were the masses. At the same time, a few people owned land and were referred to as "wealthy." There were the "haves and have nots." What contributed to the difference? I did not know, but I knew I was going to find out.

I was attempting to define the components that made a few people financially successful. It was not difficult to determine why the masses were not successful. Due to generational poverty, most thought poverty was their place in life. People in poverty had everything in common. They associated with each other and married within the poverty masses. Thus, generational poverty was perpetuated.

I developed an uncompromising attitude early in life. Perhaps one might call it pride. I don't know how it developed. It must have had a lot to do with nature. I was certainly not like those in my family in the way I discerned situations and made decisions. Others around me, although they didn't often have the necessities of life looked at me as being different, often quietly belligerent. Yet, I was going to get what I wanted, and I was willing to do whatever it took. I was not willing to take anything verbally or physically from anyone at any time or any place. As a consequence of this attitude, I was in many fights while growing up and well into adulthood.

There was no way I could afford college, nor had I ever had any encouragement from my family to do so. Being in such a state of poverty, I had no alternative other than go to work. In 1957, there were no Pell Grants or governmental programs readily available to a farm boy like me. No school counselor told me of opportunities, even if there were any. So, I took a job at Associated Grocers of Alabama, a large wholesale grocery distributor headquartered in Birmingham, Alabama. I was the lowest man on the totem pole, spending my nights unloading box cars. During my employment with Associated Grocers of Alabama, I made a measly wage of $1.27 an hour unloading boxcars.

However, by then, I had plucked my wife away from the womb of her mother at the age of sixteen to be my wife. We had eloped in Rome, Georgia the year before. She was the one I had loved even when she was a child. We moved to Birmingham across the street from Birmingham-Southern College. She and I moved into a two room basement apartment. My wife, Jackie, who was only seventeen years old by then, entered college, a frightened child, away from home for the first time and homesick. The plan was for her to finish college and then I would get my degree.

Then a letter containing my draft notice came from Uncle Sam. I had, unwillingly, been drafted into the army for two years. After eight weeks of basic training at Fort, Chaffee, Arkansas, I was based at Fort Hood, Texas. My wife, Jackie, moved from Alabama to Belton, Texas, twenty miles from the Fort Hood Army Post. This is where we lived for almost two years while she attended college at Mary Hardin-Baylor College, within walking distance of our two-room apartment.

The troops at Fort Hood were informed that President Kennedy was going to visit Dallas and come to Fort Hood to review our operations. We surmised that he was coming to give a speech touting the flexibility of the United States, its readiness, and its ability to deploy troops anywhere in the world quickly. Several weeks earlier, our division was mobilized to Germany. The operation was secretly named "Operation Big Lift." More than thirty-two thousand troops, equipment, and supplies were airlifted, exemplifying the strength of the United States Army.

On November 22, 1963, the Fort was impeccable and the troops were in dress uniform waiting for the President to arrive. Sadly, the visit and speech never happened. President Kennedy was assassinated by Lee Harvey Oswald while participating in a parade in downtown Dallas. This was a sad and lonely time for our soldiers as well as for the nation. November 22, 1963 was a day I will forever remember.

During those two years in the army, I continued to formulize my plan for success. It was a plan that I thought was close to perfection and tailored for me personally. Fortunately, I had several mentors in my supply unit that treated me as a special person and gave me very good advice.

I was promoted quickly in the military and was tempted to make the military my career, which I seriously considered. I know now that despite the pain I felt when I was drafted into the army, it was the best thing that ever happened to me. I grew up and became a man, a soldier, and a better citizen.

I chose to return to Associated Grocers of Alabama. Now it was time to follow my plan to move from the bottom of Associated Grocers of Alabama to the top within ten years. I put my plan into effect immediately, with excitement of what the results would be.

My first opportunity came when I was asked to handle accounts receivable for the company. I then moved from accounts receivable to purchasing, to supervising all purchasing, to controller, and eventually to vice president of operations, second in line for the top position.

Again, my path to success came quickly. Circumstances between the board of directors and the current president and general manager prompted him to resign from the company. I was promoted to president, general manager and board member. It had taken eight years rather than ten. I had just reached the age of thirty-four.

After my movement to the top of the company, I was well aware that things looked very different than they had when I was holding a position at the bottom of the ladder. However, after a few days I began to settle down and come to grips with the new position and its demands. I sat in the previous general manager's office and reflected on my dream that had come true. At that moment, I knew I had truly broken the enslavement of poverty. My plan was to never be in poverty again.

I was soon offered an opportunity to join another Birmingham company, Pasquale Food Company, as president and member of the board. Pasquale was not as large as Associated Grocers, but it was a public company. There were stock options and the potential of becoming a national and international company.

After becoming an international company, we were in most countries, including in all military commissaries in the world. The company had fourteen operating and manufacturing divisions in the United States, Canada, and Europe. This book is possible because of my friend and associate, John Sanford, who was a dynamo in sales and marketing.

In December of 1986, John Labatt, Ltd. purchased Pasquale Food Company, Inc., for $162 million dollars. In order to make this purchase, John Labatt required that John Sanford and I sign five-year employment and non-competition agreements. During this time, through the efforts of John Sanford, the company added $100 million to its annual sales. In 1995, Labatt was purchased by a Belgian brewer; it is now a part of Anheuser-Busch InBev. InBev is a multinational brewer and the world's market leader.

Several months after John Sanford and I resigned from John Labatt, we purchased a production facility, similar to the Pasquale divisions, in Perry County, Ohio. A few months after that, we purchased a second production facility in Altoona, Pennsylvania. In December of 1994, we were approached by The A & M Partners. After some negotiations, The A & M Partners owned forty-nine percent of the company.

I felt that I needed to be at home to support Jackie, my wife, during our daughter's perilous illness. I resigned from Perry County Foods on October 19, 1995. After I left the company, The A & M Partners took over the operations of Perry County Foods, Inc., causing it to move in a catastrophic direction.

The A & M Partners later filed a lawsuit against me for one million, two hundred and fifty thousand dollars. This was for a line of credit owed to AmSouth Bank by Perry County Foods. The A & M Partners' attorneys proposed that Perry County Foods had no value. During my deposition, my attorney, Tom Harris, allowed them to ramble on and on, knowing that they were putting their feet in their mouths every time they spoke. Tom Harris had managed to acquire a prospectus which stated Perry County Foods value was $10.2 million dollars. They had listed Perry County Foods in a Virginia prospectus. After The A & M Partners' attorneys were awed and embarrassed, the deposition ceased. After haggling for a few days, the lawsuit in the amount of one million, two hundred fifty thousand dollars dropped to zero.

As the previous paragraphs indicate, my experiences have been wide and varied. I have traveled down many roads, some quite rocky. Yet, at this point in my life, I am happily retired, spending most of my time writing about many topics of interest to the general public as well as about my experiences in my escape from generational poverty.

My intention is to convey the message to the reader that although the process is arduous, poverty can be overcome. Goals can be achieved, even against almost all odds. In order to accomplish this, a plan must be formulated and tailored for the individual. I was able to move from poverty to become president and CEO of national and international companies because I believed that I could. I used my formula to win at each level to reach the top. It is my firm belief, based on where I started in life, that anyone can achieve the same or more. I hope the reader will glean something from this book that will motivate one to look outside his or her paradigm. The magic words: I won!

ACKNOWLEDGEMENTS

I would like to acknowledge the many people who have had such a profound influence on my life. First, I want to thank my wife, Jackie, who has been with me throughout the good and hard times. She and I have three beautiful children, Kimberly, Leslie, and Les. I love all of them dearly.

I want to honor my mother, Iva Mae Alvis, and my stepfather, James Edward Alvis, who provided me with sound moral advice and gave me all they possibly could, even when I knew they couldn't afford it. They also blessed me with my wonderful sister, Wilma Ruth Reno, and my two brothers, Donald and Rick Alvis, who have been blessings in my life.

I am so thankful to those who played a role in bringing Christ into my life: Brother E.C. Moore and Martha Sue and John Sanford.

There are many others who have played a significant role in my life. Many have been my mentors. One such person was Dr. James Tanner, an industrial psychologist, who offered me harsh, soul-searching advice. It proved to be the most useful advice that I ever received throughout my business career. Unfortunately, Dr. Tanner passed away before this book was completed.

I have worked alongside many people who have been a source of support and part of the happiest days of my life. We encountered and solved critical business problems, but the laughter was always there, especially at Pasquale Food Company, Inc. Among these individuals are Neal Andrews, Jr., who hired me at Pasquale Food Company, Inc., and my friend, Doug Owen.

I want to acknowledge my high school class of '57. As I reflect on the young men and women who made up our graduating class, I have fond memories, especially of times spent with Marlin Tabscott and Joe Murphy. The years went by so quickly. I am saddened by those who are no longer with us. I often ask Jesus Christ why I have had a lifetime of near-perfect health. Most of the time I feel like a young man, except when I look in the mirror, and face reality.

Lester Nuby, Jr.

INTRODUCTION

I first met Lester in 1970 when we both were middle-level managers at a major food wholesale distributor in Birmingham, Alabama. At Associated Grocers of Alabama, Inc., Lester was a rising star in the purchasing department, and I was in personnel. We were about the same age, and our career paths were destined to parallel each other for many years as we both progressed in the food industry.

We became close friends as well as business associates. This was largely due to the years spent together, both at Pasquale Food Company, Inc. and other profitable companies. How many can say they had a seventeen-year career with one company, with laughter on the menu almost every day?

Through the years, I found Lester to possess a unique combination of integrity, intelligence, tenacity, hard work, and the ability to achieve consensus among associates. These consistent management qualities allowed him to rise through the ranks and lead several companies as CEO. He was a true leader. His formula for success, though difficult, worked for him.

If I were to sum up Lester Nuby's character in one word, it would be "trustworthy." A person earns this title through years of consistent management performance, following through on promises, and always doing more than expected.

Lester is the best manager I have ever seen. The business world is full of smart people who work hard. There are also many who are innovative and motivational leaders. However, very few possess all of these qualities. This unique combination of talents leads to ultimate business success, as in the case of Lester Nuby.

On a more personal note, for the past twenty years Lester has been an avid student of the *King James Bible* through a nondenominational Bible study group. While he does not flaunt it, when the opportunity arises, Lester will discuss his faith.

Those who read this account of Lester's life will be better for it. You will be intrigued, amazed, and informed.

It's a great read!

John C. Sanford

CHAPTER ONE

THROUGH THE EYES OF A CHILD

Although the early years of my life are dim in my recollection, I clearly remember one wintry day when the weather was very cold. The air was frigid, with a mixture of sleet and snow. I looked out the frosted windowpane I could feel the breathtakingly cold air seeping in around the glass. As I breathed on the window, it fogged up. As three and half year olds would do, I drew little images with my finger, which intrigued me. I asked others in the room to take a look at what I thought were very small masterpieces.

I didn't realize that everyone was preoccupied. They were preparing for the bone-chilling walk to Wilhite Station. My mama, grandma, grandpa, Uncles Albert, Virgil, Ralph, and Aunt Vera put hats and other heavy clothing on to fend off the bitingly cold weather. My mama bundled me up with an overcoat, gloves, and a hat that covered my head, ears, and most of my face. I had no idea where we were going.

I looked out the window again and saw dozens of people walking down the dirt road to the railroad station, which was a short distance from our big, unpainted wooden house. As we walked out of the house, we all began our journey down the little old winding dirt road from our house to what we called the main road.

We merged with other travelers. Many people had walked a long distance and were noticeably suffering from the cold weather. Only a few people arrived in cars or trucks. Some people were not dressed properly to face the harsh weather conditions. As we walked, I heard the limbs snap off the pine trees. Some were so laden with snow that, as they fell, they made the sound of a gunshot. Yet the sunlight reflected the indescribable beauty of the sleet and snow as it fell from the sky.

Wilhite Station was a stopping point for the steam engine trains to refuel and let passengers off and on. I heard the arriving train from miles away, making that peculiar, distinctive sound that passenger and freight trains make as the metal wheels hit the rails.

On most days, people looked forward to hearing the sound of the train as it came closer; that day, there was a somber feeling. People stood as if posted in stone. They were cold and uncomfortable. The precipitation and frigid weather caused ice particles to cling to their faces and clothing. Some looked like pallid corpses, their eyes filling with tears. Some were wiping tears from their eyes and faces with handkerchiefs.

The brakes of the train screeched as it slowed down and finally came to a halt. After a few minutes, the porters opened the doors. The onlookers could see through the glass windows of the warm, inviting interior of the Pullman car as the passengers gathered their belongings, hats, gloves, top coats, and scarves. As they moved slowly toward the doors and down the steps of the Pullman car, the freezing rain, sleet, and snow greeted them. Many were speaking quietly as they disembarked from the train.

Some of those who came to meet the train were openly weeping; others were being consoled by family and friends. A few people appeared to be happy; this was perplexing to me. This was something I could not understand at the moment. Most of the crowd became so quiet that I could hear the people nearby breathing slowly and intensely.

Once the passengers were off the train, men dressed in military uniform waited outside a second car with wide sliding doors. Everyone was silent as the porters opened the doors. The military men were standing at attention. The men in military uniform unloaded one wooden box at a time until six wooden boxes, each draped with a red, white, and blue American flag, had appeared. Each box was carefully placed on a wooden platform. Hearses were parked nearby to deliver the wooden boxes and caskets to their burial destination. Some onlookers were crying and sobbing as the boxes were unloaded. All the adults knew that there was a casket inside each wooden box and that inside each casket lay a son, husband, relative, or friend. The sorrow reflected was overwhelming as friends attempted to console those who had loved ones inside the caskets. One very old lady was looking up to the sky asking God to help her through this ordeal. As she stood gazing upward, the snow and sleet pelted her face.

An older, large lady I had not seen before fainted. The two men who tried to support her could not keep her from falling to the hard, frozen ground, which was covered with particles of coal, cinders, and ice. Her face was bleeding as the two men lifted her off the ground. They continued to support her as they took her to a car parked nearby. As they walked away, I could see the blood from her face as it coagulated. More blood dripped onto her coat. I was horrified. My mama saw this in my face. She told me I could walk the short distance back to our house.

When my family came home, I ran back to the window and watched as the crowd dispersed. The little drawings I did were still there. The others were eager to stand in front of the large open fireplace and "warm up," as they called it. Everyone stood around for a long time without talking or doing anything. I thought they were reflecting on what they had seen a short time earlier and trying to digest all of it. When our family was in this state of mind, I would go into an empty room and stay until their distressed and dismal moods dissipated.

As the train pulled away, I listened to the clicked-clack, clicked-clack sound of the steel wheels hitting the tracks. I could hear steam escaping, and the sound of the whistle. As the train started picking up speed, I visualized the swaying of the freight cars. Once the train had departed, in the distance I could hear the moan of the heavy engine and the sound of the whistle as it approached railroad crossings and entered small towns. Few sounds captivate the imagination like the haunting wail of the moving steam locomotive's lonesome whistle.

I conjured up the courage to ask my mama what was happening. Why were people crying? My mama said the military men had unloaded six boxes that housed six caskets with a soldier in each one. These young men had been killed in the war. Their bodies were shipped home for burial in their communities. The people that were crying were relatives of those killed in action. She said that she felt for the families, but she said that she thanked God that none of the caskets had housed her husband, Edward, or her brothers Aril and Horace.

I also wanted to know why some people were happy. My mother told me they were happy because their loved ones were coming home from the war. She said that some of the people getting off the train were civilians who had been gone a day or two and were just returning home. She also said there that other trains would possibly stop in the future to unload additional soldiers who had died in the war.

It was almost dark when I looked out the window again. The muted lighting unfortunately conjured up memories of the caskets being unloaded and the weeping of family and friends. My mama explained what had happened that day, but I did not really understand. We fear what we do not understand.

I could not get the lady who had fallen off my mind, or the blood that was oozing from her face. From that day on, I was aware day and night when a freight or passenger train rolled down what seemed to be endless tracks. As the day ended, I had a premonition that sooner or later the caskets unloaded would hold Edward, my stepfather, and my uncles, Arvil and Horace. This day afforded me a plethora of nightmares and dreams that still haunt me to this day. I doubt seriously if I will ever be liberated from the scene I witnessed that day.

CHAPTER TWO

THE EARLY YEARS

I was born in a dilapidated, unpainted wooden house on April 30, 1938, on a warm spring day on Bell Springs Mountain, Alabama. I was delivered by Dr. Lovelady, an obstetrician who came to the assistance of those who needed home delivery. At the moment I emerged from the womb, I was a little human being, luckily healthy, with no needs other than nourishment and love. My mama, Iva Mae, furnished both. I was named after my father, Lester Lee Nuby.

It was a sad time in my mama's life. My father had been murdered five months prior to giving birth to me. She had no support from anyone except her immediate family—her mother, Ethel, and her father, Charlie Millican, along with my aunt and my uncles.

My mama, Iva Mae, was an uneducated woman. She went to school in a one-room school house on Bell Springs Mountain. The school only went through the sixth grade, and there was no way for her to get to Falkville High School, which was located approximately seven miles from her community.

Mama grew up during a dismal period in America's history. The Great Depression held its ugly head over the United States and many other countries. She suffered from severe poverty, lack of education, and lack of medical treatment. Many in the Bell Springs community where she lived were in similar conditions. However, the Great Depression further served to intensify the poverty that she, her family, and her community felt, physically, emotionally, and mentally. Many people, both rich and poor, lost everything they owned.

The nation watched anxiously as President Herbert Hoover initiated numerous programs to reverse the downturn in the economy, yet hundreds of thousands of homeless people went without proper nutrition, with their basic needs not even being met. The unemployment rate reached twenty-five percent. Farming and rural areas suffered from the severe drop in the price of the products sold.

When I was born, my family, like others in our poverty-stricken community, had no electricity or running water. Bathroom facilities were outside in "outhouses," as they were called. The water came from a well or spring. In the summer months, the heat was almost unbearable. During the winter months, the only heat came from two large fireplaces. I remember the cold rooms in the winter and the cold, icy air rising between the planks of the floor. Beds were loaded down with quilts and other covers to fend off the cold. I pulled the quilts above my head and watched the white, smoky vapor as it passed from my mouth and nose as I breathed the icy air.

Most of us in our family and community wore clothing made from flour or fertilizer sacks. It was not uncommon for me to wear a shirt that had the name of a product on it. My clothes were patched several times before they were considered worn out and abandoned. My best clothing was kept to wear to church or funerals. Clothes were passed down from older children to their younger siblings. I was one of the unfortunate younger ones.

Sharecropping in those days was a way of life for my family. My grandpa was allowed to use land in return for a share of the crop, usually one half. He got his tools and farm animals from the owner of the land. The system kept our family from starving, but it was a humiliating way to live. When the harvest was poor, we often suffered from lack of a proper diet.

My grandpa was "poor, but proud." Although, governmental commodities such as cheese, powdered milk, powdered eggs, and many other items were available, my grandpa would never accept what he considered to be "handouts." Sometimes I wondered why he let us do without nutritional foods we could have had. I often heard him say, "I will never take a handout from the government or anything from anyone as long as I live." I could not quite understand his attitude. He was a quiet man who was dogmatic about politics, religion, right and wrong, and dependability.

My grandpa often spoke negatively of those who drank whiskey. My grandpa often told me stories about the "sorry" sharecroppers who made moonshine (often called liquor, hooch, mountain dew, or other names). He spoke of how sharecroppers sold illegal alcohol during Prohibition. He spoke of the "hell-bound" sellers of moonshine. My grandpa told me that it was not only immoral, but also dangerous because of the way it was made. He said moonshine often contained toxic alcohols such as methanol. He spoke of evil men like Al Capone and Joseph Kennedy who had made a fortune controlling bootlegging, production, and distribution of alcohol to sleazy establishments called speakeasies (blind pigs or blind tigers). As far as my grandpa was concerned, none of us were going to be involved in anything like that as long as he was around. Even then, I wondered what I might have done to make money if I were the man of the house. Would I have sold illegal whiskey to feed my family? I can't say. I simply don't know what I might have done to provide food for my family.

My grandpa also was adamantly opposed to smoking, dipping snuff, and chewing tobacco. My grandpa considered our family "religious folk," and we were members of the Bell Springs Baptist church. It was understood that if anyone did any drinkin', dippin', cheatin', stealin' or cursin', hell was awaiting them.

CHAPTER THREE

MY GRANDMA MILLICAN

The times were difficult for me during the early years of my life. As a young boy, of course, I needed shelter and food, but I also needed love and affection from my family. Yet, I found it very difficult to show affection toward others, for reasons still inexplicable to me. There were only three people who I knew loved me. Those were my mama, my grandma, and my uncle Ralph. My mama loved me, but unfortunately, she was much like me in that it was difficult for her to show her love.

My grandma, the backbone of our family, had a special love for me. I could see it in her eyes, hear it in the way she talked to me, and sense it the way she treated me as if I were a special child. Perhaps this was because she had known my father. She had also seen the pain and suffering my mother went through when my father was murdered. I think she always wanted to protect me from anything that would hurt me or my mother from any further pain, physically or emotionally. I did not have a father. Maybe she wanted to do all she could to make up for what I was missing in my life.

She took me to church with her, made sure I was always within her sight when we were not at home, cooked special things I liked, and made sure I was not sick. She often felt my head to see if I had a fever. She also disciplined me in such a way that I knew she cared.

Looking back, I am ashamed that I ever did anything to even slightly hurt my grandma. Yet I did. It probably caused her more heartbreak than I ever knew. When my family was living on Bell Springs Mountain, my grandma was very fond of planting, fertilizing, watering, and weeding all kinds of flowers and plants. She always planted them close to the house so that she could see them in their flowering beauty when blooming.

Once the weather started getting cold, she placed a special glass-type covering over each flower and plant to keep them from freezing. I know I did not do this because I wanted to hurt my grandma, but at this time I had a BB gun. I was curious to see how good my "shot" was. I sat on the front porch of the house and shot the glass coverings one by one until they fell apart. I will regret this deed forever. I would never intentionally hurt my grandma for any reason.

My grandma was not happy, but because of my special relationship with her, she did not say anything. I could see the pain and dismay in her face as she walked around the shattered glass and attempted to cover the plants with some of the glass that was not totally destroyed. I was ashamed, remorseful, and embarrassed, and I tried not to face her for several days. She knew I was sorry. Even today, I hurt from that asinine act.

My grandma could get riled up if circumstances warranted it. For example, I especially remember my grandma as she prepared food for the family. She always ran everyone out of the kitchen until dinner was ready. I remember watching her use lard to grease the large cast-iron skillets. She would prepare three skillets of cornbread to feed the large family and sometimes the people who worked on the farm.

Once she had placed the cornbread in the wood-fired oven, she would slightly open the oven door to check on the baking progress. Once the three skillets of cornbread were baked, she took them out of the oven and placed them on the kitchen table. The aroma of the cornbread often drew me to the kitchen to try to sneak a small piece of the warm bread. However, she did not allow anyone, even me, to get a piece of anything until the meal was complete.

All the food was placed into large bowls and onto platters and then placed on the table. Once everything was ready, my grandma put out the word that it was time to eat. The variety of food was not abundant, but we had plenty of good-tasting food. In those days, adults ate first and children last. It was difficult to glance into the kitchen and see the adults eating and talking with no concern that the children were hungry and hoping that the adults would soon finish eating. Even as a child, it did not seem right to me for adults to eat before the hungry children. I was told that the farm workers ate first so they could get back to work.

In those early years when I was a child, my family, the Millican family, was impoverished, with seemingly no way to change their plight. The epiphany of poverty manifested itself in every area of our lives. I always had that sick feeling in my stomach that something bad was going to happen; I just didn't know when or where. I was thinking constantly about how to move from poverty. It seemed that everyone around me acted and spoke as if they had given up years earlier.

CHAPTER FOUR

WILHITE STATION AND
THE MECHAW HOUSE

We moved from Bell Springs Mountain to Wilhite Station when I was approximately two years old. The opportunities for my grandpa were better economically because the farmland was fertile. My grandpa worked very hard as a sharecropper for a wonderful man who owned the land, Mr. Cornish Wilhite. Mr. Wilhite allowed our family to live in a large, unpainted farmhouse which was quite good during that era. My grandpa farmed the land. In return, he received half of the harvest and Mr. Wilhite received half of the harvest.

I often watched the other farm hands that came to help out during the harvest season. I will never forget how men working on the farm wore overalls with galluses to hold them up. The galluses were wide straps that were fitted over each shoulder and buttoned in the front to a bib with metal buttons. At the end of each day, I could often smell the sweat which permeated their bodies, overalls, and the area around them. Each night those who worked in the fields took a bath in a large metal tub to wash the stench from their bodies.

Women washed the dirty clothes on a "washboard" constructed on a rectangular wooden frame. On this was mounted a series of ridges or corrugations. The women soaked clothes in hot soapy water in a washtub and then squeezed and rubbed the clothes against the ridged surface of the washboard. Then the clothes were rinsed. This process required hard manual labor, causing the hands of women to become red and raw as they scrubbed the clothes on the board. I remember looking at my grandma's dry, red hands as she washed dirty, smelly clothes every day of the week.

I soon found out that after a season or two of sharecropping, we would move again. My grandpa purchased the MeChaw house at Bell Springs. I was really heartbroken. I had never lived in a house where I couldn't see and hear the trains close by. I suffered with his decision, but being the stubborn, serious-minded child I was, I never said a word. This was to be the third of many, many moves from house to house.

At Bell Springs, my grandpa continued to farm as he did at Wilhite Station. However, the plots of land were smaller, less level, and not as fertile as the land at Wilhite Station. In addition to farming the land, he also raised hogs, cattle, chickens, horses and mules, planning ahead in order to have food in the winter. The animals were raised and later slaughtered throughout each year.

My mama and my grandma, like other women in the area where I grew up, stayed at home, cooked three meals a day, cleaned the house, washed clothing, and took care of the children. The men and the women, working together, had large gardens. They grew tomatoes, beans, cabbage, okra, and other vegetables. They also had apple, peach, and pear trees. They picked blackberries in the woods or lowlands. These fruits and vegetables were canned and stacked in home pantries in preparation for the dismal winter months.

There was little money, and buying food was just not a way of life. Just about the only things bought were flour, sugar, coffee, and a few other items. I do remember, especially, that sweet potatoes were harvested, placed in a large hole dug in the ground, and covered and mounded with dirt. A tin roof was placed over the potato storage to keep them dry. After several months, the potato mound was opened and the potatoes were "cured," which meant they were sweet and waxy and ready to be baked or fried in brown sugar and lard. Yummy!

CHAPTER FIVE

WORLD WAR II

We continued to live with my grandparents until my mama married James Edward Alvis on December 20, 1941. I was only three and a half years old. After they married, we moved from my grandparents' house into a dilapidated, unpainted wooden house near Bell Springs Mountain. I missed my grandparents, uncles, and aunt. I was bewildered because I couldn't quite put all the pieces together. I had continued to wonder where my father was. Maybe he was in the jail house or "big house" as it was called. When I asked where my biological father was, the answer was always, "He has gone away."

My mama and Edward were married only eleven months before he was drafted into the United States Army. I had grown to love my stepfather. I knew he loved me too. He would cater to me, take care of me, and treat me as a special little boy. When he left, I was sad. My mama told me he had gone to serve in the infantry in the war. My sister Wilma was only three months old. My mama, Wilma, and I moved back in with my grandma and grandpa. Economic conditions were dire, and my mama felt it was the best and the only decision.

I kept hearing the word "Japs." At first I did not know what the word meant, because I was very young, but I soon learned that it was a derogatory term referring to the Japanese. People were talking about and cursing them as evil, saying that they were directed by the devil and all should, and would, burn in hell. This was upsetting to hear because I was not accustomed to hearing such pernicious language and strong voices.

Later, I learned that the Japanese had made a brutal surprise attack on Pearl Harbor, a United States Territory, on December 7, 1941. Thousands of American troops and civilians were killed. The next day, President Franklin D. Roosevelt declared war on Japan. After hearing what the Japanese had done, I began to understand the bitter comments and the hatred and hostility our community had toward the Japanese. Many people, my family included, said they hoped our soldiers would kill all the "Japs" and destroy their country.

Our family listened to President Roosevelt's speech delivered on Monday, December 8, 1941. I watched my grandma and grandpa and the rest of the family as their faces became gravely serious. It was if a death in our family had occurred. In this infamous speech, President Roosevelt asked Congress for their approval of a declaration of war against Japan. The speech was so important to the history of my life and to all Americans and to the world; I have included it in my book.

President Roosevelt delivered the following speech:

Mr. Vice President, Mr. Speaker, and members of the Senate and House of Representatives:

Yesterday, December 7, 1941, a date which will live in infamy-the United States of America was suddenly and deliberately attacked by naval and air forces of the Empire of Japan.

The United States was at peace with that nation, and, at the solicitation of Japan, was still in conversation with its government and its Emperor looking toward maintenance of peace in the Pacific. Indeed, one hour after Japanese air squadrons had commenced bombing in the

American island of Oahu, the Japanese Ambassador to the United States and his colleague delivered to our Secretary of State a formal reply to a recent American message. And, while this reply stated that it seemed useless to continue the existing diplomatic negotiations, it contained not threat or hint of war or of armed attract.

It will be recorded that the distance of Hawaii from Japan makes it obvious that the attack was deliberately planned many days or weeks ago. During the interviewing time the Japanese Government has deliberately sought to deceive the United States by false statements and expressions of hope for continued peace. The attack yesterday on the Hawaiian Islands has caused severe damage to American naval and military forces. I regret to tell you that very many American lives have been lost. In addition, American ships have been reported torpedoed on the high seas between San Francisco and Honolulu.

Yesterday the Japanese Government also launched an attack on Malaya. Last night Japanese forces attacked Hong Kong. Last night Japanese forces attacked Guam. Last night Japanese forces attacked the Philippine Islands. Last night the Japanese attacked Wake Island, and this morning the Japanese attacked Midway Island.

Japan has therefore undertaken a surprise offensive extending throughout the Pacific area. The facts of yesterday and today speak for themselves. The people of the United States have already formed their opinion and well understood the implications of the very life and safety of our nation.

As commander-in Chief of the Army and Navy I have directed that all measures be taken for our defense, that always will our whole nation remember the character of the onslaught against us.

No matter how long it may take us to overcome this premeditated invasion, the American people, in their righteous might, will win through to absolute victory.

I believe that I interpret the will of the Congress and the people when I assert that we will not only defend ourselves to the uttermost but will make it very certain that this form of treachery shall never again endanger us.

Hostilities exist, there is not blinking at the fact that our people, our territory and our interests are in grave danger.

With confidence in our armed forces, with the un-bounding determination of our people, we will gain the inevitable triumph, so help me God.

I ask that the Congress declare that since the unprovoked and dastardly attack by Japan on Sunday, December 7ath, 1941, a state of war has existed between the United States and the Japanese Empire.

My family and I were informed that three days later, December 11, 1941, Japan's allies Germany, and Italy, both declared war on the United States. The United States Congress responded immediately by declaring war on them. Thus, the European and South Asian wars had become a global conflict with the Axis Powers: Japan, Germany, Italy, and others, aligned against the Allies powers: America, Britain, Soviet Union and others.

A little later I learned that the United States had declared war on Germany and Italy. More often, I heard discussions that a brutal man, Adolf Hitler, a Nazi or "Kraut," was leading Germany in the war against the United States and most countries in Europe.

Hitler had initiated the extermination of the Jewish people through the use of mass killings, primarily through starvation, working them to death, and forcing them into concentration camps. Many met their brutal deaths in gas chambers. Then they were hauled into crematoriums, shoved in one on top of the other, and burned to a crisp. Their ashes burned in mass graves. Hitler held that those not representing the "perfect Aryan" or "pure" German blood were destined to be exterminated.

I never heard much was mentioned about the Italians. Occasionally, I heard the derogative term for the Italians—WOPS, a pejorative racial slur. The Italians were led by Benito Mussolini, who was credited with being one of the key figures in the creation of fascism. The Italians, Japanese, Germans, and other countries made up the Axis alliance. All of its members had one goal in mind: destroying the United States,

Great Britain, France, the Soviet Union, and the smaller countries that made up the Allies.

Our community was consumed with the stress of the war. Our family huddled around the battery-operated radio to hear the news related to the war. Gabriel Heatter, the commentator, talked about how many people were killed that week, or which battle had been won or lost. Occasionally, someone would make a comment that we were losing the war, which intensified the frustration that others already felt. Sometimes when someone mentioned we were losing the war, it would irritate people enough to start an altercation. Anyone who questioned the ability of the United States to win the war was frowned on and highly resented.

It was a time when I witnessed immense patriotism. I knew that young men and women joined the military by the thousands. Many joined one of the military branches because of patriotism, though some joined because they could not get any other job. It was obvious that Americans were shocked and afraid of another attack on the United States. Most of the news reflected that the Axis powers were winning the war.

Often, within my immediate family, there were discussions about what would happen to the United States if we lost the war. However, these conversations were few because it seemed that everyone was committed to winning the war at any cost. Deep down in most people's minds was the constant worry that Americans could be living under German or Japanese domination. As we crowded around the radio, I did not understand everything that was being broadcast. I saw the faces of those listening and heard them speaking in low voices filled with anxiety.

President Roosevelt conducted fireside chats directed to the American people, reassuring them that the nation was going to recover from the Great Depression and that the Allies would win the war. He shared his hopes and plans for the country. He spoke in simple terms that all Americans could understand. He also gave those in poverty hope.

My grandpa would often talk about the fireside chats that President Roosevelt conducted. He frequently referred to the 1932 radio address the President gave, which seemed to have made a positive impression on him. President Roosevelt used the terms "bottom of the pyramid" and "forgotten man" in his April 7, 1932 radio address. He gave hope to millions of people by referring to the "forgotten man." He held that in this distressful time of war and poverty, the building of plans must rest upon those at the "bottom of the pyramid," or the "forgotten men." He said that the unorganized but indispensable unit of economic power must build from the bottom up, not from the top down. Faith must be put once more in the "forgotten man" at the "bottom of the economic pyramid." The fireside chats continued into the 1940's until the American people began to focus on World War II. These chats gave hope to those in poverty but did little to change our plight.

I remember vividly one wonderful day when everyone in my family surrounded the radio. Today there was a feeling of happiness in the room as Gabriel Heatter; the news commentator relayed the good news that the war was possibly going to be over soon. The United States and its allies were turning the war around and beginning to have ongoing success. However, the war was not over yet.

The nation was shocked and stunned as the news reported that the beloved President Franklin D. Roosevelt had died on August 9, 1945, of natural causes. Everyone was saddened and highly concerned. Even, I as a child had an uncertain feeling as to what might happen next to our country. I could also see it on the expressionless look on the faces of my family. We had all placed such hope in Franklin Roosevelt. Now he was gone. Who would bring us hope? Who or what could end this frightful war?

Gabriel Heatter, the newscaster, informed us all that President Harry Truman immediately became the thirty-third President of the United States. He was President Roosevelt's third Vice President and had only be in office for eighty two days when President Roosevelt died. As President Truman inherited the presidency he had rarely discussed world affairs or domestic politics with Roosevelt. He was uninformed about the top secret Manhattan project which was about to test the world's first atomic bomb. If we had known the limits of his knowledge, we would have been even more afraid of what the future might bring. He learned of the Manhattan Project at a meeting with Henry L. Stinson on the day President Roosevelt died.

President Truman reported his own feelings shortly after the oath of office President Truman said to reporters: "Boys, if you ever pray, pray for me now. I don't know if you fellas ever had a load of hay fall on you, but when they told me yesterday, I felt like the moon, the stars, and all the planets had fallen on me." (Thoughts of a president, 1945, eye witness to history). I know my family was praying. When President Roosevelt died, my family looked to God for comfort in that perilous time.

The nation saw President Truman act swiftly. He gave an ultimatum to the Japanese to surrender, or the alternative would be prompt and utter destruction. My family and others rallied around him; perhaps he was the one who would bring the war to an end. When the Japanese refused to surrender, they met their ultimate demise. In early August the Japanese refused the terms of the Potsdam Declaration. On Sunday morning, August 6, 1945, at 8:15 a.m. local time, the B-29 bomber, Enola Gay, dropped a uranium fueled atomic bomb, Little Boy, on Hiroshima. Two days later after Truman's broadcast warning of further attracts, yet heard nothing further from the Japanese government, the U.S. military executed its plan to drop a second atomic bomb. On August 9, 1945, Nagasaki was devastated using a plutonium implosion-type atomic bomb, Fat Man, dropped by the B-29 Backscar. The bombs killed as many as 140,000 people in Hiroshima and 80,000 in Nagasaki.

I heard people saying that the United States should drop bombs ("bums") and destroy Japan, Germany, and Italy. The confidence that my family expressed reflected the first feeling of happiness in my family that I could remember. My grandma cried because she said Arvil, Horace, and my stepfather Edward, hopefully would be coming home and not wounded or killed. She said out loud, "God will bring our boys home safely."

CHAPTER SIX

INTO OUR OWN WORLD

Living in a dismal state of poverty was bad enough. Furthermore, World War II had also brought stress, sorrow, and dismay to my home. I felt it every day. However, I was fortunate to have a wonderful uncle who was only a couple of years older than me. He was my only friend and playmate. His name was Ralph Wesley Millican. We played from the time we woke in the morning until we were exhausted at night.

We did not have any toys purchased from a store. All the things we played with were simple toys like hammers, nails, and cap pistols. Some were handmade either by us or members of our family. Ralph and I loved to pitch horseshoes and play with handmade slingshots.

Ralph and I escaped into our own world, investigating our surroundings. We climbed trees to the very top. We considered building a tree house. We did not understand the danger of some of the things we did.

We often sat on the high bank above the train station watching the workers replenish the train with water and coal. We tried to figure out how the water from the creek got into the water tank. We were fascinated by the hoboes who rode in boxcars. Sometimes as many as twenty would "ride the rails" together, searching for work, going home, or simply running away.

I often heard my grandpa refer to them as "hoboes on the lam." To my grandpa, "on the lam" meant running away to escape punishment. Hoboes included tramps, vagrants, or people trying to get from one place to another. Some were searching for transportation to the wheat fields or other parts of the country to try to make money to send home to their families.

My mama and my grandma told Ralph and me that hoboes were dangerous and to stay away from them. The railroad companies tried to eliminate the situation, but there were so many "riding the rails" that the railroad authorities could not handle the situation. Finally, the hoboes were just left alone. Unfortunately, some met their deaths when they tried to "flip" or jump onto moving trains. Others died when trains hit them. This was called "greasing the rails" because their blood, bones, and body parts made the rails greasy. Occasionally, we would see a "possum belly," or a hobo riding on the roof of a passenger train. In order to do this the hobo would have to lie flat so as not to be blown off.

I remember the day when Ralph and I saw our first car. It was owned by Mr. Greer who lived in the area of New Hope North. He was having difficulty driving down the narrow dirt road. The dirt road had large potholes. Ralph and I were amused and awed to see the car because we had never seen one before. Everyone had always said that anyone who owned a car was considered wealthy. Having a car was everyone's dream, but they concluded they would never have one because only wealthy people owned cars. This attitude was difficult for me to understand. As a child I believed that I could have anything I wanted. I don't know why I believed that, because everything around me reflected poverty. I had nothing to compare poverty with, but I did not like the feeling of pauperism.

Our toys were made by someone in our family. One of our most wonderful toys, a truck wagon, was made by my uncle Albert. The wagon was made by sawing off the end of a log and making sure it was round after a little carving. Four of these rounds were cut, hopefully to look and be the same roundness. Each round became one of the four wheels, which were approximately one and a half inches thick. The diameter was close to twelve inches. Once the four wheels were ready, Albert used a hand drill to bore a one and a half inch hole in the middle of each one. After that, broom handles or hoe handles were sawed off to measure three feet. Albert placed the broom or hoe handles into the hole of each wheel. He adjusted the wheels on the inside and outside with long nails or screws to make the wheels roll in a straight line and not fall off.

He made the beds of the truck wagon with wooden boards. We were both so thrilled when it began to look like a little car! Albert made the guiding mechanism by attaching heavy metal wire to the inside of each front wheel axle. The guiding wires were then attached to a wheel approximately two feet up and two feet back. Axle grease was used to lubricate the wheels and axles for a faster ride. Once he made all adjustments, we were ready to ride! Ralph and I pulled the wagon to the top of the longest hill. Riding down was tremendous fun. However, pulling it back to the top of the hill for the next rider was no fun. So up and down we went until we were both tired out.

Another thing we loved to do was to play with little pigs. They were like our little puppies. However, Ralph and I found that playing with pigs could be dangerous and scary! And one day we really got scared. That particular day we were sitting on the top of the rails to watch the hogs and pigs play. We decided to walk on the wooden rail surrounding the "pigsty." While walking on the wooden rail, I accidentally fell in with the pigs and hogs. Hogs, as most people know, love to live in an environment that is truly filthy. The "pigsty" was a cesspool of mud, water, and hog feces. I started screaming for help. Luckily, some of the farm hands pulled me out. When we got back to the house, I was "stinking like a pigsty." My mama and grandma gave me a thorough scrubbing to get rid of the foul odor. My grandma really alarmed us when she told us that if the large hogs got the slightest taste of blood, they would eat us.

Ralph and I continued to play with the little pigs, just being more cautious about climbing on the wooden rail. We played with the piglets until they were grown, some to two hundred and fifty pounds or more. They were our pets and all were given names.

One wintry day when I was five and Ralph was seven, we learned a very difficult "life lesson." As I said, we loved those pigs, especially since we played with them from the time of their birth. I sometimes reflect on what I saw that day and have an empty, sick feeling. It was something I wish I had never experienced.

Even though the weather was cold and the ground very icy, Ralph and I wanted to go outside and play. We bundled ourselves up as much as we could and ran outside to play. As we were leaving the house, my grandmother said loudly, "Do not go near the barn today!" Of course, hearing this only sparked our interest about what was happening at the barn. We couldn't see the barn from the house, so we ran about two hundred yards to see what was going on. We got close to the barn without being seen and hid behind a wooden fence that was covered with foliage.

There were six men, including my grandpa, in the barnyard. Ralph and I were aghast to see a hog hanging from a hoist that had been built for one purpose—to slaughter hogs. We knew this hog by name, and all the other hogs, too, because we had watched them grow from little piglets. The hog was dead with his hind feet attached to the hoist; his head was almost hanging to the ground. All of our pet and friend's hair was removed with scalding water and sharp knives.

Then we saw one man with a sharp knife slice the hog open just under his neck down to the bottom of his stomach. Blood and intestines were flowing everywhere. While this was happening, another hog was pulled from the barn, squealing loudly as if he knew his fate. He ran quickly from his assassin. Ralph and I secretly hoped the hog would get away. However, the hog was caught and positioned. One of the men with a smaller knife stuck the hog, hoping to hit the jugular vein in his neck so he would quickly bleed to death. The hog struggled but quickly died. The other hogs watched, squealing, awaiting their fate.

As Ralph and I watched, we knew there was nothing we could do. We both stood there crying. Yet we never talked about what we saw that day because it hurt too much. Again, this experience was one I wish I had never had, because even now I can hear the squealing of the hogs as they were killed. I can see them struggling to get away. Several years ago, I saw the movie "*The Silence of the Lambs.*" The things Ralph and I saw that day was the "slaughtering of the piglets."

CHAPTER SEVEN

SAYING GOOD-BYE

Ralph and I were also fascinated with the Bell Springs cemetery, which was located a short distance from our house. It was eerie to see the cemetery, and we had ambivalent feelings prior to going there. Although we were afraid, we were curious about the tombstones and flowers placed on the graves. We could see the cemetery and the gravestones from our house. We walked through the gravesites and looked at the names carved on the headstones.

People said the graveyard was haunted, especially at night, and referred to "haunts" walking in the graveyard, especially on rainy nights. Someone told us that if we went there at night, we could see little flags moving up from the graves. The idea of each of the graves housing a person who once lived gave us something to ponder.

Almost every month someone died and was buried in the cemetery. Ralph and I often got close enough to the cemetery to watch one or two "gravediggers" dig the grave. The next day we would watch a hearse arrive, followed by several cars and trucks. People got out of their vehicles and watched as the back door of a large ambulance was opened. Six men pulled the casket housing the corpse out and placed it over an open gravesite.

After the people assembled around the gravesite, the preacher from a local church gave a short speech, mainly directed to the family. We watched while the family and friends wept. After he finished speaking, he asked the onlookers to move away as the casket was lowered into the grave.

Once the casket was lowered into the bottom of the grave, men started filling the site with dirt. The leftover dirt was used to form a mound. It was then decorated with flowers. Most people slowly drifted away; however, some people lingered until sunset.

Sometimes there was a military funeral, which was different and very interesting to Ralph and me. The casket was draped with an American flag. Usually there were six military men in dress uniform, there to represent the branch of service in which the deceased served. The six military men were referred to as the honor detail. At a specific time, all six men would fire three shots from their rifles simultaneously. At the end of the burial, taps was played by a military bugler, and the American flag was folded and presented, by a military chaplain, to the next of kin of the deceased. The military funerals always seemed sadder because of the taps played at the end of the burial.

Ralph and I went home after we watched burials feeling perplexed and fearful. Often we silently looked out the window toward the cemetery. We usually did not talk about what we had seen for several days. Finally, Ralph and I would get up enough courage to go back to the gravesite. The beautiful flowers had been blown off the grave, and the live ones now looked terrible.

Death was a subject that we did not understand. However, at our ages, death was something that happened to someone else. Yet each time there was a death and burial at the cemetery, both of us had sad, empty, and uncertain feelings. Now that I am older, I still have mixed feelings about life. I often think of a song written by Ann Murray and Jan Arden. It has been one of my favorite songs since I heard it several years ago. It is meaningful to me because most of the lyrics focus on that fact that somebody is always saying goodbye. As a small child I vividly remember young men volunteering or being drafted into the military services during World War II, with tearful people saying goodbye. In many cases, it was the last goodbye.

Years after experiencing the scenes of death, burial, and grieving, I have been at railroad stations, bus stations, and airports when someone was saying "goodbye." If one has experienced this emotion, he or she can understand that inexplicable feeling.

However, I have complete confidence in my belief that death is saying goodbye only for a short period. Many know the wonderful feeling of being saved. They know that Jesus Christ is in the hearts of those who have accepted his death on Calvary as payment for all of their sins committed in the past, present, and future. Death is simply moving from the darkness of this world to our graves, awaiting the Rapture. Those dead in Christ will meet the Savior to reign with Him forever. Those still alive who have accepted Jesus Christ as their Lord and Savior will be raptured after the dead in Christ.

"SOMEBODY'S ALWAYS SAYING GOODBYE"

Railroad station, midnight trains

lonely airports in the rain

and somebody stands there

with tears in their eyes…

"IN LIFE AS IN DEATH

SOMEBODY'S ALWAYS SAYING GOOD BYE"

CHAPTER EIGHT

ANOTHER CHANGE

I was dismayed when my mama informed me that the three of us—my mama, my sister Wilma, and I—were moving down the road into a little house she had rented. My stepfather Edward was in Germany during this time. She said we needed to live in our own house. One day Edward would come home, and we would need to live there as a family. She took me to see the little house, which was only a short distance from where we were living with her parents. I was concerned, however, because although the house was near the rest of my family, I would have to walk past the cemetery to see the rest of my family and to play with Ralph.

Within a short time, we moved into the house, and for the first time we lived by ourselves. I was happy about the move and house, but at the same time, I missed my grandma, Ralph, and all the rest of my family. At night I was afraid someone would break into our house and kill us.

I also had dreams about my uncles and my stepfather Edward being killed in the war and brought home for burial. I also dreamed about how it would be if death occurred in my family and I stood at a distance as the caskets were lowered and covered with dirt. These scenes stayed in my thoughts and dreams for several months.

After a short time, I became comfortable and could walk by the cemetery to play with Ralph. Sometimes my mama and Wilma would go too. I was beginning to understand that it had been necessary for my mother, Wilma, and me to live with her parents and family because of our circumstances. We had no money of our own until my mother married Edward, my stepfather. I understood that she wanted a place of her own.

After we had lived there one and a half years, my mama announced that she had purchased a house over on Highway 31, across the highway from a grocery store owned by Madison Hart. Mama had saved some of her military allotment money and made a sizeable down payment on the house. This house was the best house I had ever been in. I was going to live near the highway, across from a grocery store, and be able to see cars and trucks driving up and down the highway and activity everywhere. I considered this to be the best thing that had ever happened to me. It was a beautiful little white house in great condition; it inflated my ego just looking at it.

My mama purchased the house from Mr. Glynn Anderson, who owned motels near our house. He was well respected, intelligent, and wealthy. He had a reputation of being good to everyone and people had a certain admiration for him and looked up to him as being better than most folk.

While we were living in this little house, Uncle Tasker, my great uncle, came and spent several days with us. He was a small, distinguished man who always dressed as if he were in a Broadway play. Every day he wore a suit, white shirt, tie, and shined shoes, with a small handkerchief in his coat pocket. He enjoyed telling stories and listening to baseball games and big band music. He especially liked the music of Bing Crosby. He was so different from everyone in our family. I was fascinated with his appearance, style, and how he expressed himself. He is one person I will never forget! I thought he represented someone I might like to be immolating one day. He certainly did not reflect the poverty that surrounded us daily.

CHAPTER NINE

THE WAR IS OVER!

When I was seven years old, on August 15, 1945, we heard the news that the war was over. The Japanese signed an unconditional surrender to the Allied Forces on September 2, 1945 aboard the deck of the battleship, the USS Missouri. People were laughing, celebrating, congregating, sounding car horns, and embracing each other in a manner I had never seen before. This meant that Horace, Arvil, and Edward would be coming home from the war. However, it did not mean Horace, Arvil, and Edward would be coming home soon. It was going to take several weeks or months for the military men and women to make it home from various areas around the world.

The time came when families received notices stating the date that each soldier would be home. Everyone waited anxiously for a family member, friend, or neighbor to return home to celebrate. Then one evening there was a knock on our door. My mama opened it and there stood my stepfather in military uniform.

I was happy to see him in an awkward way. He had been gone for three years, and it was difficult to remember much about him because I was so young when he was drafted into the Army. It seemed that I was meeting a stranger that I had heard something about. He brought me several gifts. I was awed because I was not accustomed to getting toys or gifts. I still have the special gifts he bought me in a small cedar chest.

My mama was very happy to see him. They were only married a short time prior to his going into the Army. I felt to some degree she was having difficulty interacting with him. But, as I went to sleep, my mama was bringing him up to date on what had happened over the past three years. He was very happy to see his three year old daughter, Wilma.

After a few days I realized it was going to take a long time for Edward to adjust to civilian life. In the days and weeks after he returned home, my stepfather and mama had many conversations about what he was going to do to make a living. After a month or more, my stepfather went back to work for the L&N Railroad where he had worked prior to going into the military. The demands of this job were not only hard physical work, but he had to leave home on Sunday night and return home Friday night. After being in the military three years, it was difficult for him emotionally. This was not an ideal situation, and the schedule began to wear on my mama and Edward.

After living there two years following his return from the Army, my mama and Edward decided to sell our beautiful little white house and move to another house and take up farming. Even as a child, I knew this decision was not a good one and would be a long-term mistake. When our house was sold, we moved over near my grandma and grandpa. This house was not as nice as the one we left, and once again I lived near a cemetery.

CHAPTER TEN

VETERANS ARE HEROES

Most people in our community thought of veterans as heroes, but not all. A few months after Horace, my uncle, returned from the Navy, Ed Cole, who owned a large truck, came to my grandpa Millican's farm to pick up a load of cotton from the barn. It would be taken to Gordon's cotton gin in Falkville, Alabama to be processed, baled, and sold. I watched as Mr. Cole backed the truck adjacent to the barn so the cotton could be loaded onto the truck. While the cotton was being loaded, Mr. Cole, who never served in the military, started making negative remarks about those who served in the military. He said that veterans got benefits from the government while those who did not serve in the military got nothing. He said this was very unfair because folks like him had suffered through the depression and war just as the veterans had.

I never knew what prompted this man to make those remarks. Before I knew what was happening, Uncle Horace jumped upon the back of the truck where Mr. Cole was and grabbed him by the neck. Horace hit him a few times in the face. Blood gushed from Mr. Cole's nose and mouth. After giving him a good "licking," Horace threw him off the bed of the truck onto the ground. He also had a few choice words for Mr. Cole concerning veterans' benefits. One of the things I distinctly remember was that my Uncle Horace called him an ignoramus. At the time I didn't know what the word meant, but I was very proud of my uncle.

I do not know what happened next because I was so scared that I ran as fast as I could to the house, almost out of breath and barely able to speak, to break the news to my mama and grandma. Once I got enough nerve to return to the barn, things had settled down and they continued to load the truck. Needless to say, Mr. Cole had nothing to say. He quietly loaded the truck. That was probably the last time he said anything derogatory about veterans.

Later in life, I learned that many men had dodged the military draft because they had political ties. Some contended that they had some sort of ailment, some even pretending that they were insane. It was unforgiveable for men to find a loophole to stay out of the military. Those who found a way not to serve in one of the military branches were able to secure the best jobs. A large number of military personnel returning from the war could not find a job. As stated earlier, people would often say, "The war will eventually end but poverty will endure." This was true. Nothing changed once the war was over. Poverty continued as it had for generations. It is often said that "War is Hell." Those who used political connections, lied, and found other non- legitimate reasons to stay out of the war may find out what hell is really like, if they end up in "Hell."

CHAPTER ELEVEN

GRAMMAR SCHOOL DAYS

My mama kept me out of school until I was seven years old. I have never received a justifiable reason for this decision. She claimed later that the "whooping cough" was going around and she wanted to keep me "out of harm's way." But I never really understood this because it would put me back a year. I would graduate at nineteen rather than eighteen. It was like losing a year that could have been devoted to college or work. I was the only one in the first grade who was seven; everyone else was six.

In those days, children who lived in our area walked over to highway 31 to catch the school bus. The first day, I walked with Ralph and several other children. Most of the parents who lived in the community went with their children to catch the bus and were there to meet them when they returned from school. I did not let anyone know, but I was scared and did not know what to do, or where I was going, or if I could get back home. I was also concerned that neither my mama nor stepfather mentioned seeing me off the first day. My parents never mentioned seeing me through the first day of school, but I was adamant that I would do it alone. No one was going to know how I felt.

I think my mama and stepfather were so preoccupied with the day to day economic restraints that they did not realize they neglected some important issues. As the years passed, the pattern set that day never changed. Throughout my years of grammar school and high school, no one in my family ever visited the school for any event. They did not even attend my high school graduation.

That morning when I got on the yellow school bus, I knew it was going to be the most dreadful day of my life. As I looked out of the school bus window, I saw places I had never seen before. I had never been on a bus and had only been to Falkville once with my stepfather.

The bus arrived at the school and the students slowly disembarked. I followed the rest of the students in who looked like they were in the first grade. Luckily, I found the first grade classroom.

At that time, classrooms had few supplies. I did not have any other than what the school supplied. We did not have books to take home to study. We did not even have enough for every person in the class to have one. That was a good thing for me because there was no way that my mother and stepfather could have bought them for me. I was lucky to get the fifteen cents it cost to pay for my lunch in the lunchroom.

The best thing about the day was my teacher, Mrs. White. She was so kind, like an understanding mama. She reminded me of my grandma Millican. I think if it hadn't been for that wonderful teacher, I might have run away and never come back!

I still felt lost and afraid from the time I arrived until I was on the bus going home. I was so afraid I would not be able to find my bus. I remembered that a boy on my bus told me to remember the school bus number. He said it was always parked near the grammar school swings. Fortunately, after worrying all day, I looked for the grammar school swings, found my bus, and survived my first day of school.

After approximately one week, I settled down, and catching the bus in the mornings and getting back on the bus in the afternoon became routine. Mrs. Easter Column, who was my bus driver, lived close to me. She looked out for me and the rest of the students on her bus. However, she was very strict and enforced proper conduct while on the school bus. She was a very unique lady; I know I will never forget her. Mrs.

Column was our bus driver from the time I entered the first grade until I graduated from high school.

Our class had thirty-nine students. One teacher was in charge of all of us, regardless of the subject matter. I gradually began to feel better when I developed a limited friendship with some of the boys. In fact, I was beginning to even like school.

However, I did really enjoy the two weeks that school was out in the fall. That meant it was "cotton pickin' time," even though children also helped their families harvest corn and other products. For Ralph and me, it was a vacation time. It was two weeks to play, sleep late, and, in general, do nothing.

I dreaded the day when the two weeks were over and I had to go back to school. But the day came, and I caught the bus and started the routine that lasted until the end of May. School was out until the end of August.

After completing the first grade, I was more comfortable. I had learned the system and toured the high school, football field, and all the other facilities. Additionally, as the year went by, I had more friends. Some of them came over to Ralph's house to play baseball. We played baseball in a large open field until almost dark. I never had homework because we couldn't take books home. I probably would not have done it anyway. No one ever promoted much "book learnin'" in my community.

It was not long before I started to notice girls. They were also watching me and the rest of the boys. It was a strange, awkward feeling because at that age I was shy and reluctant to even let girls catch me looking at them. Trying not to let them know I was watching them, I quickly narrowed down the few that I thought were pretty. I wanted to say something to some of the girls, but I just could not do it.

At the tender age of nine, Shelby Wilson and I were sweethearts, which did not mean anything. We were both too shy to talk. Besides, we did not even know what to talk about. We passed notes while in the classroom, but it was not long before the teacher stopped that activity.

One of the things I found out quickly when I was in grammar school was that in every class, there was a bully or two who intimidated anyone who would let them. I was a proud young child. I was not willing to accept any bullying from anyone. One day I had the opportunity to prove that. A large boy tried to intimidate me. I accepted a little of it but then when it continued, I punched him with my fist between the nose and cheek. I will always remember seeing blood drip out of one side of his nose. After that, he never bullied me again. The word got around that I was to be left alone.

I knew that there was a good possibility that there were bullies in every grade. I gave some thought about how to handle each one, and that was to punch the bully in the face with my fist landing on the temple of the head or between the nose and cheekbone. I don't know why I took that approach, but I knew from that moment through the rest of my life that I would never be bullied by anyone. The procedure in handling a bully was to punch first and punch hard.

MY CREED

I will never accept verbal or physical abuse

from anybody, anyplace, or anytime

as long as I am alive.

I will never allow another person to be

physically or mentally abused.

I will never allow animals to be abused.

When I became older, I became interested in just why someone would want to bully another person. Why were they aggressive and intentionally want to hurt another person, physically or mentally? I believe now that the person doing the bulling really has a lack of self-confidence. They want to gain power over another person because they feel arrogant and narcissistic. Some use bullying as a method to conceal shame or anxiety to boast self-esteem; by demeaning others, the bully feels empowered. There are many good books on this subject.

CHAPTER TWELVE

THE NUBY VISIT

While I was in my early years of grammar school, my mama, my grandma Lilly Nuby, and one of my aunts showed up at school to pick me up. I happened to be out on the playground when they got there. My mama beckoned me to come over to the car. My mama told me that they had come to school to pick me up. This was the first time I had ever seen my grandma Nuby, and I could not even remember hearing her name until that day. It made me a little nervous because I do not know anything about any of the Nubys. As far as I was concerned, my grandma and aunt had never been a part of my life. Why were they showing up now? My mama introduced me to them as if they were strangers, and in my mind they were.

It was already about 1:00 pm so I just left school without telling anyone. I did expect to have a problem the next day. Luckily, no one even missed me. Looking back, I am not so sure I was lucky that no one noticed I was gone.

My grandma Nuby and my aunt spent the rest of the afternoon with us. During their visit, I learned that there was a Nuby side of my family of which I had never heard and that did not know. I did not really care one way or the other. Even if I had cared, I would not have ever let them know it. I would have been too proud to open up to them. When we got home, I went out to play. I never really talked to them.

After my grandma Nuby and my aunt left, I did not see any other person on the Nuby side of the family until I was almost out of grammar school. That time, they showed up just about the time school was out. They spent the afternoon with us again--well, not really with us, because I ignored them and went out to play as soon as we got home. After that day, I never saw my grandma or aunt again. I did meet my uncle Lloyd Nuby one time. I also saw Oliver Nuby, another uncle, a couple of times. I never met my grandfather George Nuby.

As I look back, I have never understood why the Nuby side of my family did not include me in their lives when most of them lived within a short distance of my home. I have thought, at times, my mama over-protected me and did not want me to be influenced by, or to spend time with, the Nuby family.

I have wondered if I did not miss something by not developing a relationship with them. The time slipped by and they have passed, and I will never know the answers to those questions. But I will always have questions about my grandpa Nuby, who lived with my brother Donald Alvis and his wife Brenda, for some period and died while living with them. Donald's wife was my first cousin and my grandpa's granddaughter.

After many years, I almost completely blocked the Nuby side of the family out of my mind. I did have lingering tinges of resentment and bitterness toward them. I don't know why they were not interested in seeing me, especially my grandpa and grandma Nuby.

Today, when I think about their lack of concern for me, I wonder if they had other important things going on in their lives that prevented them from seeing me. Maybe they didn't ignore me because they were apathetic. Perhaps they wanted to block the murder of my father out of their minds. Maybe seeing me conjured up memories they had rather forget.

I think my mother might have made it difficult for them to get to know me. I often wonder why my brother and his wife Brenda never mentioned that my grandpa lived with them. He died while living with them, but I never heard anything about it? It continues to haunt me that a grandpa and grandma would not find, look up, or contact their grandson. Adults have a responsibility to do this; children do not!

THE YEARS MOVE QUICKLY BY

During my years in grammar school, we moved a lot. This time, Edward started working in the construction industry, building houses. Our economic situation improved. Yet with things seemingly better financially, my mama was no happier. She seemed to be searching for something or trying to relive the past. One of her personality traits was a sadness I never quite understood. Perhaps she reminisced about my father and his death. It was only a short time until she wanted to move again. Edward always wanted to please my mama. So it was not long until we moved back to the other side of the mountain again to the same house we had just left.

This house was one we had lived in before, and one that brought sadness to me as we moved there. I remember at night walking in an open field looking up at the stars and moon and trying to see the little city which was in the distance. This little town was Falkville. This was the saddest time in my life. Looking back, I was depressed for several months. I often wondered if my mama and stepfather gave any thought to the negative effect moving so often had on me, my sister, Wilma, and my brother Donald who was born on June 7, 1945.

Despite where we lived, when August came, we all dreaded going back to school. August came and it was time to go back to school. All my friends dreaded going back, but after the first day we were fine. Yet we always looked forward to May. School would be out again and Ralph and I could play.

We did the usual things, along with the other boys that lived in the neighborhood. We played baseball all day ever day. We did not realize it at the time, but all the baseball playing would place us far ahead of others. Those interested would try out for baseball in the eighth grade. We were improving at hitting the ball, catching the ball, and throwing the ball. We were pretty certain all of us would make the starting team in the eighth grade and play high school baseball four years or until we graduated. Even though we would often explore caves, bluffs, the woods, and other areas of interest, but we always got back to baseball.

CHAPTER THIRTEEN

BASEBALL AND DREAMS

During the summers, baseball remained "my game." In our community, that was only game available. We made our baseballs by starting with a small rubber ball. A needle was stuck through the rubber ball with a lot of thread. Heavy duty thread was wrapped tightly around the rubber ball, always keeping it round. Once it was the correct size, the ball was sewed several times around and around to keep it tight and round. Baseball bats were made by selecting the correct piece of wood and carving until it became approximately the size of a regular bat.

In addition to making the baseballs and bats, I decided to make a catcher's mitt. In order to do this, I guessed at the size of the ones sold in stores. I used cloth to make the front and back, leaving space inside to fill it with cotton. Once this was completed, I left a small opening to stuff cotton in and move it around uniformly. When this was done, I used leather to cover the inside and outside of the mitt.

Many farmers in the area had animal hides. One of the farmers gave me a large piece of cowhide. The leather was trimmed to make the mitt look good. I sewed the front and back leather together and was ready to try it out. First I took my fist and pounded out the area where the ball would be caught. Ralph would throw the ball as hard as he could to get the mitt to conform to the ball. After a few days of catching the hard balls, the catcher's mitt fit my hand and was comfortable.

After about a week, for reasons unknown, my mama seemed irritated and made a statement that I all I did was play ball. I did not understand because there was nothing else to play. One day when Ralph and I were throwing the ball back and forth, my mother asked my sister, Wilma, to grab the catcher's mitt and run inside the house with it.

I thought about it for a minute and then ran into the house to get it and resume throwing it back and forth. I entered the house and ran into the kitchen as fast as possible. The wood burning stove eye was open, and my mitt had been stuffed into the stove eye and was burning up. I never knew why the mitt was burned up and never asked. I will always remember that it broke my heart and placed my mind in limbo for several weeks. I was twelve years old at the time and had dreamed of eventually having a catcher's mitt, because, initially, being the catcher was the spot on the team I wanted.

As I started in the eighth grade I was excited to find out when the baseball season started. I was not certain, but I believed that, because I had played baseball almost every day of the year since I was six years old, I could make the high school team. Of the three sports at Falkville High School, football, basketball, and baseball, baseball was the sport in which I believed I could excel and make the starting team.

All of us who played baseball became better as time moved on. We learned the technique of pitching the ball and how to stand to hit the ball better and farther. I did not realize it at that time, but baseball would become my best sport. I would be one of the best players at Falkville High School from the time I was in the eighth grade until I graduated. My bailiwick was pitching and hitting.

I had dreams of being on a minor league team after graduation. Maybe I could move on to the major league. I knew I was good enough. However, living in a state of poverty with no mentors, I had no one to tell me exactly how I could achieve that goal. Reluctantly, I put my dream on the back burner.

CHAPTER FOURTEEN

GUITARS AND MUSIC

I dreamed of having a guitar. I wanted to learn how to sing and play the guitar, as well as the other instruments that made up a rock and roll, country, or, gospel band. However, having a guitar was the most important of all. I listened to the radio when possible. At that time most of the music was big band and country. I loved all of it and sang the words when no one was around. I tried not to think about it; unfortunately, I could not think of any way to get one. Because of the way we lived, in poverty, I could not see being able to purchase a guitar or much of anything else.

Despite our economic plight, my stepfather ordered a guitar from the Sears and Roebuck catalogue for Christmas. I was startled. I had no idea where the money for such a wonderful gift could come. It was the best Christmas. At the age of twelve, I was actually holding a Silvertone guitar in my hands. As I wrote previously, although Edward was not my biological father, he treated me as well as or better than my biological father could have. I don't know how he was able to pay for it, but he knew I was extremely thankful.

Now that I had a guitar, what could I do with it? There were not any people that I knew who played the guitar, so I had to find a way to learn to tune it and to understand the cords. It was very confusing to have a guitar and not know anything about it or how to play it. I tried to find out if there was anyone who lived in our area that played the guitar or any musical instruments. I could not locate anyone.

One day I was extremely lucky. I happened to notice a small advertisement in a magazine. The ad was about the U.S. School of Music. The company indicated that all I needed to do was to fill out an application with my name, my address, and the name of the musical instrument of my choice. The company would send some very basic information, thinking I would order their full program, which was quite expensive. I quickly filled out the information requested and mailed it to the company.

In approximately two weeks, I received a package of information. Thanks to the U. S. School of Music, I had information to learn how to tune the guitar. They also sent a page with a graph of cords outlining where to place my fingers on the neck of the guitar with my left hand, and how to strum the strings of the guitar with my right hand. Once I had conquered the cords, G, C, and D, I was ready to try playing the cords to a simple tune which was "You Are My Sunshine." This was an exhilarating moment. After this momentous breakthrough, I knew I was going to learn to play my Silvertone guitar.

Ralph was awed and wanted to learn to play the guitar too. So we shared the one guitar and continued to improve on the basics such as cords and timing. What we really needed was to meet some people who knew how to play. As time went by, we located other young men who played the piano, the guitar, the bass, and other stringed instruments. We were improving but needed a lot of practice to be around these individuals who could really play.

We were so fortunate that Mr. Hart, the caretaker of Bell Springs Baptist Church, allowed us to practice in the church building. This was a tremendous advantage for us. Since we had a practice space, we asked Carl Williams, an excellent piano player, and others, who played various instruments, to meet us at the church twice each week. As a small group we became pretty good playing the songs we had selected. We were actually a small country and rock and roll band. As time went by, our opportunities to sing and play came frequently. Our small band played anywhere we were allowed to play.

However, our popularity was overshadowed by a rock and roll band from Hartselle High School. We were envious of Bob Cain and his band because they were very good.

The band was headed up by Bob Cain, who went to Hartselle High School. He could sing and play the piano and trumpet. Gary Hargett played the piano when Bob was singing. His band was so popular that after Bob Cain graduated from high school and college, he opened the "Cain Break" in downtown Birmingham. A night club that was open all night except Sunday night, it was an overnight success. Consequently, he was not only popular in Birmingham; he became known statewide as well as out of state. He appeared on the Johnny Carson show and other national shows. I felt fortunate to play with Bob's band one night at the Cain Break.

Bob Cain's story was inspiring. With the help and support of his wife, Penny, Bob changed his life and accepted Jesus Christ. Approximately twenty years after the Cain Break was opened, Bob drove to his night club, looked at it, and drove away, never to return.

After he abandoned the club life and secular music, Bob went through several years' reassessment of his life. Then another door opened for Bob. He was asked by one of the Blackwood Brothers Quartet members to come to Nashville to be a guest on the Gaithers' gospel music show. Bob was a huge success and became a regular on The Gaithers' Show.

As part of the Gaithers', he toured nationally and internationally. One of the Gathers' CDs features Bob singing "Why Me Lord," written by Kris Kristofferson. The version that Bob sang has been touted as the best version of this song ever performed or recorded. Hearing Bob sing this song touched my heart.

The last time I talked to Bob was at the Vestavia Country Club in Vestavia, Alabama, a suburb of Birmingham. He not only performed but also gave his testimony and how he came to know Christ as his personal Savior. At that time Bob knew he had cancer. Approximately three years later, he passed away. Yet his gospel music lives on.

I tell this story about Bob Cain because his dream was much like mine. However, I chose to take a different route. I look back now at "the road not taken" and wonder how my life might have turned out. It would have been a risk financially because I knew it took many years for most musicians to become successful. An excellent example of this is the band "Alabama."

I wanted to be a musician more than anything else. After suffering through the decision, I knew I could not live without working for several years, so I reluctantly decided that I had to go to work and make music my hobby. There is a positive to not fulfilling my dream. If I had gotten into the music industry, I might have missed the most important person in my life-my wife.

CHAPTER FIFTEEN

HIGH SCHOOL

In August of 1951, I started high school. It was different because I didn't know anyone except those who were in my sixth grade class. Now there were more than two hundred in the high school. It was easy to see that the older boys considered seventh graders as second-class citizens, and they did not have much to do with us.

In high school there were bullies, just as there were in grammar school. It did not take long until the bullies surfaced. Most of them were in the eighth grade through the twelfth grade. At first, the bullies just made derogatory remarks. Every day it was just a little more, until the name calling turned to shoving and pushing. I took some of this harassment because I did not want to have problems starting my first year in high school.

A chubby young man in the eighth grade was one of the leading bullies. Of course, I was one of his targets. By that time, I had decided that I did not care if I got into trouble. The next time this young man verbally abused me, I punched him in the mouth as hard as I could. He fell to the ground with a trickle of blood oozing from his mouth. He reacted with tears. He never bothered me again.

At my age, that was the only way I knew how to deal with bullies. The way I handled bullies quickly spread around the school. I had earned a reputation. There were a few more incidents, but I always came out on top of each situation. Generally, other guys just left me alone. If they did not have anything positive to say to me, they moved on to others who would take their intimidating remarks.

One day after school Cecil Williams, Charles Summerford, Ralph, and I were riding horses when we ran into an experience that none of us had encountered before. We were riding near the new I-65 highway, on the road that lead to Wilhite Station, when one of the horses suddenly stopped, reared up and started backing away. We knew something was wrong and we moved the horses away and tied them up. Cecil, Charles, Ralph and I walked toward the area where the horse stopped. The four of us were shocked to see a man off the side of the dirt road, lying in the tall grass. We had never seen anything like this before, but we knew the man was dead and had been there for several days. The summer heat had transformed his body into a condition that was three times the size of a normal body. We were noticeably shocked and dismayed after looking at the body which was covered with ants, maggots, and other insects. We moved away quickly because of fright and the indescribable smell. This event quickly drew a crowd of people. The police were there in a few minutes because someone had called them. Once the police were there, the area was isolated by using yellow tape along with several police officers standing by. The police asked the four of us a few questions and suggested that we go home. We untied our horses and were leaving as an ambulance was pulling into the area where the body was located.

Rather than going home, we all went to Charles Summerford's house, which was in the area. Once there, we talked about what we had seen and speculated about who would do something like that. We asked each other, "Who would murder another person?" What we saw was heavy for a young man to see. We tried to talk about the gruesome sight, but we could not find words to express our feelings.

After an hour or so, we went home and attempted to tell our parents about the horrendous situation. Our families were shocked and dismayed that someone had murdered a man in our general neighborhood.

Several years later, the murderer was apprehended, tried and found guilty. He was sent to prison without the possibility of parole. The murderer had picked up a hitchhiker and murdered him. This happened in a small community and highlighted an alertness that it could happen again. It has been many years since the murder, and nothing has happened like that again.

After school, Ralph, Jackie Johnson, and I were standing in front of the grocery store located in Lacon, Alabama, when another unbelievable event took place. A man was standing on the side of the highway as cars were speeding by. As we were standing there observing the various cars passing, the man stepped out, as if to cross the highway, when a car hit him head on. The car was going fast enough that it left an imprint of the man on the front of the car. Obviously, the man was killed instantly. Again, it was a horrendous site to see, because the man body was crushed and left in a deformed state, and blood was everywhere. The driver of the car was in shock, as well as the drivers of other cars that stopped. Someone in the grocery store called the police, and within a few minutes they were there as well as an ambulance. The police asked everyone to leave the scene of the accident. The three of us were ready to move away and go home. Once home, Ralph and I went into detail describing the horrid situation that we had witnessed.

CHAPER SIXTEEN

UNCLE VIRGIL

Virgil was diabetic. Diabetes mellitus, often referred to as diabetes, is a group of metabolic diseases in which a person has high blood sugar, either because the body does not produce enough insulin or because cells do not respond to the insulin that is produced. Virgil had type-1 diabetes and had to give himself an injection of insulin three times a day. He also had to stay on a restricted diet. Should his diet or insulin get out of balance, he would go into shock and be unconscious until he received sugar or juice.

He would stay unconscious until the sugar got in to his system. Everyone is the house was alarmed at his condition until he started responding. Every time he went into shock, all of us thought he was going to die, and this was constantly on our minds. My grandma had to consistently plan the meals for him. Also, it was difficult to get the insulin he so desperately needed. We had little or no transportation. Virgil's illness was one that was always on everyone's mind with concern about whether he would live or die because of the complications diabetics have.

With everything going on in the family, my grandma was the strength behind everyone, and she was the one directly responsible and willing to take care of Virgil. He had to have the insulin and a specified diet or he would die, and all of us were fully aware of the ongoing dilemma that my grandma endured every day. It was like waiting for something very bad to happen but not knowing when or where.

I loved Virgil and just kept hoping he would get well and not have any illness or have to take insulin and be on a restricted diet. But this was just a little boy dreaming and hoping the dream would come true. I knew that Virgil was not going to get well and that at some point the diabetic condition would kill him.

On December 1, 1952, Virgil was transported from home to the Decatur General Hospital. Previously he had had injuries or infections that were difficult to heal because he was diabetic. This time he had appendicitis, and before the operation his appendix burst. Due to the inflammation and his being diabetic, there was no chance for him to heal. The doctor alerted the family that due to his condition, he was not going to live. I was able to visit him but, he was in a coma, with a tube that drained fluid from the incision. The experience was beyond anything I had seen before. I was fourteen years of age and this was overwhelming to see and hear.

On December 4, 1952, he died while in the Decatur General Hospital. I cried until I couldn't cry anymore. He was only thirty years of age, and I loved him very much. Once the casket was brought home for viewing, I cried so hard and long that I thought I was going to die. I remember a minister coming into the back room of the house. He consoled me, talked with me, and helped me get through the moment. Virgil was transported from Decatur General Hospital to the funeral home, and then home. In those days, it was common for the body to be brought home, and the casket would be opened for viewing the body that evening until approximately 8:00 p.m.

Virgil was the first immediate family member to die. It was my first experience of enduring the grief and pain that death brings, especially when it is one you love

People who lived in the community brought in all types of food so the family would not have to be concerned with cooking. It was an act of kindness and sympathy toward the family. Several people stayed up all night. This was called the "wake" because people stayed awake all night looking over the body.

The next day, Virgil's body was moved from home to Bell Springs Baptist Church, where the funeral service was held. He was then transported to Bell Springs cemetery for burial. Our family was weeping as the burial process took place. Ralph and I had observed this several times, before but we did not know the people. This time we felt the loss of Virgil, and we all cried until there were no more tears.

Again, we all cried over and over, and then we went home with heavy hearts, stunned that Virgil was gone. I could not believe it and had a feeling that he was gone but would come back home. As the days and weeks passed, reality set in, and I accepted that he was gone and was not coming home. I loved him and will never forget how he treated me. I was so happy to have him visit us, and I will always remember the fun we had while he was there. I look forward to seeing him in heaven.

He was different from others in the family. His personality was different, and the way he dressed and carried himself was noticeable. When he visited us, while not living with my mother's family, I was thrilled to see him, and he paid a lot of attention to me and spent time playing and talking with me. His death left a void in the family that could not be filled.

Virgil's death almost killed my grandma and I think contributed to her death a few years later, coupled with the lack of medical attention. She died almost five years later, on September 6, 1957. She was sick and worn out, in need of medical attention and prescription drugs. I think personally she died from a broken heart. I know that she was saved; she had accepted Jesus Christ as her Lord and Savior. This gave me a wonderful peace of mind and still warms my heart. I have often wished that I had been old enough to work while she was alive. I would have made sure she received the care she deserved, and it would have been such a thrill to give her things that she needed or wanted. When she died, I felt as if a part of my heart died with her. It took a very long time for this feeling to dissipate. One must share this feeling to truly understand it. I would like to have shared my faith in Jesus Christ with her. I look forward to being raptured with her if I am dead, when Christ is seen in the clouds or, if I am alive, when Christ returns. I can see my grandma's grave open as she moves up into the clouds to meet Jesus Christ.

The death of my uncle Virgil, and a few years later, the loss of my grandma, were my first experiences of losing someone I really loved, and I knew they loved me. I was still a teenager, and the death of these two family members was very difficult. They were my first experiences with "saying goodbye.

CHAPTER SEVENTEEN

WORKING DURING SCHOOL

Beginning in the eighth grade and throughout high school, I worked to have personal money. I worked each summer doing various jobs that were available. Each summer for approximately three months, I worked doing the following jobs: cleaning out septic tanks, cleaning grease traps, building fences, baling hay, and other available jobs.

I think baling hay and unloading it in a barn loft was the most difficult job. The particles of hay would fall down as the bales were tossed to another person in the loft of the barn. I suffered with allergy and sinus problems. The hay only intensified the problem and caused me to have an unrelenting headache. I was sure that I did not want to do any of these jobs the rest of my life.

The people for whom I worked paid in cash. Even though I was in poverty, I managed to have cash when needed. I never forgot the formula that I had been working on since I was seven years old. Every night I reviewed my notes and updated them, sometimes adding new ideas. Becoming financially successful was the goal that I had thought about and worked toward for years. I discovered that poverty was magnified once one enters school and other activities and places outside the circle of generational poverty.

One summer I worked tearing down old houses in Birmingham. It was hard work, but the worst part was removing the roof shingles. The temperature was ninety degrees on the ground, and it felt like one hundred and twenty degrees on top of the house.

I spent the summer before entering the twelfth grade working in Atlanta, Georgia. My Uncle Bill and Aunt Vera Arnett asked me to live with them during this time, which was a wonderful thing for them to do. My Uncle Bill had arranged for me to work for a construction company. I had no idea about what I was getting into. The first day, the construction foreman assigned me and two other employees to dig a basement under a large house. Obviously, the two other employees were used to manual hard work. At the end of the first day, I was almost paralyzed from the digging and shoveling of dirt all day. I was young and strong, but I had never done any work as hard as this. The next morning I had to roll out of bed with every muscle sore from the previous day's work. After taking a very long hot shower, I felt better, but I became concerned as to how I would get through the day.

Fortunately, when I arrived for work the foreman wanted me to place siding on a house that was under construction. I felt like a miracle had occurred. The siding job was much easier, but it took me almost a week to recover from the digging and shoveling.

Bill Arnett was someone I admired. I will never forget the positive effect he had on my life. If we had lived closer to him, I feel certain that he would have been my mentor. He was liked and admired by those who knew him. Unfortunately, within a short time of retiring from one of the major airlines, he and his wife Vera were in an automobile accident that left Bill paralyzed and Vera in serious condition for months. Bill lived several years, but sadly he has passed.

During the three months I worked in Atlanta, I saved every cent of money I made without anyone knowing. When I came home and entered the twelfth grade, I had money and worked on the weekends when there were jobs. Eventually, I opened a bank account, and each time I made money, it was deposited. Once the three months were over, I caught a greyhound bus back to Alabama and home.

CHAPTER EIGHTEEN

DATING AND HAVING FUN

Since my family was still in poverty when I started dating, I had a very difficult time having the money to take girls out. I only had the little savings I had accumulated working during the summers and was miserly in spending it. Besides that, I did not have a car of my own. Our family had to share one car, a fifty-five Chevrolet. My stepfather needed it for work, so I was not able to drive it very much. Besides, it was costly to put gas in the car. Driving was a necessity because I did not date girls in my community.

I was very particular about who I dated. I certainly was not about to date girls from the Bell Springs community. They were living in a state of poverty, and that is the one thing I was leaving behind. As mentioned before, I knew that poverty begets poverty. So why take a chance?

I attracted many girls. I think that some of their attraction to me related to being a musician. At any rate, I had no problem attracting girls. However, I gave full credit for any popularity I had to my guitar.

I was often criticized by some boys and girls for only dating girls with money. A lot of the criticism came from people who lived in my community. Of course, this meant that they came from wealthy families. Their fathers were doctors, dentists, or had some noteworthy occupation. This criticism usually came through a third party. If someone had criticized me directly, I would have had some issues to take care of with that person. Each time I heard criticism, I handled it with arrogance and defiance. I knew that exclusively dating girls with cars and money who were pretty, or relatively pretty, would draw attention. I will have to admit that some of them were not as pretty as others, but they had good personalities. At that time in my life, I did not care what anybody thought about me.

As I look back now and evaluate the dating years, I am embarrassed that I took advantage of the dating scene. In most cases the dating was because the girls had cars and money, and were from affluent families. However, I treated the girls I dated with respect, and I think we had a lot of fun.

When dating the girls mentioned above, I took my guitar and sang a song performed by Phil Philips and other artists. The name of the song was "Sea of Love." When I was with one of the girls, I would pull my guitar out of the back seat of the car and sing the song as follows:

SEA OF LOVE

Come with me my love

To the sea…The sea of love

I want to tell you

How much I love you…

But when I was alone, I substituted, "I want to tell you…how much I love your new car." I know the above is shameful, but I was young – God has forgiven me.

In May of 1957, I graduated from high school. During my grammar and high school years there were some rough times, but overall I had a good time. However, I often think of one event that continues to haunt me, and causes a feeling of ambivalence. The event I am referring to was our senior class trip to Florida. As far as I know, everybody made the trip except me. There were some expenses that this trip demanded, and I did not have the money, nor could I get it. As I remember, I searched every possible resource to get enough money to make the trip, which at the time seemed like the greatest thing a senior could do. However, I recovered from missing one of the most important events which I had dreamed about. I quickly chalked it up to poverty, which added fuel to my determination to break the iron clad boundaries poverty inflicts.

CHAPTER NINETEEN

FIRST FULL-TIME JOB

Several months after graduating from Falkville High School in May, 1957, I went to work at Associated Grocers of Alabama, a cooperative grocery wholesaler company that distributed groceries, produce, tobacco products, candy products, frozen foods, and meat products to independent grocery supermarkets in Alabama, Tennessee, and Mississippi. Associated Grocers of Alabama, founded in 1927, is one of the oldest grocery wholesale cooperatives in America.

The day I reported to work, the company employed three hundred and seventy employees. I became number three hundred seventy one. I was at the bottom of the advancement list. However, when at the bottom, there was only one place to go—up. My first assignment was unloading boxcars of product. The product was loaded on wooden pallets. A forklift operator carefully lowered the forks and slid them into the pallet and moved the product into the warehouse.

The other person who worked with me was Willie Norris. He was very muscular and looked like an athlete. He probably weighed two hundred and fifty pounds, compared to me at one hundred seventy pounds. I was envious of the ease he seemed to exert in lifting one hundred pounds of animal food or sixty pounds of sugar. I admit that this job was much more than I could do, but I never gave up, and after several weeks it became easier because I was getting stronger. I suffered through many days before I could handle the job. The difficulty and hard work reminds me of a quote by Lyndon B. Johnson, who said, "Sometimes you just have to hunker down and take it like a jackass in a hailstorm."

Willie and I became good friends. We worked side by side. We occasionally had problems with other employees. There was one employee who worked in the warehouse that intruded in our area almost every day. He made comments that were not acceptable to Willie or me. This man had worked for the company for several years and had either brought with him or developed a big mouth and a bad attitude. Every time he came into our area of work, Willie told me that sooner or later one of us was going to have to knock him on his ass. I asked Willie to let me handle the situation.

When he came into our area the next day, I walked up near his face and punched him in the mouth as hard as my right fist could hit. I felt good watching him fall to the floor with blood oozing out his mouth and nose. Once he got up off the concrete floor, he left our area and we did not see him for a few days. I did not want Willie to be involved in any fights, because in those days the company would have been much harder on Willie because he was colored. At age twenty, I looked forward to anyone doing anything to provoke a fight. I don't know why, but I relished a good fist fight.

A few days later, the employee was back, to our surprise, complaining and making derogatory remarks about colored people. One day, when he was spouting off about colored people, I walked up to him as if I was going to talk with him. Instead, rather than talk, I used my right fist to punch him several time in the mouth, nose, and face. He was almost knocked out, but eventually got up off the floor looking as if he had been through a sausage grinder. He was dazed and said he was going to the company officials and turn me in for picking a fight. I told him I was going with him to report the incident, which would give me another opportunity to knock the other side of his nose off.

He left our area and we never heard anything about him again. This man was racist and received satisfaction in belittling colored people. At the time he referred to colored people as "niggers." In most cases, the supervisors did not care because he was expressing what they felt but refused to say. Someone said he resigned from the company. I felt good about the one-way fight and hoped that I possibly changed his life for the better. I did not realize he had left the company when I sent word to him that I could be hazardous to his health. If I saw him again, I would inflict havoc on his life. My experience reflects that bullies don't change.

Willie and I continued to unload boxcars. The company was gaining sales and the boxcars were beginning to back up because we could not unload them fast enough. Someone in the company recognized this, and two additional employees were hired. One of the two individuals spoke in the third person; that was annoying, but Willie and I just listened to it day after day, and the man never stopped talking. His first name was Jimmy. Jimmy made statements such as that Jimmy went fishing last weekend, Jimmy had a date with a new girl last weekend, and Jimmy hurt his foot while hunting, Jimmy was not making enough money for Jimmy to "get by monetarily." Willie and I talked about the situation and concluded that we could not take much more of Jimmy. We decided to stop the "Jimmy Stupidity." The next day was going to be Jimmy's last Jimmy.

When he came to work, Willie and I could already hear him talking about what Jimmy had done overnight. I walked up to Jimmy and asked Jimmy how he would like to have his arm "jimmied." He asked me what this meant. I explained to him that a jammer was usually a short crowbar to pry something open or break into it. He quickly became angry and stated he did not like the criticism from Willie and me. He wanted to take issue with what I said, but I moved up very close to his face and asked him how he would like an old fashioned ass-kicking. I was ready and expecting anything to happen. He backed off and went to see his supervisor because he said he did not want to work around Willie and me. He received a transfer to work in the freezer, which was always ten degrees below zero. Willie and I laughed, and said now Jimmy is getting Jimmy's ass frozen off.

My stepfather, Edward, worked in the same area that I usually worked in, but he never understood my short temper, fighting, and taking issue with almost everything. He was an amicable gentle man who talked, laughed, and joked with everyone, and everyone liked him. I regret to say that his position in the company never changed. He was always a fork-lifter. He loved his job and did not mind working until he could hardly walk. He had a great deal of energy and was constantly on the move.

Noah Chandler was the warehouse supervisor and made several changes in the manner in which the warehouse was operated. I was moved from the day shift unloading box cars to the night shift, pulling or selecting orders. This job was easier, but working all night was the most difficult thing I had ever done. After working all night I could only sleep a few hours during the day. When I returned that night, I was already so tired and sleepy I could hardly stay awake, knowing I had ten to twelve hours of hard work ahead of me. After several months, I was moved to the day shift doing the same thing I had been doing at night. I was happy because I could sleep at night.

All employees were happy to see Mr. Chandler leave the company. He was from the old school of autocratic management. Mr. Chandler was bald and had a wen on top of his head the size of a golf ball. Shortly before Mr. Chandler left the company, he screamed in his very high pitched voice at one of the relatively new employees. The employee was in his face and told him he was going to knock the growth off his head with his fist. The employee was fired for insubordination. However, Mr. Chandler never said an unkind word to me. If he had screamed at me as he did the other employees, I really would have relieved him of that wen. At this time in my life, I didn't care if I was fired. Mr. Chandler was eventually replaced by Claude Farley.

During the first two and half years, I was moved to several positions, including being a tow motor operator. This was much better, but the motors were run using gasoline, meaning the warehouse was filled with pollution. The fumes were so great that all warehouse workers suffered from burning eyes and headaches. I kept trying to break through the warehouse jobs and move into the office area. I knew I had to get into the office in order to reach the level in the company that I was determined to reach. The big question was how I was going to reach this goal. I had been there long enough to understand it was going to take a very unique approach to get where I wanted to go in the company. At night I reviewed the day and thought about how to improve my formula. My thoughts were focused on what I must do to move from the warehouse into the office. I knew if I could reach the office level, in any capacity, I would move through the ranks to the top.

CHAPTER TWENTY

DATING AND MARIAGE

It had been approximately four years since I graduated from high school, and I had the desire to visit my old school. In visiting the school, I set up a date with a girl in the eleventh grade. The date was set for Friday night, but prior to the date she had to cancel for some reason... When this happened I went back to the high school the next day, and I quickly remembered Jackie Freemen, whom I had liked when she was in the seventh grade and I was a senior.

I remember looking at Jackie while standing in the hall near the radiator. The same classmates stood there every morning, including Joe Murphy, Marlin Tabscott, Cecil Williams, and me. This was where we observed the girls as they walked by, even though we said it was to stay warm. I was attracted to Jackie even when she was a child. She told me later than she had been infatuated with me from the first time she saw me. I did not know it then.

I remember when she was in the seventh grade, a group of boys and girls of all ages rode in the back of a pickup truck driven by Charles "Chicken" Summerford. Our destination was Sportsman Lake. We participated in all the rides, including the Ferris wheel. I made sure that I was fortunate enough to ride with Jackie. I thought it was quite funny when I rocked the Ferris wheel from the very top. She was scared to death. I know we only rode it once. When we rode back home in the back of the truck, somehow I managed to sit by Jackie again. When I put my arm around her, I felt that she really was pleased.

Even in the seventh grade, Jackie was the most popular girl in school, and she remained so through grade twelve. She was a cheerleader, was voted most popular, and was chosen Miss Falkville. She had other honors and was a top student. I always felt that some people were envious and resented her. However, with her personality she was unstoppable.

This time, when I saw her, she had grown up and I was instantly in love. I tried to think of how to approach her because I was nervous and did not want to make a mistake. I finally had the nerve to talk with her and ask if we could go to a movie. She said she did not know because she had to ask her dad, who was very strict. This conversation left me very concerned because I had heard from others about her dad. He had retired from the Navy at age thirty-eight and was an honorable, but tough, man.

I was really worried to the point of feeling sick, but finally I called Jackie from a telephone booth on the side of highway 31, in downtown Falkville, which boasted one red light. I dialed Jackie's number: 133-J. She answered the phone and informed me that her dad approved of our going to the movie on a Friday night, but that we must be home by 10:00 p.m. I was overly happy, and felt like I had just won a million dollars. I was floating on air. After receiving that call from Jackie, I spent full time thinking about her. I remember asking myself what had happened to me, who had repeatedly made the statement that I would never marry.

Friday night finally came, and I drove to her house to pick her up, paranoid about facing her dad and mother. I walked up to the front door and lightly knocked. Jackie's dad opened the door. He was a short, strong-looking man with a very clear and distinctive voice. I introduced myself to him, and he stated that he was Jackie's father. He emphasized that he understood we were going to a movie in Decatur; I agreed. Then, he emphatically said "Be back here by 10:00 p.m." I said, "Yes sir!"

Jackie came from upstairs looking amorous. We were on our way to Decatur to see the movie "*The Shaggy Dog.*" I was so infatuated that I barely remember anything about the movie, other than it starred Dean Jones, a distant relative of Jackie's family. I was in love and tried to understand the feeling. In order to get Jackie home by 10:00 p.m., we had to leave before the movie was over. We left the movie with time to stop at the Dairy Queen in Hartselle, Alabama, and had something to eat and drink. We did get back to Jackie's house by 10:00 a.m.

Her dad was up, waiting to see if we returned at 10:00 p. m. as he had specified. As I was leaving, he said he knew my father and other relatives. I was in a hurry to leave because I was afraid of Jackie's dad. However, meeting Jackie's parents gave me a more comfortable feeling about them. I concluded that if I conducted myself properly, and adhered to Mr. Freeman's rules, I would possibly date Jackie again. I did not tell anyone, but I knew that I was going to see, date, and marry Jackie, regardless of the difficulties. There was nothing that was going to stop me! I had not expressed my ambition to anyone at this time, but my mind set was, that I was going to have anything in this world I wanted.

Beginning the next Friday night, we were allowed to be together each Friday night, to go to a movie, the boat harbor, or stay at Jackie's home. On Sunday afternoons, the whole family would sit inside the fenced area adjacent to the house and just talk. Jackie's dad did most of the talking and joke telling. It was a wonderful time because it was an opportunity to be with Jackie, as well as an opportunity to get to know Jackie's parents and her little brother Mark.

Mark was the center of attention. He was two years old and one of the cutest little boys I had ever seen. Jackie loved him very much and was proud for me to meet him. I also met Jackie's brother, Mack, who was enrolled at the University of Auburn. He was dating Jamie Hardin, who would later become his wife.

I also met Jackie's maternal grandfather, Luther Lafayette Payne, who was obviously of Native American decent. He was a wonderful, small man who always said Jackie was his favorite granddaughter. Her grandmother Myrtle Iduma Payne had passed. I don't remember

Mrs. Payne, but of all Jackie's relatives, Mrs. Payne was her special grandmother. Sometimes, Jackie reflects on the special love she had for her grandmother Payne, and the positive affect her grandmother had on her.

On Jackie's father's side of the family, I met her grandmother, Zula Beatrice Freeman, who was a very nice person. She did not talk much, making it difficult to communicate with her. Jackie's grandfather Luther P. Freeman had passed. He was an entrepreneur who owned a retail clothing store, houses, and apartments. In those days he was a well-known, respected businessman. However, due to the Great Depression, along with thousands of businessmen, investors, and entrepreneurs, he lost everything he owned. Mr. Luther Freeman died at age fifty-seven. Some relatives think he died from certain ailments, but also of a broken heart.

I eventually met Jackie's uncles, Herman and Bryan, and Jackie's favorite uncle, John. All of the Freeman siblings were intellectuals. When they were together, they talked about politics, books, and other things that were thought-provoking. They were all Yellow Dog Democrats who praised Franklin Roosevelt for all the good things, and the blamed the Republicans for all the bad things. According to them, all the mess and confusion in the United States was because of those damn Republicans! If I disagreed, I kept my mouth shut, because there was no chance of changing anybody's mind. Jackie's dad and her uncles, Herman and John, were all musicians. John and Herman could have gone far in music if they had pursued their talent.

I had fallen in love with Jackie, and I tried to understand the feeling. What is love? I knew the question had been asked for centuries. There is still no definitive answer. Years later I learned about Robert Sternberg, a Yale University psychologist, who developed the "triangular model" of love-one of the most encompassing views to date. His model is like a triangle that has three sides: passion, intimacy, and commitment. The motivational side of the triangle is passion, the spine-tingling sensation that leads to intimacy. The cognitive and willful side of the love triangle is commitment. Commitment looks forward toward a future that cannot be seen, yet promises to be there-until death. It creates a small island of certainty in the swirling waters of uncertainty. The state of being in love is like no other; it causes one to lose all perspective. Over the years I have continued to review the definition of love, but eventually concluded, "It is not explainable, but you know it when you have it."

There are few conditions to which more books and movies have been devoted, and few subjects that fascinate us more, than falling in love. We think about it, talk about it, hope for it, fantasize about it, go to great lengths to achieve it, and feel that our lives are incomplete without it. But we really don't understand it. Research has revealed which parts of the brain are stimulated when we are "in love." Most of us know how it feels to fall in love. But we don't understand why we fall in love or perhaps more importantly, why we seem to fall out of love with distressing regularity.

In order to understand falling in love, we must first understand the most important human need. The most important requirement for our emotional health and happiness is to feel loved. Our souls require feeling loved in just as real a way as our bodies require air and food. Not just any kind of love will do. The only kind of love that can fill us up and make us whole, emotionally, is Real Love. Real Love is caring about the happiness of another person without thought for what we might get for ourselves. It is Real Love when other people care about our happiness unconditionally. With Real Love, people are not disappointed or angry when we make foolish mistakes, when we don't do what they want, or even when we inconvenience them personally.

When the word "happiness" is used, it does not mean the brief and superficial pleasures that come from money, sex, power, and the conditional approval we earn from others when we behave as they want. Nor does it mean the temporary feeling of satisfaction we experience in the absence of immediate conflict or disaster. Real happiness is not the feeling we get from being entertained or making people fulfill our desires. It is a profound and lasting sense of peace and fulfillment that deeply satisfies and enlarges the soul. It doesn't go away when circumstances are difficult. It survives and even grows during hardship. True happiness is our entire reason to live, and it can only be obtained as we find Real Love and share it with others. With Real Love, nothing else matters; without it, nothing is enough. Walter Render, in his book, "Love is An Attitude," states it best: "Love cannot be begged, bought, borrowed, or stolen; it can only be given away. "An anonymous quote: "Love is a tickle around the heart that you can't scratch."

One time Jackie had the audacity to ask me the names of girls I had dated. My mind went blank, and I could not think of the correct answer. Rather than answer, I drove off the road, distracting her for the moment. During this event, she forgot the question. However, I knew it would rear its ugly head again. This is one of those situations when one should use his inner recesses of the mind in order to give the correct answer. I gave some deep thought to her question and almost decided there could not be an acceptable answer. Realizing the question would surface again at some point, I decided to answer Jackie's question with the lyrics of a song performed by the Platters. My guitar was always within reach, and I was prepared to sing the song, if necessary.

ONLY YOU

Only you can make this world seem right

Only you can make the darkness bright

Only you and you alone can thrill me like you do

And fill my heart with love for only you…

I thought it was enough to skirt the question. However, there are some questions to which any answer is just not good enough, and this question—which girls I dated in the past–falls into that category. This is a great song, dedicated to the only girl I ever loved, and it is still my number one song to her. However, if the song did not do the trick, I was prepared to say, "I don't remember." However, if she had demanded to know who I had dated, I would have acquiesced, and named everyone that I had dated and some I thought about dating. This statement proves how gullible men are when they are in love.

While dating Jackie, I continued to work for Associated Grocers of Alabama from 6:00 p.m. to 6:00 a.m. five nights each week. The physical work, long hours, and working at night were taking a toll on me, but there was not anything I could do about it at that time. Sometimes I would work all night and then drive to Falkville to see Jackie, or just to talk by telephone. By the time I drove back to Birmingham, I only had a few hours to rest and, hopefully, sleep.

After several months of working all night five nights each week, the hard work, and sleepless nights were taking a physical toll on me. I was driving to Falkville one or two days per week after working all night. I had lost weight, and soon was in the Hartselle Hospital. I was sure my illness was caused by fatigue without enough rest and a poor diet. Dr. Block diagnosed my illness as being caused by an intestinal problem prompted by amoebas. I did not believe that, and I was released from the hospital and as soon as possible went back to work.

The day I was released from the hospital, I started improving my diet and getting more rest, and I changed my pace to one that I could handle. Being in love could have been part of the problem, because I wanted to be with Jackie every minute, and this was a continuous concern. Being in love causes a certain type of insanity that is difficult to see and understand. I disliked working in Birmingham and being seventy miles away from Jackie.

After dating for almost one year, when Jackie was only in the eleventh grade, we decided to get married. On April 22, 1960, we eloped, along with Robert Winkles and Nina Partlow. Jackie and Nina put their wedding dresses in a car that I had borrowed from my Uncle Albert. We were married at the courthouse by the Justice of the Peace in Rome, Georgia. Because Jackie was underage, I changed her birth certificate, which was very obvious. I had used blue ink rather than black ink. The Justice, who married us, looked at it and looked at me. He knew the certificate had been changed, but he did not say a word. That was a relief. Whew!

Once back in Birmingham, Jackie went home and I went home. We kept our marriage secret for a few months until Jackie's mother figured it out. She and Jackie drove to The King Pharr Cannery in Cullman, where I worked at that particular time, to confront me and to confirm the truth. This confrontation with Jackie's mother was shocking. It was frightening to think about confronting Jackie's father. I became dizzy just thinking about it.

The most unexpected thing happened. Jackie's mother and dad did not say anything negative to me or about our eloping. And from that time until they passed, neither ever mentioned the elopement and marriage. Then and today, I have a deep hurt because, in retrospect, I know I should have talked to them and asked for permission and their blessing to marry Jackie. This is something I will always regret.

A short time prior to Mrs. Freeman's death, I talked with her about this, and told her I regretted handling the situation the way I did. I also expressed my appreciation of how she and Mr. Freeman accepted me and never mentioned our elopement situation. I also thanked her for a life-time of never having an unkind word from either of them. At times, I hurt when thinking of eloping with their sixteen-year old daughter, who was still in high school, and not talking with them prior to the marriage. I often feel I highly dishonored them by the way I handled everything. I was twenty-two and Jackie was only sixteen years of age. I should have shown more maturity and care for their feelings. Now, having daughters of my own, I know how they must have felt.

After being around Jackie's mother and dad for a while, I learned that her father was witty, funny, and always telling a joke or some line that was humorous. Mr. Freeman played the guitar and piano and could sing all the old standard music which I enjoyed. Both of Jackie's parents were very intelligent. They produced three intelligent, successful children. Mack became a prominent architect, Mark an Industrial Psychologist with an earned PhD, and Jackie, my wife, a full professor with an earned doctorate. Once the news became known of our marriage, Mr. Payne, the principal of the Falkville High School, took issue with Jackie being married, and wanted to strip her of her various titles. Moreover, he wanted to expel her from school. Jackie's mother became involved in the situation and I stayed out of it. Even though Mr. Payne caused us a lot of grief, Payne, Jackie completed the eleventh grade and graduated from the twelfth grade. She gave up being a cheerleader and other honors. Mr. Payne thought he was doing the right thing and what was expected of him as principal. Looking back, Mr. and Mrs. Payne were genuinely good people.

Dr. Jacqueline F. Nuby

Honey, you are my shining star

Don't you go away

Wanna be right here where you are

Until my dying day....

Song recorded by the Manhattan's

CHAPTER TWENTY-ONE

LIFE ABOUT TO CHANGE
UNITED STATES ARMY

After Jackie graduated from high school, we moved to Birmingham, where she enrolled at Birmingham-Southern College. We rented an apartment across the street from the college. It was extremely small, but furnished. Our apartment was in the basement of a large brick house. There was a second basement apartment next to us where a Birmingham Barons baseball player and his wife lived. Even though it was furnished, all was not good. We slept on a twin bed. Our rent was $35.00 per month, which now sounds like so little, but then it was a lot, and we did not have or make a lot of money. I don't remember Jackie purchasing any additional clothing while we lived there. I made just enough money to live in a very lean manner.

Despite our lack of money, we were happy and did not spend time thinking about what we did not have. Even at that time, and at the level I was working at Associated Grocers of Alabama, I was sure that in the future we would eventually have anything we wanted. This truly was a positive view of the future, but I had very strong feelings about being financially successful. The formula I had been working on was beginning to come together, but I still needed some time in the workplace, to refine and test it. I did not know that after years of struggling on this project, I was getting closer to putting my plan into effect.

Jackie went to school during the day, and I worked all night at Associated Grocers of Alabama. Our schedules were not ideal, but it was the best we could do at the time. On the weekends we spent our time walking the streets in downtown Birmingham, going in and out of the stores, just looking at the clothing and other things that we did not have. At that time, we did not have money to spend other than to pay for the essentials. Downtown Birmingham was new and interesting because we had not been exposed to the large stores and restaurants and to all the people walking the streets and the stores. We would stop in Newberry's and have a Coke and maybe something inexpensive to eat. At that time we didn't did not have anything monetarily, but we had and loved each other.

While spending our time together in downtown Birmingham, we noticed that restrooms were identified as White Only and Colored Only. We learned that colored people could not eat at the same restaurants as whites. Water fountains were labeled White Only and Colored Only. We faced a new situation that neither of us had ever confronted before. After a few days of evaluating the city, we learned the city of Birmingham was highly segregated. Colored people had to sit at the back of buses, and they had to give a white person their seat if the bus was full.

I was sixteen years of age when I saw the first colored person, and I had not developed a feeling of difference to the races. Jackie's dad was in the Navy for twenty years. He and his family had lived in various parts of the United States and Jackie was not prejudiced or judgmental toward colored or whites. Now that we lived in Birmingham, we were beginning to see injustice up close. Both of us had a difficult time understanding this ugly situation that we discovered was prevalent throughout the South and the nation.

After experiencing segregation up close, I tried to define what it was and came up with the following definition. Racial segregation is the separation of different kinds of humans into racial groups in daily life. It may apply to activities, eating in restaurants, drinking from water fountains, using bathrooms, attending school, going to movies, and the rental or purchase of a home. It was also prevalent in the workplace, social clubs, country clubs, and throughout our society. Even though it was difficult to see, underground segregation prevailed in many areas of society. One could feel the tinges of acrimony between blacks and whites.

Both Jackie and I were amazed and horrified as we listened to George Wallace after he lost the election in 1958. He made many acidulous remarks slanted to hurt the blacks who lived within the state of Alabama as well as outside Alabama. After the election, Wallace's aide Seymour Trammell recalled Wallace saying, "Seymour, you know why I lost that governor's race? I was 'outniggered' by John Patterson. And, I'll tell you here and now, that I will never be 'outniggered' by John Patterson again." In the wake of defeat, Wallace adopted a hardline segregationist stand. He stood up to his word and used that stance to court the white voters in the 1962 gubernatorial election.

After George Wallace's landslide election in the state of Alabama in 1962, he took his oath on January 14, 1962, standing on the gold star marking the spot where, 102 years prior, Jefferson Davis was sworn in as President of the Confederate States of America. In Wallace's speech, he used the phrases for which he is best known:

In the name of the greatest people that ever trod

this earth, I draw the line in the dust and toss the

gauntlet before the feet of tyranny, and say

segregation today, segregation tomorrow,

segregation forever.

I think biographers Dan T. Carter and Stephen Lesher sized George Wallace up correctly as "the most influential loser" in the 20th century of the U. S. politics. The above conviction Wallace held was renounced later in life, after an assassination attempt left him paralyzed; he was confined to a wheelchair the rest of his life.

I heard a lot about many local activists led by Fred Shuttlesworth, a fiery minister who organized demonstrations consisting mostly of young people. Shuttlesworth became legendary for his fearlessness in the face of violence. During this time, there was a string of racially motivated bombings that damaged many black churches. The most devastating bombing was at the Sixteenth Street Baptist Church, in downtown Birmingham. Four little black girls were killed in that bombing. The world looked at this event with horror. It was especially noted because television stations ran footings of the demonstrations. For the first time, the world would see that black children could be hosed down to the ground by policemen and dogs used to push back the demonstrating crowds. This bombing and numerous other events earned Birmingham the derisive nickname "Bombingham."

Fred Shuttlesworth really wanted Dr. Martin Luther King, Jr., and the Southern Christian Leadership Conference (SCLC), which Shuttlesworth had co-founded, to come Birmingham to assist him in his efforts. Dr. King was a Baptist pastor, and an advocate for social justice. When he finally did come to Birmingham, they jointly launched "Project C," a massive assault on the Jim Crow System.

Those of us who lived in Birmingham, especially Jackie and me, were well aware of the Jim Crow laws that had been in place from the late 1800s. The intent, segregationists said was to provide "separate, but equal" status for black Americans in public facilities. In reality, this led to treatment and accommodations that were usually inferior to those provided to white Americans, systematizing a number of economic, educational, and social disadvantages.

I watched intently as Dr. King, along with many other local and national leaders, led marches in many cities. Violence was cropping up everywhere. Dr. King opposed violence, but emotions were running high. In some cases, he could not keep violence from taking its course. Some white people participated in the marches that were led by Dr. Martin Luther King. The nation was highly segregated, and the President of the United States was about to enter the picture. Jackie and I were not aware of how serious the situation was. We could not believe that segregation, bigotry, hatred, injustice, and prejudice existed in the United States or anywhere else. We were beginning to see that our world, especially mine, had been a tiny speck in the United States and the world stage of reality.

This was a very sad time, not only for the nation, but especially for the city of Birmingham. Due to the insane actions taken by Theophilus Eugene "Bull" Conner, the Public Safety Commissioner of Birmingham in the 1960's, the city of Birmingham was the focus of national and international news. Conner became a symbol of bigotry and the icon of racial intolerance. Even today, Birmingham continues to be known for the brutality that took place under his watch. However, I truly believe that his brutality served as one of the catalysts for major social and legal change in the Southern United States and, in large measure, assured the passage of the Civil Rights Act of 1964. One could state that "Bull" Conner was an uncompromising defender of racial segregation.

Dr. Martin Luther King, Jr. wired President Kennedy from Atlanta stating that he was going to Birmingham to plead with Negroes to "remain non-violent." But, he said that unless "immediate federal steps are taken" there will be "in Birmingham and Alabama the worst racial holocaust this nation has ever seen."

During all of this dissention, Dr. King berated Wallace by wiring him that "the blood of four little children…is on your hands." The wire stated that Wallace was irresponsible and his misguided actions had created in Birmingham and Alabama the atmosphere that has induced continued violence and now murders. (United Press International, September 16, 1963)

The most disgraceful part of this sorrow and shame lay at the hands of J. Edgar Hoover, Director of the FBI or Federal Bureau of Investigation. Hoover knew who the conspirators were but left them alone. J. Edgar disliked Dr. King, but the Director alleged to have other reasons, too. He was reluctant to reveal his informants and questionable wiretapping in court. William Falkner was correct when he wrote that in the south, "the past is never dead: it isn't even past." (Article written by David J. Garrow, Newsweek, July 21, 1997. "Birmingham bombing.")

One man who stood out following this turbulent period in the nation's history was Bill Baxley, who served two terms as Attorney General of Alabama from 1971-1979. At the age twenty seven was the youngest to hold that position in the United States. He served one term as lieutenant governor of Alabama from 1983-1987. During this time, in politics, Baxley aggressively promoted the state's first African American assistant attorney general, Myron Thompson, who later became a federal judge.

It was later reported to the public that Baxley's tenure incurred the wrath of the Ku Klux Klan when he opened the case of the 16th Street Baptist Church bombing. In a letter, the Klan threatened him, compared him to John F. Kennedy, and made his an honorary "nigger." Mr. Baxley responded on official state letterhead "My response to your letter of February 19, 1976, is—kiss my ass." As attorney general, Baxley was made famous for his most prestigious case against the Ku Klux Klan when he prosecuted Robert Chambliss in 1977 for bombing of the 16th Street Baptist Church. However, Civil Rights activists blamed George Wallace, Governor of Alabama, for the killings. Only a week before the bombings he had told the York Times that to stop integration Alabama needed a "few first class-funerals."

Alabama Attorney Baxley stated to the press, "We know who did it." In 1977, he was noted for his most prestigious case against the Ku Klux Klan, in his prosecution of Robert Chambliss. In the first trial Chambliss was found not guilty. The case was unresolved until Bill Baxley requested the official Federal Bureau of Investigation files on the case and discovered that the organization had accumulated a great amount of evidence against Chambliss that had not been used in the original trial. In November, 1977, Chambliss was tried once again for the Sixteenth Street Baptist Church bombing. At the age of 73, Chambliss was found guilty and sentenced to life imprisonment. On May, 2000, the FBI announced the church bombing had been carried out by a splinter group, the Cahaba Boy's. It claimed that Robert Chambliss, Herman Cash, Thomas Blanton, and Bobby Cherry had been responsible for the crime. At this time Herman Cash was dead;

however, Blanton and Cherry were arrested, tried, and convicted. (Killers of innocents–commentary Birmingham World, dated September 16, 1963). It is my belief, and that of many others, that J. Edgar Hoover, head of the FBI knew who the killers were and covered it up from the beginning.

Bill Baxley should be applauded because he stood up against fierce opposition from the Ku Klux Klan and many white racists to bring those who bombed the 16th Street Baptist Church located in Birmingham, Alabama to justice. He stood up for justice when others sat down.

THE WORST IS ABOUT TO HAPPEN

During the first years of our marriage, I had not forgotten my vow to break the chains of poverty. I had this oath ingrained in my mind from the time I was a small boy. I continued to isolate the ingredients that made some people successful. I noticed food brokers that were more successful than others. I observed employees, the differences in personalities, work ethics, and how they interfaced with other personnel. I was beginning to narrow down the ingredients that made some successful. I noticed that working hard rarely led to success. However, a few were successful. I charted the differences between the "haves and the have nots." I was not able to develop the exact formula that I wanted to follow or thought would work for me. I would never give up on trying to figuring this out, and I knew there was an answer which might be different for different people.

Bill Lawrence, a large food broker, got my attention because he seemed to have everything it took to be successful. He was a distinguished gentleman approximately forty-five years of age. He dressed with style, spoke in a dignified manner, was friendly, treated everyone well, and had a certain aura about him that solidified his success. Mr. Lawrence was a role model, as well as a few other people such as Mr. Mobley and Mr. R. C Riley. As I continued to search for the formula to be successful, I eventually realized I had to create a formula that was tailored just for me. At this time I started rewriting most of the formula I had worked on for years. Yet the old notes and ideas were helpful.

I was working diligently to move up the hierarchy at Associated Grocers of Alabama. Mr. Mobley was the President and General Manager, and Mr. R.C. Riley was second in command as Vice President and Assistant General Manager of the company. Frank Helms was a Vice President. There was a large number of office personnel because the computer system was archaic, demanding a large number of personnel to maintain the system. A "tub file" housed cards that were pre-punched and loaded into the computer to run the items ordered by the customer and printed out on an invoice. Most of the employees worked in the warehouse, the frozen food department, the meat department, and the candy and tobacco department, or as product checkers, drivers, and supervisors.

Everything was moving along fine at Associated Grocers until mid-December 1962, when I received a letter from the United States Government notifying me that I was to be at a specified location in Huntsville, Alabama on a certain date. The purpose was to catch a bus and be transported to Montgomery, Alabama, for a physical examination to determine if I were physically and mentally fit to meet military requirements. This was an alarming letter which sent all kinds of negative thoughts through my mind.

I drove to Huntsville on the designated day, caught a chartered bus along with many others, and rode back through Birmingham on to Montgomery, Alabama. Once we reached Montgomery, we were given a short orientation about why we were there and the procedure that we were going through that day.

As a team of doctors stood by, approximately fifty of us were examined thoroughly by the doctors. We were asked numerous questions about our health. Then we were asked to drop our pants and underwear for a more personal examination. At first it was embarrassing, but then I realized that everyone was standing naked. This was an uncomfortable situation to be standing with fifty naked young men in the same position. The examination went rather quickly, and it was comforting to pull my shorts and pants up and get dressed.

We were quickly loaded back onto the bus that brought us. We were headed back to Huntsville, Alabama, where we started. The bus went back through Birmingham. I wondered why the deportation point had to be Huntsville, realizing I would spend two hours or more driving back to Birmingham. When we arrived in Huntsville, I could not wait to find my car and drive home to Birmingham to see my wife. It took more than two hours to drive home to Birmingham.

As I drove home from Huntsville, I was troubled about the letter I had received and the trip to Montgomery, wondering if I had passed the examination or failed it. I did not want to have a disease or anything wrong with me, but deep down in my heart I hoped I had failed the physical examination. Maybe I had flat feet or was not intelligent enough to be in the military. I was happy to see Jackie. It was as if I had been gone for a year although it had only been one day.

My hope of not passing the physical and mental examination did not materialize. At the end of December 1962, I received a letter from the United States Army stating that I had been drafted. My orders directed me to be at the Birmingham Train Station on January 16, 1963. This letter was more disturbing than anything that had previously happened to me.

It was going to be a drastic change that included leaving my wife, job, and the area. Jackie would have to drop out of Birmingham-Southern Southern and move back to Falkville to live with her mother and dad. But for me, the thought of being away from Jackie was more disturbing than anything I had ever confronted. I had never been away from home, other than living in Atlanta with my Uncle Bill and Aunt Vera Arnett while working in construction during the summer, when I was in the eleventh grade.

My letter from the United States Army stated that my eight weeks basic training would be at Fort Chaffee, Arkansas. Late in the evening on January 16, 1963, I boarded a passenger train that would take me to my destination, Fort Chaffee, Arkansas. As the train picked up speed, I took inventory of the other young men on the train with me headed to the same destination. I was mentally and physically worn out and felt that I could go to sleep. As the night moved on, many of the draftees started playing cards and shooting dice getting louder and louder, which made it impossible to sleep. I could not understand why many of the draftees were seemingly so happy and I was sad, confused, and thinking about being away from my wife. After observing most of them for a while, I believed they were going to a better place than they were leaving.

It took all night, but the train finally arrived in Pine Bluff, Arkansas. It was still dark when we got off the train. We loaded onto buses that were seconds away from the train. As we were driven to Fort Chaffee from Pine Bluff, Arkansas, I could feel I was entering the twilight zone.

I was not wrong. The drill sergeants were talking as loudly as they could and making harsh remarks. After not sleeping during the night, I was in a mental daze, trying to get a grasp on what was going on and what to expect next. In order to get mentally prepared, I remembered the quote I had used during my first days at Associated Grocers: "Sometimes you just have to hunker down and, take it like a jackass in a hailstorm." This quote was made by Lyndon B. Johnson.

From the moment we stepped off the bus at Fort Chaffee, Arkansas, all of us knew we were going to go through hell for eight weeks. We were immediately lined up and fitted with uniforms, clothing and boots. Some personal supplies were issued to us until we could go to the PX, or Post Exchange, and purchase additional needs. Once the clothing was issued, we were herded to our assigned barracks and bunks. I felt fortunate to get the lower bunk. We received foot lockers and were told how we had to fold and pack each item the military way.

As these simple instructions were being carried out, the drill sergeants continued to shout out instructions, making denigrating remarks to all of us. Those who took the most abuse were the young men who looked different or stood out as fat, tall, short, or who were in any way "different." All the drill sergeants were using intimidation with our group. I felt certain all new arrivals were enduring the same. I was trying mentally to put this eight-week experience in perspective and figure out how I could cope with a complete change of life. The life I had known was gone for at least eight weeks. After that, there were an additional twenty-two months that I was obligated to the United States Army. However, it was possible to be in the Army longer than two years, depending on the situation in Cuba, Vietnam, or other potential military conflicts.

The drill sergeants had a job to do, and they were certainly doing it well. The mental and physical exhaustion of each recruit was noticeable. As the days and weeks went by, I started understanding the tactics they were using to break us down. They sought to teach us discipline as we had never known before. We were taught that we were to perform as a unit and to have respect for each other and the officers. We were beginning to realize that harsh training and discipline we were receiving could save our lives should we be unfortunate enough to be in a battle. However, there were times when I wanted to punch the drill sergeants in the mouth as hard as I could.

The Fort had been closed so long that it was in ill repair. I could sit on my bunk and see through the wood planks all the way to the ground. It was degrading for recruits to pick up cigarette butts or anything else on the ground. We never had enough food to eat. Because of this I ate things that I had never liked before.

Inspections during the middle of the night were something that we did not look forward to. The drill sergeants came in at midnight and dumped all foot lockers. However, all foot lockers were expected to be in perfect condition when we were awakened at four-thirty to start a new day. The worst duty was working in the mess hall. It was referred to as "KP," which meant Kitchen Patrol.

It was hell, but looking back on the eight weeks of basic training, it was good for me because I suffered through it. When the eight weeks were over, I came home to be with my wife, who was the most important person in the world to me. I think, while gone, I wrote a letter to her every night and received a letter from her every day.

Some soldiers were counting the days by using a calendar, marking off each day as it went by. Soon we had been there four weeks, which seemed like a lifetime, but the end was in sight, and I was planning to go back to my wife, who was living with her mother, father, and Mark, her little brother.

After four weeks, or half way through my basic training, Jackie's mother drove her to Fort Chaffee, to see me. I can't remember a happier time in my life! My wife was there and was going to spend the night and drive back to Birmingham the next day. Seeing Jackie lifted the heavy burden of all that had happened in the first four weeks of basic training, and I knew I could endure the additional four weeks. I always had a special feeling for Jackie's mother for making this drive, which was approximately six hundred and fifty miles round trip, making it possible for me to see my wife.

When Jackie and her mother drove away, I was saddened, but I knew I could survive four additional weeks. The training was becoming easier every day because I was becoming stronger, tougher, leaner, and gaining a more positive outlook. Additionally, the drill sergeants were becoming more normal, and we spent more time in class being taught the tactics of war and battles and how to kill another person in various ways. I was already becoming brainwashed.

Finally, it was time to leave Fort Chaffee and go home for a short period of time before being assigned to one of the other Forts in the United States, or some other place in the world. In leaving Fort Chaffee, I remember how cold it was when we arrived there in January.

After getting home to Jackie's mother and father's house, I was given a thirty-day leave before reporting to Fort Hood, Texas. After reading my orders, Jackie and I looked at a map to determine where Fort Hood was located. We found that Fort Hood was adjacent to a little town, Killeen. There was another small town nearby, Belton, where a college was located. That would be good because Jackie could continue to go to college.

There was one thing I had not thought about. How was I going to get to Fort Hood, Texas? Over the next few days I found out that one of the young men in my Fort Chaffee unit was going to Texas, but to a different post. We talked by telephone and made arrangements that he would let me ride with him to Fort Hood.

I did not know quite what it would be like at Fort Hood. I quickly found out that Fort Hood was and is the largest active duty armored post in the United States, and the only post in the United States capable of supporting two full armored divisions. Fort Hood is a three hundred and forty square mile installation. The post stretches twenty- six miles from east to west and twenty-four miles from north to south. Killeen is directly adjacent to the main cantonment of Fort Hood, and as such, its economy heavily depended on the post and the soldiers and their families stationed there.

When I got there, I checked in and was directed to my unit. The assignment that I would have for that time, and hopefully for the next two years, was "Hell on Wheels," the Second Armored Division, and Battery D. It turned out that I had been assigned to a supply unit.

The first day was a disaster because I had not slept very much in the car from Birmingham to Fort Hood, Texas. We only stopped for gas. Once I arrived at my Battery, I asked a sergeant for directions. He assigned me KP, which meant kitchen work.

That night we were informed of the sleeping arrangements, how many would be in each area, and how many showers and beds there were, and we were given overall advice on what to expect. Our sleeping quarters had approximately thirty soldiers in one large open room. It was the first time in my life that I met Mexicans, colored people, and people from various parts of the United States with different accents, along with a few people from other countries that were U. S. citizens. When we were in our sleeping quarters everyone had a radio on, very loud and on different stations. It was definitely a new experience for me. Fortunately, at 10:00 p. m. the lights were out and all radios were turned off.

Within ten days, we were out in the field for three days on my first maneuver. We carried everything that was needed as if we were in battle. Our battery "D" was the second armored divisions supply unit and support for anything that fell into the supply category.

The personnel that made up our supply unit were Warren Officer Robinson, Master Sergeant Vevercica, Staff Sergeant Morgan, and me. These three men treated me as a son. They helped me in any way they could, giving me advice and directions when needed. We worked together as a unit. When I first joined the unit, I did the duties of a clerk, typing, filing, and placing orders to replenish the par inventory. It was so easy that I was surprised until we went out on maneuvers for several days or a week. That was difficult, with very hot weather, bug bites, hard work, and never enough food. Sometimes some of us went through the chow line twice if nobody noticed.

After I had been at Fort Hood for approximately one month, Jackie came out to live with me off-post. I notified my commanding officer that I was moving from the barracks to Belton to live in an apartment with my wife. We rented a small apartment, which was really part of an old house. The weather was extremely hot. I remember that Jackie said the sidewalks were hot enough to fry an egg on. We did not have an air conditioner or fan. Even so, it was wonderful coming home to my wife. The only exceptions were when I had guard duty or was out in the field for a few days.

At the end of my first year, Jackie and I drove home from Belton to Birmingham and on to Falkville to visit her parents. The drive was exhausting. We did not stop other than to get gasoline, a Coke, or something to eat. We arrived in Birmingham first. My family had moved there to be closer to Edward's job at Associated Grocers. We were very tired and really did not know where my family lived. We did have an address so we finally figured it out. We were happy to see them after such a long time.

The two weeks were up, and we headed back to our little apartment in Belton, Texas. I remember while driving back we did not talk very much. I think we both were reminiscing about the past and not sure about the future. The Vietnam War was escalating; this concerned us because there were some career soldiers in our unit who had speculated that we would be sent to Vietnam because our division had tremendous firepower. I could not think of being sent to Vietnam and tried to keep it off my mind. I did not share my concern with Jackie.

When we made it back to Belton, I went back to Battery D, reported in, and continued the same job I had before I left for Alabama. Jackie went back to school at Mary Hardin-Baylor. Both of us dreamed of the day I would be discharged. We could go back to our normal lives.

I would go back to work at Associated Grocers, and Jackie would be in school again at Birmingham-Southern. That would be on January 17, 1965, if everything went as planned and the Vietnam War did not become more serious.

During our two years in the Army, Mack, Jackie's brother, while attending the University of Auburn, was in the ROTC. While driving through North Carolina, he was in a serious accident that came close to taking his life. His head had hit the top of the car, resulting in a serious head injury. During the time he was in the hospital, Jackie's mother and dad were there around the clock.

I know Jackie wanted to North Carolina to be with her family. She didn't go because I did not want her to leave me. We did not have the money for her to go, but I am sure her parents would have helped us pay for the trip to see her brother. I know she has always regretted not visiting him. I did not realize the seriousness of Mack's injuries. It was a very selfish thing for me to do.

CHAPTER TWENTY-TWO

OPERATION BIG LIFT TO GERMANY

Time was now moving on, and I was beginning to count the months to when I would be discharged from the Army, which would be on January 17, 1965, still more than a year away. Near the end of August 1963, there were rumors that the Second Armored Division would be air-lifted to Germany for a month to six weeks, conducting maneuvers. The code name was "Operation Big Lift." We did not hear much about it because it was to be a secret maneuver, but the change in planning and internal discussions let us know that something big was in the making.

Our division was notified in writing that at an unknown time, the second Armored Division, Hell on Wheels, was going to be air-lifted to Germany. Unfortunately, I was one of the soldiers named to the advanced party, which meant that we would leave a week earlier than the other troops. We were given special orientations about the necessity of an advance party. We needed to prepare for the bulk of the troops to arrive one week later. We understood, but we did not like the idea.

It was a massive undertaking to prepare for thirty-two thousand troops. Everything had to go, including all the armored vehicles, tanks, ammunition, small arms, and so forth. Everything had to be loaded on special planes to be airlifted to Germany. We were notified of when we were leaving and where to pack everything we had that was related to the military.

As we were on the buses, the soldiers who were to make the trip later were shouting out, "Don't worry, we will take care of your wives while you are gone." These comments and similar ones brought out the worst in those on our bus. There was cursing, vulgar terminology, and other comments that I'd rather not repeat or write. Some personnel on our bus shouted that they had already had affairs with the wives of those who were shouting outside our bus. As the buses were slowly moving toward the departure location, I felt as if I would never see Jackie again. She was the strength that kept me moving, and having her to come home to each night was like looking forward to our first date.

We were bused to a large aircraft hangar where we, as usual, waited and waited until we were exhausted. Finally, the announcement came that we were departing, and we were soon loading on an aircraft tanker. The plane was an old cargo plane which had no windows, and the seats were made of heavy net. They were very close because so many men had to be on the plane. Right away everyone could see and feel it was going to be a very uncomfortable eight or nine hour flight to Frankfurt, Germany.

Once in the air I tried to sleep, but this plane was not made for comfort or sleeping, so I took a nap now and then and just listened to the loudness of the plane. After nine or ten hours in flight the pilots were preparing for landing. Everyone was anxious to get off the plane, and quickly started gathering their belongings. All duffle bags had been shipped, hopefully, on the same plane. I had some concern about finding my duffle bag at approximately three in the morning. A mountain of duffle bags was lying on the ground, ready to be picked up. Fortunately, it did not take long to find my bag. I was relieved that it was not lost. I quickly opened the bag and took out one of my coats.

We were then driven to barracks, where all of us fell onto cots and slept until awakened the next morning. We were surprised because it was too easy. All we did was stay in the barracks, talk, and do some planning for the troops that were going to be there in a few days. Life was leisurely for a few days, and we hoped this was the way the four to six weeks would be. Most of the men were talking about wanting to get away from the barracks and go into town. Some mentioned they wanted to go to Paris, but the restrictions and time schedule prohibited this from happening. However, we were informed at the end of the maneuvers that we would be allowed to leave the barracks with a written pass and a time to report back. Many took advantage of this opportunity.

The maneuvers were difficult. After we left the barracks; we were in the field for three weeks. After the three weeks, we stopped at a small city that had barracks. We were able to take our first shower in three weeks. The weather was frigid. By the time I could take a shower, all the hot water was used. My only option was to take a shower in extremely cold water. But, after drying off and dressing, I felt very good. We were fortunate to sleep inside a building with bunk beds for two nights. After two days, we were back on the road slowly making our way back to Frankfurt, Germany. I rode in a supply truck that did not have a top to cover the driver and me. I got so cold that I got into my sleeping bag, and covered myself with army blankets. After a day of freezing in the front of an open truck, we arrived back to Frankfurt Germany. It was wonderful to get back, take hot showers, sleep in a warm room, and have plenty of food.

Within a week we were taking care of undone business and getting ready to pack up everything we took. We would get on the same or similar plane and fly back to Fort Hood, Texas. When the time arrived, we suffered through the flight and arrived at Fort Hood. As usual, in the military solidified the term to "hurry up and wait." Unloading the soldiers, their duffle bags, and other materials seemed to take forever, especially when one was in a hurry to see his wife after being gone five weeks.

Eventually we were off the plane, had our belongings including our duffle bags, and were walking to the aircraft hangers for debriefing and instructions. Those who lived on post went to their barracks. Those who lived off post went home.

Jackie was waiting for me at Fort Hood. We drove to Belton, where we lived. It was one of the happiest moments of my life. Being gone only for five weeks made me realize how much I loved her, needed her, and, appreciated her. I am sure being alone while I was gone, with no relatives within six hundred miles, was difficult for her. At that time Jackie was only eighteen years old.

Almost every day I thought the Vietnam conflict, as it was called, though it was quickly becoming a war regardless of what the Kennedy and Johnson administration called it. I hoped and prayed that I would reach January 17, 1965, and receive my discharge before the Vietnam military conflict became a full-fledged war. Officers and enlisted men constantly talked about the Vietnam situation, and all asked the same question: "Why are we there?"

I was scheduled to go before a panel of officers the third week of January 1964. The purpose of the meeting was a review for possible promotion. I knew that after the review I would be asked if I had considered "re-upping" as it was called when one re-enlisted. I knew there were bonuses available, and other perks such as an offer to enter college and graduate as an officer. I was considering all options: I could make the military a career and go to officer's candidate school. I could move back to Birmingham and go back to work for Associated Grocers of Alabama, or I could find another job. After weighing all the options, I knew I was not going to do anything that would keep me away from my wife.

As time moved on, I never gave up on my dream of being financially successful. What ingredients make some people monetarily successful and some not successful? At that time, I had concluded that different things worked for different people, but I was narrowing down the things it was going to take for me to receive the monetary success that I wanted. Each day I made notes of the things that I learned growing up, in school, in basic training, and now as a United States soldier. I set a personal goal that I would hone my skills before I was discharged from the Army.

Jackie and I knew we were poor financially, but we were rich in all other areas. I also knew that if I had continued in the military we would do well, but I had been thinking and planning to go back to Associated Grocers of Alabama. I had put together my plan to move through the ranks, and get to the top of the company in ten years. I was confident the plan that I had spent years on would work for me.

CHAPTER TWENTY-THREE

ASSASSINATION OF PRESIDENT JOHN F. KENNEDY

After returning from "Operation Big Lift" to Germany, our division was working to get back to normal. On November 21, 1963, all Fort Hood military personnel were notified that President John F. Kennedy was going to visit the military post on November 22, 1963. Prior to visiting Fort Hood, the President and his entourage were going to visit Dallas, Texas coupled with a large downtown parade. Visiting Fort Hood meant the two divisions had a short time to prepare for the visit and military parade. The Fort was abuzz because we knew that Fort Hood had to be in first-class condition, and everyone worked very hard to accomplish this goal with limited time. Once the goal was completed, the commander and officers signed off on the readiness for the President's visit. We spent some time practicing for the parade. The President of the United States visiting Dallas, Texas was going to be a big event, not only for Dallas but for Fort Hood.

The local, national, and international news continued to broadcast his visit to Dallas and continued to elaborate on how tight the security was and how it would be enforced by personnel from other cities. This event caused the local, regional, and international news coverage to focus on Dallas. Fort Hood was the largest military post in the United States, and it was highlighted in the news.

November 22, 1963 arrived, and the President of the United States was at the Dallas airport. Due to security measures, it would take several hours before the President's motorcade would wind down the streets in Dallas. While the President was at the Dallas airport, the thirty-two thousand troops were parading in dress uniform waiting for his arrival. Everyone looked forward to the President visiting the Fort, but hoped he would get there early in the afternoon, because everyone was fatigued.

A few hours later, a silence fell over Fort Hood as the horrendous news spread throughout the thirty-two thousand soldiers that President John F. Kennedy had been killed by as assassin's bullet as his motorcade wound its way through the crowded streets of Dallas. Everyone was stunned and in a state of disbelief. It was difficult to believe and impossible to understand that the President of the Unites States had been assassinated. Everyone was hurting, with a silence that spoke louder than words. Everyone in my unit was devastated by the President's death. Some people were asking what was going to happen next. This was a time that brought the nation together regardless of whether you liked or disliked President Kennedy. A sergeant in our unit made the statement, "It really did rain on our parade today."

President Kennedy was sworn into office on January 20, 1962, and he was assassinated on November 22, 1963. He was born on May 29, 1917, in Brookline, Massachusetts. President Kennedy was the youngest man to be elected President; he was also the youngest to die in office.

In a speech slated for November 22, 1963, President Kennedy planned to tout the successful airlift to Germany. He wanted to state that the nation was "prepared as never before to move substantial numbers of men and equipment in surprisingly little time to advanced position anywhere in the world." The address, however, was never given. However, Operation Big Lift to Germany demonstrated the capacity, strength, and resolve that helped the United States and our NATO Allies eventually win the Cold War.

Fort Hood was unofficially closed. I went home for several days. The on-post personnel just stayed in their barracks. The news reflected that the country was in shock. The conspiracy theorists and the President's assassination dominated the news.

The same day that President Kennedy was assassinated, Vice President Lyndon B. Johnson was sworn in as President of the United States on Air Force One as he flew back to Washington. Lyndon Johnson became the thirty-sixth President of the United States. Spiro Agnew was named Vice President. At the time, most people did not know who Spiro Agnew was and did not care.

Lee Harvey Oswald, the assassin, was charged with the crime, but he was killed two days later by Jack Leon Ruby. It seemed there was more to the overall situation than the American people knew. This caused more shock, panic, and concern about what was happening in the United States. The conspiracy theorists kept the Mafia, Cuban retaliation, and a certain member of labor unions as possible suspects in the assassination of President Kennedy.

After approximately one week, Fort Hood was functioning again, but with a cloud of uncertainty hanging over it and the personnel. I found that staying busy was the best thing I could do to keep the President's assassination off my mind. Everyone was attuned to what had happened and was braced for something worse to happen, just as the nation was waiting for something else to fall. Many soldiers were deeply concerned about what kind of a President Lyndon Johnson would be. Everyone was aware of the situation going on in Vietnam. Everyone was also aware that Lyndon Johnson supported the involvement of the United States in Vietnam and was noticeably concerned. Most soldiers thought President Johnson would escalate the United States' involvement in the Vietnam conflict.

President Johnson settled into the White House and outlined everything he intended to accomplish, including the priorities of President Kennedy. President Johnson's theme for his administration was "The Great Society." The conspiracy theories continued and linger in many people's minds today. The country was in turmoil, with other harsh revelations on the horizon.

CHAPTER TWENTY-FOUR

PLANNING FOR THE FUTURE

The New Year arrived: 1964. For the first time, I started thinking that in one year and two weeks I would be discharged from the army and would be going back to Birmingham. The army and my superiors were working on me pretty hard to stay in the military. I had received several promotions and was a couple of months away from being promoted again, which was highly unusual for someone who was in the army a little more than one year.

It had only been thirty-nine days since the assassination of President John F. Kennedy. This lingered in my mind and continued to leave negative images and thoughts of the president's death but also of the military. The question of making the military my career became more dismal.

The third week in January, I went before a panel of officer who asked me about Operation Big Lift and my evaluation of the exercise. I was asked about the Kennedy assassination and how it affected me and the troops. Then there were general question about current events. The last question was whether I had considered re-upping, which meant that at the end of my two years, I would continue in the Army for an additional three years or more. I stated that I had given this some though but needed additional time to think it over and discuss it with my wife. At the end of the meeting, one of the officers presented me with staff sergeant stripes and asked me to have them sewn on all my uniforms. I reflected my appreciation and left.

I was learning, gaining additional knowledge and experience that, at some point, I would use to define and refine my formula for success. I had learned so much at Associated Grocers of Alabama, and now in the army, and in the three years of army reserve obligation when discharged. Associated Grocers of Alabama, the only company I had worked, was run autocratically. I did not like that management style, and I kept thinking about different management styles that should work better. The army was also run autocratically, so I really did not have a model to look at or examine. But I knew I would figure out the answers once I was out of the army.

In September of 1964, I was called before a panel of officers and questioned about the military and current events, and asked questions on how certain military operations should be handled. Near the end of the session, I was asked to give an overview of what I thought of military life. I summarized my answer to this question, and one of the officers made some remarks about the rewards of a military career. Again, I was asked about re-enlisting or re-upping in the Army. Again I told them I was giving serious thought and would make a decision in December of 1964.

As I drove home to Belton, I was formulating again and again the ingredients that I must have to achieve the success I wanted. Becoming a Staff Sergeant gave me additional confidence. I had figured that in the Army I could move past ninety-five percent of the enlisted men rapidly. I realized that about four or five percent of the enlisted men had the drive, ambition, work ethic, and passion to achieve, but I was thinking I had an additional ingredient that few, if any of them, possessed.

Each time I received a promotion I told Jackie about it. Then we both asked the question, "Does it mean any more money?" It did, but I couldn't remember how much it would increase my small monthly check. This was important because we left for the army with one thousand dollars. We had saved and still had it, but could not add to the amount because it took every cent we received from the military to barely live. We went to the commissary a couple of times each month and purchased the things that would last us approximately two weeks. We would go back a second time to purchase our needs for the balance of the month. After paying for rent, utilities, gasoline for the car, insurance on the car, and food, we did not have a cent left over. My clothes were furnished by the army, and Jackie did not purchase anything. We lived frugally and sometimes it was hard, but overall we were happy. Our rent was $35.00 per month and gas was $.18 per gallon. I don't remember Jackie purchasing any clothes during the two years we were in the military. We were poor, but managed to pay our way without incurring any debt. Our favorite song was "Our Day Will Come."

We went to church, to Belton Lake, and into stores, and we watched three channels of television, and that was our recreation. But most importantly, we had each other. We had some involvement with a couple of military men and their wives, but we did not join the military activities.

We lived in three different small apartments in Belton, but the last one was the best. It was upstairs over another apartment, but it was within one or two blocks of Mary Harden-Baylor College. Jackie could walk to school and come home at lunch if she chose to do so. The shower was so small that I had to stand side–ways to fit into it and have room to take a shower. I was in top physical condition and weighed one hundred sixty-eight pounds. The apartment was small, but we loved it. Belton was a small town with a lot of western flair that was visible by the clothing men and women wore: cowboy hats, western jeans, and boots. There was also horseback riding and parades on Saturdays. It was an ideal little town to live in, and we were beginning to like it.

CHAPTER TWENTYFIVE

DEPARTING THE U. S. ARMY

During the ten days prior to January 16, 1965, I spent a substantial amount of time considering a military career. The important question I had concerned the negative aspects of a military career. As I was considering a military career, I was also thinking about moving back to Birmingham. At that time, I was not sure I could go back to Associated Grocers of Alabama. But within a couple of days, I found out that the company where I had previously worked was obligated under law to take me back and give me the same position or a comparable one. But I was not sure I wanted to go back to work for Associated Grocers of Alabama.

I knew the military had brainwashed me, because, almost twenty-four months earlier, I was boarding a train to Fort Chaffee, Arkansas, for basic training. This was the most painful thing that I had faced to date. I hated the thought of leaving my wife, leaving my job, being away from my family, and losing two years of my life, when I wanted to move up the latter of success. It was amazing, reflecting on the slow train from Birmingham to Fort Chaffee. Now, I was seriously considering staying in the army for twenty years or more. It was phenomenal how two years in the United States had changed my initial outlook.

On January 12, 1965, I had considered all the options. I could move back to Birmingham and go back to work for Associated Grocers of Alabama. There I could continue my plan to work from the bottom the company to the top. Or I could move back to Birmingham and find another job and seek success there. I could go to college and work part-time, or I could stay in the military and make it my career. I decided to move back to Birmingham and go back to work for Associated of Alabama. The decision was easy, because I knew that I was never going to make any decision that would keep me away from my wife.

After my decision was made, I started packing all my belongings and going through the process of departing from the Army on the morning of January 16, 1965. As I looked at the office where I had spent almost two years and talked to the three soldiers who were my superiors, I had a deep feeling of sadness. After doing this, I got in my car and drove to Belton, where Jackie was waiting for me. Prior to loading our car, we went to the bank and withdrew one thousand dollars, the same amount we had when I was drafted into the Army.

Everything we owned was packed in our 1958 Pontiac. We had developed a special fondness for Belton. I am sure Jackie had enjoyed attending Mary Hardin-Baylor College. Both of us had ambivalent feelings as we were driving away from the little town of Belton, where we had lived for almost twenty-two months. I felt sad that we would never return; and we haven't yet. Leaving the Army and Belton, Texas was bittersweet, but we felt it was the right choice for us.

We drove to Birmingham without stopping, other than to purchase gasoline, eat and drink something, and make a few restroom stops.

While Jackie and I were driving from Belton, Texas to Birmingham, Alabama, I had ample time to reflect on my life and analyze some of the good, bad, and ugly decisions I had made. I focused on several major issues. What are the psychological effects on generational or culture poverty? I had been there, lived it, and felt it, and was a long way from breaking these debilitating circumstances.

In analyzing the effects, I knew poverty crushes the spirit. Poor people feel powerless to change their circumstances. Failure to improve is often because they do not have the tools to succeed financially. It is thought that generational poverty is the worst if one lives in a country surrounded by images of success. These images crush the spirit. After spending two years at the lowest level at Associated Grocers of Alabama and two years in the United States Army, I knew education was the usual way out of poverty. In order to move out of poverty, one has to leave that broken spirit behind. If one brings that broken spirit along, he is likely to be less successful that those who were somehow shielded from the spirit-crushing nature of abject poverty.

I had spent most of my live formulating my plan to be the first in my family to break down the wall of generational poverty. My spirit was maybe wounded, but never crushed. I was ready to tackle anything that would move me toward my goal. That goal was to use my formula and move to the top of Associated in ten years or less. I was willing to pay any price to reach my goal.

CHAPTER TWENTY-SIX

RETURNING TO ASSOCIATED GROCERS & CONFLICT

Once in Birmingham, we were exhausted, and we slept until rested. We visited our parents and spent some time with them prior to looking for an apartment near Birmingham-Southern College. Jackie only had one more year of college.

We moved across the street from Birmingham-Southern College into an apartment complex, which made it easy for Jackie to walk across the street to school. It was a very simple apartment. We were so excited when we were able to go to Sears and Roebuck to buy our first furniture. Jackie often spoke of how wonderful it was when we were finally able to buy a washing machine.

I went back to work at Associated Grocers of Alabama. It was still located in the Birmingham Food Terminal, which was only two miles from our new apartment. I went back to the same job I had when I was drafted into the military two years earlier. I was disappointed to return to the same job, because during the two years some personnel had been promoted to better positions while I was serving my country.

However, after approximately two months, Mr. R. C. Riley, who was a Vice President of the company, asked me to come to his office. Even though I did not know why I was there, Mr. Riley made me feel comfortable. There was some talk about my military experience and other mundane matters. Then he asked me would like to move into the office to handle the company's accounts receivable. I had no idea of what the job entailed but I quickly said "Yes." He explained what was involved in handling this position and that he would personally help me for a few days. He then handed me a job description. I thanked him and left his office very happy, because I knew this was my first step toward the top of the company. At the end of the day, I went home to tell Jackie the good news. However, I did not tell her of my ambition to move to the top of the company within ten years. If I had told her, it would have seemed like an impossible dream.

While I was working hard at Associated Grocers, Jackie attended Birmingham-Southern College and was going to graduate within a couple of months. In the fall of 1965, she graduated and took a high school teaching position at Tarrant High School. This prompted us to think about moving closer to Jackie's place of employment. Because Jackie was close to her Uncle John Freeman and his wife Aileen, who lived in Center Point, we rented a house on Birchwood Street in Center Point.

During this time, Associated Grocers of Alabama had moved from its Finley Avenue location into its new two hundred and fifty square foot warehouse on Vanderbilt in Tarrant, Alabama. The move to Center Point made the travel to work closer for both of us.

As this was happening, Mr. Riley asked me to come to his office. I had been handling accounts receivable for approximately nine months. As I entered his office, he looked at me and asked me if would like to move into the buying department. I was silently overcome with joy and told Mr. Riley that I had been waiting for this opportunity.

In a week, I moved down the hall to where all the buyers were located. I had a larger office with secretarial help and was enthusiastic to get into the job. There were eight buyers; in addition, Mr. Mobley, Mr. Riley and Mr. Helms purchased. I was assigned a segment of the grocery department buying. However, this was another step toward the top. As I immersed myself into the buying of the three thousand items assigned, I began to think of buying for each department and eventually supervising all buyers.

After renting the house on Birchwood Street in Center Point, we purchased a house that was less than one year old at a good price. The house was located in a subdivision off Carson Road. The house was perfect for us, and we were very proud of it. We had to purchase some additional furniture to keep the house from looking empty. It was on a corner lot with a beautiful lawn. At this time, Jackie started to teach at Erwin High School because it was closer to where we lived.

After three years, we decided to sell the house we loved and purchase a larger on Tyler Road in Vestavia, Alabama. We were fortunate to sell the Center Point house for twice the amount we paid for it. The new house in Vestavia was exactly what we wanted.

During this time, I was moving up at Associated Grocers and keeping my formula on my mind every day. At this time I had moved into buying for other departments and was spending some time in the meat and produce department. Every day I was looking for an opportunity to move up another notch.

Jackie took a teaching position at Pizitz Middle school, and she taught there for half of one year before resigning because she was pregnant with our first child. At that time, once a woman was noticeably pregnant, she had to discontinue teaching until after the birth. On February 13, 1970, our first daughter, Kimberly Jacqueline Nuby, was born. I just could not believe we were parents and had a little baby girl. I remember standing outside the window where I could see all the newborn babies, but I saw only one baby, "my baby." This was a life-changing event for me! Then, on May 20, 1971, our second daughter was born. She was named Leslie Paige Nuby and, again, I looked through the glass where all the newborns were, but I could only see, "my baby," Leslie. Having children was a traumatic change in our lives, because we were married ten years before our first baby was born. I quickly realized that all the attention from Jackie was now shared with two babies. It was a change and I had difficulty adjusting.

As all this was happening, I continued working at Associated Grocers of Alabama. I had my formula in place, and it was working well. During this time, I had moved through the ranks. I moved through the ranks of the buying positions and soon became the head buyer for Associated Grocers. This made me the fourth or fifth person in line for the top position. I could sense that I was resented by some people in the warehouse, in the buying department, and on the level above me. I was fully aware of this every day and handled it in a harsh manner. The resentment did not go away, but it went underground. It was known that I would have issues with any person who criticized anything I was doing.

Mr. Mobley, President and General Manager of the company, liked me, and he often talked to me in his office, which to me was a wonderful thing for him to do. He was a mentor and inspired me to move through the ranks of the company as fast as possible. He did many things to help me in addition to sponsoring me to join the Masonic Lodge, in Woodlawn. He suggested that I should get involved in activities outside the company. I became a Rotarian and was one of the founders of the Oxmoor Rotary Club. Mr. Mobley was truly a good man who had been a grocery retailer, a motivational speaker, a Christian, and a compassionate man. He had spent many years leading Associated Grocers through many changes, including relocating into a new warehouse.

In 1968, Mr. Dave Mobley, who had been President and General Manager for years, retired from the company. Mr. Grant Myers served as interim President and General Manager. He could have taken the position of President and General Manager if he had chosen to. He had that much support from the board of directors. However, Mr. Myers knew the difficulties the person in that position could potentially face. After a few weeks, he declined the offer because he had a number of convenience stores he wanted to expand. It was probably one of the best moves he could have made.

In 1968, Mr. George Little became President and General Manager of the company. He had the ability to motivate those around him to do their very best. He was "a mover and a shaker" and initiated tremendous changes in the company. Among these innovations was retaining an industrial psychologist, which would play a great role in selecting and evaluating the personnel of the company. Initially, Dr. James Tanner gave a battery of tests to those considered in "top management" positions. I was one of the lucky few selected. At the time, I did not realize that the results of the interview and testing would have such a positive impact on my future.

A schedule was given to each person outlining the time and place to meet Dr. Tanner. Once my day arrived, I drove to Dr. Tanner's office and met with him for the first time. He gave me an overview of what the schedule would be for the next four hours. I was surprised that I would be with him for four hours. For the first time, I felt concerned.

He spent the first hour and half conversing with me, occasionally interjecting questions. He asked me about my childhood, schooling, and family. I explained to him what it was like growing up in poverty, and I told him about the murder of my biological father. He also asked about my immediate family. He wanted to know if I was married and had children, and what my relationship with them was like.

However, the majority of the questions were about how I saw myself, my ambitions, and my goals, my current position in the company, my salary, where I planned to be in five years, and how much money I planned to make at that time. He asked how I evaluated the company and its management and top personnel. He asked if I had the ability to handle tough situations. He inquired about what I knew about the board of directors of the company and its functions. Then he went on to ask me if I could handle the diversified group of retailers.

Once the questioning was over, I was escorted to a small room with a table and chair. Over the next one and half hours I took a battery of tests including an intelligence quotient (IQ) test, an aptitude test, Myers-Briggs Type Indicator, and the Rorschach, or ink blot, test. After taking all the tests, Dr. Tanner spent thirty minutes talking with me. He assured me that I had performed excellently during the discussions and testing. He stated that once he had evaluated the tests, he would prepare a formal report for the company and me. He also said he would discuss the report in detail with me.

In a few days, Dr. Tanner come to my office and went over my report in detail. I was very happy with the report, and I asked Dr. Tanner if I could ask him some questions that were pertinent to my improvement. He said he would be happy to answer any questions, yet he seemed surprised. He stated that he rarely had someone ask how they could improve personally and in their job performance. He said most people cannot accept the truth because it is often considered criticism.

I often think of the movie, *"A Few Good Men"* when I remember how I asked him to offer suggestions. He looked at me and asked, "Do you think you can handle the truth?" I looked at him dead in his eyes and said, "Dr. Tanner, I can handle the truth. I welcome anything you can tell me that will help me become a better employee." I wanted to be the best I could in every way possible. I trusted Dr. Tanner to advise me. He began by giving me the "hard truth" and some things I must do to fulfill my goals at Associated Grocers. I wanted to be at the "top," regardless of what it took. I will admit that some of the things he suggested stung and hit some sensitive nerves. However, I wrote down everything he suggested and immediately started making the changes he deemed necessary for me to achieve my goal.

Within a short time, I had changed most of the things he suggested, and I was working on the others. Dr. Tanner was on a retainer, and he paid a visit to the company once each month. After two months, he was surprised to find that I had substantially made all the personal improvements he suggested. Dr. Tanner became my mentor and continued to give me advice and direction. I was able to confide in him and receive feedback on my concerns and problems. He guided me through several situations and helped me for many years. Later, he was the person who guided me to Pasquale Food Company, Inc.

In addition to retaining an industrial psychologist, Dr. Tanner, things at Associated Grocers were changing quickly. George Little was responsible for starting Key Insurance Agency, managed by R.C. Britt, which offered all insurance coverage to retailers, employees, and anyone else that needed insurance. He also spearheaded the opening of Images, Inc., an advertising agency and printing shop. He acquired Associated of Chattanooga, Tennessee, and Bama Brokerage Company. He spearheaded a construction company, purchased half of WAQY radio station, an institutional sales division, and a few other companies. This was exciting, yet perplexing because it took personnel to run these entities. Many employees were hired to run each entity. It was difficult or impossible for these new entities to become profitable. Generally speaking, most of the new companies eroded the base of the parent company.

George always had some plan in the works. One day he called Phillip Watts, John Sanford, and me into his office. He had come up with a plan for us to present our wives with mink stoles (of course paid for by the company). He asked us to bring our spouses to his house for dinner on the following Friday night. His plan was for us to give our wives mink stoles as if we had bought them. However, our wives knew that none of us could afford to buy a mink stole, but we played along with the plan. George was happy about the show we all put on.

One day George asked me if I belonged to the Vestavia Country Club and, of course, I said, "no." He made a call to A.J. Virciglio while I was in his office. After that conversation, he handed me two thousand dollars for the fee to join the club. He asked me to go over to Vestavia Country Club, fill out the application, and pay the two thousand dollars for the initiation fee. Within a week I was notified by letter that the board of directors had accepted me as a new member of the club. At the time, the monthly dues were $30.00 per month.

Joining this club, thanks to George, my family experienced a lot of happy days enjoying the various activities that the Vestavia Country Club offered. We continued to be members until 1999, at which time we rarely went to the club and our children were in or out of college and did not use the facilities. At that time I wrote a letter reflecting appreciation for being a member for thirty-one years and the enjoyment the club had given our family.

CONFLICT BEGINS

In March of 1972, the tension between George and most of the board of directors became strained. George had been in the top position for four years. That could be considered a long tenure in the cooperative food business, which was owned by the members. George was on vacation at a lake house when Mr. Heard called me, and asked me to meet him at Central Bank. He asked me to bring the company's accounts receivable, accounts payable, income statement, balance sheet, and cash flow statement. Once I had gathered the information, I called Mr. Heard at his office and told him I would meet him at Central Bank at 2:00.

When I arrived at the bank, I was escorted to Mr. Lloyd Rains' office; Mr. Rains was the president of the bank. Mr. Harry Brock, who was CEO and chairman of the board, was also in attendance. I gave Mr. Heard the documents. He opened the large package and took a few minutes to look over them. Once he finished, Mr. Rains brought up the bank loan pertaining to Associated Grocers. He referred to the amount of the loan and the board of directors' concern about the manner in which Associated Grocers was being operated under the leadership of George Little. He made it clear that his remarks were no reflection on me personally. I could sense there was a serious problem between the bank and Associated Grocers of Alabama.

When Mr. Heard spoke, I knew he had met with the bank personnel and that a decision had already been made. Mr. Rains, Mr. Brock, and Mr. Heard indicated that the company had written checks that the bank had no deposits to cover. As a consequence, Mr. Brock, Mr. Rains and Mr. Heard asked me to find another bank as soon as possible. This was shocking because George was not present and the burden of finding another bank was a challenging situation for me to encounter.

I left the meeting, went back to my office, and closed and locked the door. I called George and gave him an overview of exactly what had happened. He did not respond as I thought he would. Instead, he told me he would call Mr. Heard and take care of the situation.

Later that day I received another call from Mr. Heard informing me that George would not be coming back to Associated Grocers. As I listened, I had a sick feeling in the pit of my stomach. It was a difficult decision for me, but I felt I should call George again and tell him everything I knew, including about the recent conversation with Mr. Heard. When George answered, as calmly as I could, I related my conversation with Mr. Heard. Mr. Heard had emphatically made the statement that George was not coming back to the company. From George's response, I could detect his feelings of frustration and anger. He told me that he was going to make some calls and would call me back.

After a few hours, he called back. From the tone of his voice, I could tell that this was not going to be a pleasant conversation. George had apparently made some calls and did not receive the responses he had anticipated. It was clear that he was extremely angry. He made some very harsh statements about Mr. Heard and the board of directors. He went on to tell me all of the things he had done for me, personally, for the other employees, and for the company, as a whole. He said he was coming back to the company to terminate everyone he had helped.

I did not understand what he was talking about as far as the employees. I did understand that he and the board were at odds concerning several issues, because I attended the board meetings. His conversation left me stunned. I quickly surmised that George thought that we all were part of a conspiracy to have him terminated. Of course, this was not the case. All of the employees liked George and had admiration for him.

This situation was definitely getting out of hand. However, because Mr. Heard called me to gather certain documents and meet him at Central Bank, I had an obligation to keep George informed. Later in the day, I felt compelled to call Mr. Heard again to relate the harsh conversation I had with George. He assured me once more that George was not coming back to the company. None of the employees would be affected. He asked me to take control of the company until he and the board could meet. I did as Mr. Heard had asked me, without letting the other employees knowing what had transpired. I only depended on Bill Pore, the company's financial officer, to assist me in this situation.

Mrs. Gordon, George's secretary, knew what was going on. The concern and shock were reflected in her eyes. I knew that I had to talk to her as little as possible because she was very close to George. Anything said would be relayed to George in a matter of moments. I felt that I was caught between George, who had been very good to me, and the board of directors. I wanted to do the right thing, but everything was happening so fast that it was difficult to keep my sanity.

George did not come back to the company. I never really knew all the details. I did know that most of the board members did not agree with the way George had been running the company. Some thought he was deceptive as well as too close to Mr. Heard. This was not actually the case, because all of George's initiatives had been approved by the board of directors.

One might assume that George Little's involvement with the company was over, but it was not. He caused further dissension by calling and visiting members who were not on the board of directors. I received calls from dozens of these people. However, I did not want to talk or meet with them. I wanted to stay out of the situation as much as possible.

CHANGES TO COME

In approximately one week, the board of directors named me as President and General Manager. It was an unusual feeling to take the office that Mr. Dave Mobley, Grant Meyers, and George Little had occupied. It was a large office with furniture, a bathroom, sitting room, and a small office adjacent for the secretary to work. It was overwhelming and humbling to sit in that office, because I had spent most of my life getting there.

I had spent thousands of hours from the age of six until age thirty-four trying as hard as I could to achieve monetary success. It almost brought tears to my eyes to reflect on what it took to sit in that office. As I closed my door, I kept thinking, "It's a long way from unloading box cars to this office." It was possibly the first time that I silently said, "Thank you, God, for seeing me through poverty, the Army, and the various levels within the company to reach this point." I asked God to forgive me of my sometimes brutal, hurtful, and offensive behavior toward many employees, suppliers, board members, and other members of the cooperative. My formula had worked for me, but others around me had suffered because of my actions. I had my plan in place, and there was no stopping me from achieving success. But now, I wonder at what cost this success had been.

After becoming President and General Manager, there were several articles about me in supermarket publications and in the local newspapers. I must say it felt very good to read these articles. I still have a file containing articles and letters from Dave Mobley, R.C. Riley, Frank Helms, and many other people congratulating me on achieving the new position. The article that I liked best was in Supermarket News. It reflected my promotion and gave information about Associated Grocers of Alabama, and said that at thirty-four, I was the youngest president and general manager in the cooperative food industry. I received a great deal of recognition locally, regionally, and internationally. It often was awkward, embarrassing, and humbling to talk about my success with those in which I interacted.

DR. JAMES TANNER

I chose to keep Dr. Tanner as a consultant. He continued to spend a day each month at Associated Grocers. During that time, I sought advice from Dr. James Tanner often. On his one-day visit to the company, he observed various departments and talked with supervisors and employees. He would report back to me with an update on the happenings of the company. Although he did not point anyone out in particular, this information gave me the ability to zero in on problems or potential problems.

I told Dr. Tanner about all of the things that bothered me about Associated Grocers. I had concerns because Associated Grocers of Alabama was a member-owned warehouse. Warehouses such as this offered an unstable future. The makeup of the board of directors was not of the highest caliber. Most had little or no knowledge concerning the duties of a board of directors. The only expertise they had was in managing small, independent grocery stores.

It was very difficult for board members to give any meaningful input as far as business planning, contingency planning, capital improvements, cash flow, and long-range planning. Out of fifteen board members, there may have been three that were truly qualified to sit on the board. Most of the board meetings focused on trivial things. They were concerned that the warehouse was discriminating in the pricing formula. They grumbled over shortages in products. There were also highly concerned about the prices at Food World, a new chain. They also questioned the honesty of the warehouse management, staff, and employees. I often wondered if those obsessed with questioning the honesty of others were usually dishonest themselves.

Board meeting were like a zoo, starting at 7:00 p.m. on the first Tuesday night of each month and sometimes lasting until after midnight, with little or nothing accomplished. The only good thing that came from these meeting was the delicious apple pies furnished by Mr. Charlie Larocca, who was a board member.

Dr. James Tanner had been around long enough to know that my concerns were on target. He and I talked about the necessity that I have more security than Associated Grocers could offer. When I was at the very bottom of the company, the top looked easy. It appeared as if I could spend all my time devoted to the running of the business. But once I was at the top, it was a very different ball game. At least fifty percent of my time was spent dealing with the politics of the groups and independents. I considered this wasted time.

Mr. Inos Heard was chairman of the Board of Directors of the company. Most board members detested Mr. Heard because he co-owned, with Mr. A. J. Virciglio, fifteen Western Supermarkets, and was the largest customer of Associated Grocers. Additionally, Mr. Heard was a strong, outspoken leader who was dealing with a group of neophytes. It was obvious that the lack of intellect and business common sense represented on the board irritated him. I often asked how these people got on the board of directors of a sixty-eight million dollar company when most were uneducated in business and lost in the board's function.

However, when I became president and general manager, I was determined to succeed. I started gathering all reports pertinent to the operation of the company. Reviewing these reports kept me up-to-date on sales, gross profit, items marked out to our customers, delivery cost, analyzing the size of each order, the number of personnel, and the labor cost per shift and sales. Additionally, each department was measured against a budget. In the meat department, shrinkage was measured due to bone dust, seepage of moisture, and the fact that the fat content was trimmed.

The dollar amount of damaged product that occurred during the night shift was astounding. The product could be repacked and sold to retail outlets that specialized in purchasing damaged product. However, this had not been happening. Someone had been selling the damaged goods to an independent retailer and pocketing the money.

The first stockholder meeting was scheduled in May of 1972. I spent a tremendous amount of time preparing for every phase of this meeting. The meeting went fine, and the company was starting a new year, one which would bring dramatic changes.

Mr. Heard and I, with the board's blessing, drove to Montgomery to meet with Billy Graden, who ran Bama Brokerage Company. After some discussion, we gave Bama Brokerage to Mr. Graden. There was really no benefit in keeping it.

We dismantled the construction company, which was a tremendous cost to the company. We eliminated the fifty percent of ownership in WAQY radio station and Images, Inc., an in house advertising agency. Neither company had any possibility of making any profit. Key Insurance Agency was doing well, so it was left in place. Other entities that were draining money from the parent company were also dismantled.

Associated Grocers of Chattanooga, Tennessee was more complicated to phase out. Howard Noble and I decided to take a small aircraft, owned by Associated Grocers, to assess what might be done to get the inventories of both companies sorted. The inventories of both companies had been combined. We met with Jack Holloway, the general manager of Associated Grocers of Chattanooga to discuss the details.

On the way back from Chattanooga, the weather became turbulent. Even though the aircraft was piloted by Ray Chaney, an experienced pilot, we all grew more alarmed when the light aircraft began to struggle.

The plane was dropping as the turbulence took its toll. The plane rocked and bumped constantly. Lightening was hitting and bouncing off the plane. I thought the end of my life was close at hand. I made up my mind that if it was time to go, I was ready to die. Meanwhile, Howard Noble held tightly to the arm rest and prayed. I truly believe that our pilot, Ray Chaney, was preparing himself for a crash, which would be our demise. However, we were able to fly on and into the Birmingham airport. I still believe that it was because of the grace of God that we were spared.

John Burns, who headed up the company's meat department, and I continued to meet at the King's Inn in Homewood for breakfast with Mr. Heard, Mr. A. J. Virciglio, and Ron Richards to write the Western Supermarkets ads. The ads were usually written thirteen weeks in advance, giving Associated Grocers buyers time to purchase the product and have inventory in house to cover the ads. All other groups gave the company a copy of their ads.

GEORGE'S CONTINUED INVOLVEMENT

While at Associated Grocers, George started an SBIC, a company designed to make loans to small businesses. George wanted to purchase the small company from Associated Grocers. After evaluating it, the board of directors decided to just give it to him. He opened up an office in the Bank for Savings building which was located in downtown Birmingham. The mission of the small business investment company (SBIC) program was to improve and stimulate the national economy and small businesses by supplementing the flow of private equity capital and long term loan funds for the sound financing, growth, expansion and modernizing of small business operations. This would tend to maximize participation of private financing sources.

After a few weeks, George called me and stated that he could borrow ten thousand dollars from Monty Adams, the president of C. F. Sauer Company. George was close to Monty and several of the top people at this company. He explained that he needed my help in accomplishing his goal. It would not obligate me in any way or cost me anything.

George told me that Monty Adams would make a ten thousand dollar loan to him if he would sign a promissory note. However, in order to satisfy his board of directors at C.F Sauer, the check for ten thousand dollars needed to be made out to me. This was because Associated Grocers purchased product from C. F. Sauer, and it would not be questioned by his board if done in this manner.

I gave this request serious thought before making a decision. But because George had been very good to me and had helped me many times, I felt I should do this in order to assist him. So I called Monty Adams and told him it would be fine if he sent the check to me after George signed the promissory note. Once the note was signed and returned to C. F. Sauer, the check would be made out to me and I would endorse it, and deliver the check to George. Monty assured me that I had no liability in this matter and both of us were doing this to only help George.

The promissory note came, and I took it down to George's office for him to sign. I kept a copy and mailed the originals to Monty Adams. In less than a week, I received a ten thousand dollar check made out to me, which I endorsed and delivered to George at his office in the Bank for Savings building.

GEORGE & LONE STAR INSURANCE

During this time, George called and asked if I would fly to Dallas, Texas to meet with the Lone Star insurance company executives. I already knew the personnel there because they had conducted business with Associated Grocers through Key Insurance Agency. I talked it over with R.C. Britt; he advised that he had discontinued doing business with Lone Star because of what he called "unethical business transactions."

However, George insisted that I go to Dallas, Texas to meet with him to discuss some business matters. We met at an elaborate hotel and had dinner in a room that was nicer and more elegant than any place I had ever been. Lone Star was holding a big party in honor of my presence. There was dinner, alcoholic drinks, dancing, and fine foods. Moreover, the room was filled with beautiful women.

It only took a few minutes to decipher the reason for this overwhelming gathering. The purpose was to make sure there was enough wine, beer, or hard liquor to make me intoxicated, or at least tipsy. That would be enough to get me involved with one of the women and perhaps wind up in her room. George's plan was to "have something on me" so that I would be obligated to do business with Lone Star Insurance Company. I did not realize it at the time, but George was already a part of the Lone Star Insurance Company.

I did not get tipsy or intoxicated and did not end up with one of the women. This was truly a setup. Even after George and the top people at Lone Star knew the setup had failed, George was not discouraged. He tried to get me to have drinks in another part of the hotel with one of the secretaries. I used the old slogan, "I am too exhausted and need to go to my room to sleep." The next day I caught a flight back to Birmingham early in the morning and went to work.

The pressure to use Lone Star Insurance Company through Key Insurance Company did not stop with my trip to Dallas. George continued to call me. He tried to make me feel guilty because while at Associated Grocers, as President and General Manager, he helped me by increasing my salary and promoting me, and he had made several perks available. This was all true, but I could not defy the wishes of R.C. Britt, the President of Key Insurance Agency and the board of directors, who did not want to do business with Lone Star Insurance Company. After four or five weeks I had to tell George that the company was not going to do business with Lone Star. This angered him tremendously.

THE LAWSUIT

After several years, I found that George Little was not out of my life. I received a certified letter from C.F. Sauer naming me as a third party in a lawsuit pertaining to a ten thousand dollar loan going back a few years. The principal, interest, and attorney fees had increased the initial ten thousand dollars to almost thirty thousand dollars. I immediately called George, whose office was in the old Fine Arts Building downtown. Mrs. Gordon answered the telephone. I asked if I could speak to George. She explained that George was out of town in Dallas, where he was spending most of his time. I asked her if she was aware of a lawsuit from C.F. Sauer and a ten thousand dollar loan George had received several years ago from Monty Adams. She acknowledged that the lawsuit had been received, but said that nothing had been done about it yet.

I was overheated with anger. I asked Mrs. Gordon how in the world I could be named as a third party to this case. Obviously, she did not know, and she said she would have George call me when he was back in town. I did not wait for George to call because I did not think he would. He never called, so I obtained an attorney, Dale Corley, and asked him to handle the case. It dragged on for months, but finally, after spending more than one thousand five hundred dollars, I was dropped from the case. This situation really hurt me and further tarnished my feelings toward George.

CHAPTER TWENTY-SEVEN

LEAVING ASSOCIATED GROCERS
JOINING PASQUALE FOOD COMPANY

In mid-July of 1973, the board members, their wives, and Jackie and I went to Las Vegas for four days and nights. Each year there was a convention which all of Associated Grocers and Affiliated Foods attended. The convention featured industry leaders who indicated how the industry was changing, motivational speakers, what was new in the industry, and some entertainment. There were a total of thirty-two people making this trip. It was like most seminars, a vacation for those on the Board who had at least given their time, discounting their value to the company. I don't remember any board member other than Inos Heard discussing anything learned at the Las Vegas Convention.

Mr. Frank Schifano, a board member, and his wife invited Jackie and me to stay with them in Las Vegas because they had a large suite there. The nights were miserable because Frank had emphysema and had extreme difficulty in breathing, but it was very nice of Mr. and Mrs. Schifano to ask us to stay in their suite. The suite was very nice with several large rooms, a hot tub, a fireplace, and many other amenities. I will always remember Mr. Schifano and his wife for treating Jackie and me as their guests. But I could hardly wait to get back to Birmingham to work.

After returning from the Las Vegas convention, I had a visit from Dr. James Tanner. He had learned of a company located in New Orleans that was searching for a President and CEO. The name of the company was Consolidated Foods. The company basically did the same business as Associated Grocers. Dr. Tanner asked me if I was interested and whether I would I like to explore the possibility of running the company. He related as much as he knew about the company; it was owned by one man who was not active in the business, but had two sons in the business. However, according to the information Dr. Tanner received, the father did not think that either son had the ability to run the business successfully, nor did they want to run it.

I told Dr. Tanner that I was interested in discussing the company with the owner, and I asked him if he would set up a call for me to meet with the gentleman. The next day I talked with the owner by telephone. Both of us agreed the next step would be for me to fly to New Orleans to meet him and tour the facility. So, in August of 1973, I flew to New Orleans. I was met by the owner, whose name I unfortunately cannot remember. He was a distinguished man, dressed in horseback riding attire because he had just finished riding. We went to his home, which was a large, elegant house, located in the best area in New Orleans. During the time at his house, he explained the company, its operation, and the situation with both sons. Obviously, I had concern about the role I would play in the company as President and the role the sons would play.

We drove to the company, met his sons, and toured the company. It was an older facility, but in excellent condition. I sized the sons up as having been reared in wealth and having attended the best universities. However, they were not as hungry to succeed as I was. One of the sons was an attorney, and he planned to start his own practice or join an existing firm. After leaving the company, I felt much better because I did not see the sons as competition.

After my trip to New Orleans, I thought about the things I had heard and seen while visiting there. I talked with the owner several times in order to gain additional knowledge about the company, the compensation, bonus requirements, benefits, and an employment agreement for five years. There were no problems with the questions I asked; all would be worked out if I wanted the position. At that time, he offered me the position of President and CEO of the company, only reporting to him.

I told him I needed a week to think through the offer and all it entailed. I wanted to talk to Jackie and give some thought to moving and giving notice to Associated Grocers. After that telephone conversation, I had a lot to think about. It was difficult to consider leaving the company I had been with for fourteen years, having moved from the lowest level to the top. I had a certain love for the company, even though it was a difficult company to manage.

After a week, I had a telephone conversation with the owner of Consolidated Foods. He asked me if I had evaluated everything and made a decision. I told him I needed a few more days to make a decision, and I said that I would call him. I had already spent a lot of time evaluating the move from Birmingham to New Orleans—what it would be like living in New Orleans, especially being away from my extended family and Jackie's family.

Dr. Tanner came by the company for his monthly visit. After he had made his departmental visits, he came to my office and gave me an update as usual. Then he said, "There is a small company in town that is making a lot of money, a public company that needs someone to run it." At that time he told me that Neal Andrews, Jr. was the majority stockholder of the company but not a manager or administrator. He said that Neal was an entrepreneur, but that he needed my organizational skills and other talents to make the company as profitable as it had the potential to become. He said Neal was not at the company as much as a manager should be and that the caliber of the employees was poor. He said I might be interested if I were willing to put in the effort and time to revamp the company.

Dr. Tanner said I could derive stock and stock options, plus a good salary, bonuses, a furnished car, a relocation allowance, and other perks based on performance. I did not know anything about Pasquale Food

Company, Inc. When Jackie and I first moved to Birmingham, Tommy Turrentine, a supervisor at Associated Grocers, invited us to lunch at the Pasquale located at Eastwood Mall. This was not only the first Pasquale we had had ever seen, but it was also the first pizza we had ever eaten. Tommy Turrentine spent time with Jackie and me to show us around the city. We never knew why he treated us so well, but we appreciated everything he did for us, and we will always remember him.

Before leaving my office, Dr. Tanner said that if I had any interest at all, I should call Neal Andrews. He gave me Neal's telephone number. He said Neal was a wild man and had a very rough reputation in the Birmingham area. He also said that Neal could be a "son of a bitch." I told Dr. Tanner I could certainly work with one SOB because I had been tolerating a large number of SOBS for years.

Near the middle of September, 1973, I called Neal and arranged to meet him at The Club to talk for the first time. We met on a Tuesday night. He introduced himself, and we conducted small talk before getting into the subject of Pasquale. He told me the type of person he was looking for to run the company. Neal gave an overview of the company and told me how he first became a franchisee and opened several pizza restaurants in Tuscaloosa and Birmingham. In 1968, he purchased the company, which was located in Cincinnati, Ohio. He explained how the company was currently operating. The company sold franchises and the necessary equipment for the restaurant and charged a fee for installing the equipment. The company sold the franchisee the opening food order, and continued to sell and ship products weekly to the pizza restaurants. In addition, the company collected a royalty on the retail sales.

Neal explained how the company operated internally. The company produced pizza crusts, processed and cooked various types of sausage, and made pepperoni, meatballs, and all the sandwich meat. Plus, the company produced the buns for the sandwiches and supplied the franchisees with all other food products and equipment needed to run a retail pizza restaurant.

Within a few days, I called Neal to set up another meeting. I informed Neal that I was interested in the position and would like to talk with him about compensation, benefits, bonus program, a company car, and my authority to run the company. Neal was more generous than I expected. At that meeting, I accepted the position and discussed giving Associated Grocers a thirty day notice. Everything we agreed on was written on a paper napkin by Neal and confirmed with a handshake.

Neal said there were weaknesses in some important areas within the company and that it needed qualified personnel. I told him I would make all the changes necessary to elevate the company to a professional status. I would quickly terminate anyone who did not or could not measure up to my standards. I asked Neal if there were any employees that were "sacred cows." He said there was only one, and that person's name was Pat Marino, better known in the company as "Papa Pasquale." He said that Pat started when he opened his first pizza restaurant in Tuscaloosa, Alabama, and that he had assisted in opening many other pizza restaurants. Now, Pat was helpful in retail promotions, running errands, and other miscellaneous things. I told him I understood, and that Papa Pasquale would be with us all the way.

The thought of leaving Associated Grocers of Alabama was difficult. I had spent a total of fourteen years there, less two years in the military. I had an opportunity to move from the very bottom of the company, through almost all departments and levels to finally fulfill my first major goal. It was also another opportunity to put the formula into effect that I had worked on for many years. My formula had catapulted me to the top. I had been through all of the ranks. I had been in the union and had worked side by side with those who were doing the hardest labor and who would probably never move upward. Even though I had fights and numerous problems with people working in the warehouse, freezer, and cooler and with the personnel in produce, the drivers, the mechanics, and other non-office personnel, I felt a deep compassion for them.

The first thing I did the next morning was call the owner of Consolidated Foods in New Orleans. This was one of the most difficult calls I have ever made. I think the owner and two sons were convinced that I was going to take the job. I had a difficult time explaining why I wasn't taking the job, because they had agreed to everything I had asked for and more.

I think the owner was convinced the two sons would do the things they wanted to do, and the father would have someone there who could run the business. Again, it was very difficult to say no, because of the professionalism they had shown during our meetings and telephone conversations. I do not think I will ever feel good about this conversation. I do not think they ever understood. I probably came too close to taking the job.

The next day, I delivered a letter of resignation to Mr. John Davis, who was then chairman of the board. His office was in Edgewood, across from Dixie Supermarket. Mr. Davis was a good man and seemed to be saddened by my resignation. We reminisced for a while and briefly discussed Pasquale Food Company. We discussed the mechanics of turning over everything I had that belonged to Associated Grocers, including all company files, reports, books, other data, and the company car.

I continued to work for three weeks rather than a month. I left a week early because there was nothing left for me to do. I also believe that once I had made up my mind to leave, I was "mentally gone." It was difficult to say goodbye, especially to those who had endured battles and wars with me. As I cleaned out my desk, and boxed everything up belonging to me, I had ambivalent feelings that were impossible to describe. My decision brought tears to my eyes.

I had gained a tremendous amount of experience, knowledge, and wisdom during the fourteen years I was with Associated Grocers. I became seasoned and could deal with difficult people and difficult situations. I had moved from the bottom of the company, unloading boxcars, to the top. This is something that can't be expressed in words. My formula had worked to perfection, and I had reached my first major goal in life, with many more already outlined.

I knew that I had broken the "Yoke of Generational Poverty," and I was the first in my family to achieve this goal. I also knew I would never return to the "death hold" that poverty has on people who are trapped within its grasp. There is one enigma in moving from poverty to wealth that I will never forget: I would be highly resented by some members of my family, extended family, friends, and other people. I am happy to say I did not let this nonsense deter me, even when I heard comments such as, "He has forgotten where he came from," or "He has forgotten his 'raising.'" To break free from the claws of poverty and to become successful financially means never being able to meet the expectations of family and friends. Enough is never enough once they know you have wealth. This creates a conundrum that has no answer. Some people have problems with people who move from one level of Maslow's hierarchy to the next level. I was keenly aware of the resentment at work and away from work and handled it with an air of defiance, or I just ignored it.

On Monday, October 19, 1973, I was at the Pasquale Headquarters earlier than any one who worked in the office. I went through the warehouse to get into the office. Once there, I waited for others to show up for work. I waited for employees to arrive at eight o'clock. No one showed up. Instead, they were arriving at eight-fifteen, eight- thirty, and later. It was obvious to me that my style was going to be difficult for current employees to accept. I knew at that moment that there was a plethora of problems and that this was a company that was out of control. I was fully aware that the employees were going to experience an aberration in my management style once I had time to dig into every area of the company.

The first day was a disaster because I had been accustomed to organization. Pasquale did not have any organizational structure as far as I could determine. Three ladies who worked in the computer section just walked out without warning. The same day, I contacted Dick Langford, the president of Time Share. He was able to keep us in business until his company had time to write programs that were tailored for Pasquale. Dick had been the warehouse manager and supervisor at Associated Grocers of Alabama while I was there.

The first thing I focused on was getting the orders in on time, loading the outgoing trucks properly, and getting the trucks to leave on time. This was the lifeline of the company's success. The restaurants depended on almost one hundred percent of their supplies from Pasquale. This should have been an easy task, but the warehouse had no organization. The same products might be located in five or six different locations. This had to change immediately. I made sure that the warehouse was racked (placing the product off the floor in an organized manner), that an order puller was filling an order, and that the product was slotted in the order of the pull ticket or invoice.

Pasquale had an unacceptable climate and a lack of leadership in all departments. To get Pasquale under control, I needed a large number of qualified personnel. In order to accomplish this, I terminated many employees. Some employees left for other reasons. This was not an easy transaction, because some of the personnel had been with the company a long time.

One of my first moves was to hire George Sutton from Flowers Bakery to supervise our bakery, which included par-baked pizza crusts and hoagie buns. Roy Laney was hired to run the warehouse, which meant he had control over receiving and shipping. Robert Waldrop was hired to run the meat department. I hired Bill Pore, who was the financial officer at Associated Grocers of Alabama, to run the finance department. Doug Owen was hired to handle customer services, and later became the purchasing agent.

Once Pasquale was staffed properly, with an organizational structure and accounting system in place, a short, a mid-term, and a long-term plan had to be devised and implemented. This was time consuming because the company did not have a base plan from which to begin. I started a ground zero in all areas of the company.

R.C. Riley, my long-time advocate at Associated Grocers, was hired as purchasing agent. However, much to my dismay, after being with Pasquale for approximately one year, Mr. Riley died from cancer. It was a shock for me because he was diagnosed with cancer in January and passed away in March. He had been looking forward to the time when he could retire and move to Logan Martin Lake. He wanted to spend quality time with his wife, children, and grandchildren. He was a very good man; he had helped me in the past so much because he had faith in my abilities. He was one of the greatest mentors I ever had.

Personnel changes were slower than I had planned, but we eventually had a core of personnel that could do their respective jobs and were dependable. As I think back, it seems I terminated everyone except Neal

Andrews and Papa Pasquale. As mentioned earlier, Neal Andrews was the majority stockholder.

Neal Andrews and I, as part of our plan, wanted to employ someone who could head up the retail operations, which included franchised and company stores. We evaluated a few inside personnel and reviewed a tremendous number of resumes. Then I remembered John Sanford, who had worked for Associated Grocers of Alabama. John had resigned from Associated Grocers of Alabama to take over sales and marketing for the Super-Valu division located in Anniston, Alabama. Once he joined Super-Valu, he became very important to the company because he increased their sales dramatically. I mentioned John to Neal; however, our concern was that he had such a good position at Super-Valu that it would probably be difficult or impossible for him to leave that company.

The next day I called John and told him about Pasquale, its internal and external operations, and how his expertise might prove valuable in increasing sales at Pasquale. John had some questions, but did not seem overly motivated to leave Super-Valu because he did not know much about Pasquale. I told Neal about our conversation. We discussed the situation in more detail, such as John's salary, bonus, company car, and other perks. We decided that it would be a good idea to drive to Anniston and meet with him personally.

I called and confirmed the date and time that we would be there. Neal and I arrived and met John's family. Then we secluded ourselves with John to seriously discuss Pasquale Food Company. We intended to get him interested in joining Pasquale as Vice President of franchise and company store operations. After our visit and several telephone conversations, John decided to join Pasquale.

During everything that was going on in the company, Jackie was at home taking care of two babies, Kim and Leslie, who were born only one year apart. She was also pregnant with another child. When our son Les was born at the Baptist Medical Center on April 18, 1974, we were overjoyed. Naming him was easy; he was going to be named Lester Nuby, III. Prior to his birth, many people asked me if I wanted a boy because we already had two girls. I always said it did not matter. But in my heart, I really wanted a little boy. He was a wonderful, handsome little boy, who was easy to manage and who had a great attitude. I remember when he was almost three years old, I was leaving for work and, as I backed my car out of the garage, he was standing at the door crying because I was leaving. This touched my heart and still does. In life, how often does one have this experience? He may not ever forgive me for naming him after me.

In the fall of 1974, John arrived at the company and assumed the role of Vice President of Operations for the company. During the first few months, he spent time on the road visiting and assessing all of our franchisees. He also discussed his evaluation with Neal and me. The picture was mixed, but leaning toward the negative side, because most of the pizza restaurants were old, with no continuity of menu, signage, or buildings. Most did not have a franchise agreement that stipulated that the company could collect a royalty fee. This void had been offset, because in the early days a majority of the restaurants purchased a substantial amount of their food and equipment from Pasquale Food Company, the franchisor. Therefore, the company made its money off the sale of food and equipment. However, the laws were changing, and it became unlawful to force a franchisee to purchase from the franchisor. Mandatory purchasing was effective if one had a formula that could not be duplicated. It was also mandatory for the franchisee to purchase product that, if not from the franchisor, was comparable to the product specified in the addendum to the franchise agreement.

John Sanford also discovered that some pizza restaurants were selling hot dogs and other non-authorized product. He quickly realized that he had a challenge. John made improvements and converted most franchisees from their old franchise agreements to a new agreement that was legal and enforceable. He held franchisee area meetings, developed advertising groups, and improved the franchisee and company store situation. But there were some things that were unchangeable, such as the lack of continuity in the structure of Pasquale stores, signage, and menus.

In 1975 and 1976, we started talking with design companies to develop a new building, signage, and uniform structure of the interior of each Pasquale. After talking with several companies and evaluating their designs and ideas, Pasquale selected Lippincott and Margulies, a New York-based company, to handle the new restaurant design.

In 1977, William D. Hasty, an attorney with Liberty National, was hired as Pasquale's in-house attorney to streamline the company's franchising agreement and related documents. Additionally, "Bill," as he was called, handled or coordinated all legal issues pertaining to the company. He was also an asset to the company in many other areas such as preparing documents for the Securities and Exchange Commission and annual reports and keeping the company in compliance with regulatory entities. Bill did an outstanding job for the company.

Bill also had a unique brand of humor we enjoyed. After a long week it was not unusual for Neal, John, Bill, and me to consume a bottle of Dubonnet or Harvey's Bristol Cream Sherry. However, this was always after hours when all of the other personnel had left the building. I consider Bill a friend and one of the best men I have known.

The design of the new pizza and pasta restaurant was going to be unique and give continuity to the Pasquale chain. In doing so, we could compete with incoming pizza franchises. The cost of each Pasquale was one hundred and seventy five dollars up to two hundred thousand dollars. Additional features and upgrades pushed the cost higher and higher. Once the building design and signage were completed, the cost of construction was too high for franchisees to build and justify their return on the investment or "ROI." Only two restaurants were built, which were company-owned units; one was constructed on Valley Avenue in Birmingham, Alabama, and one in Hoover, Alabama. Due to the cost of construction and the high interest rates, the company could not sell the newly designed unit to existing or potential franchisees. During this time, very high interest rates, ranging from eighteen to twenty percent, not only had an adverse effect on our company, but on other companies as well.

SUPERMARKET PIZZAS & PASTA

John Sanford had been with Pasquale for approximately four years, and had spent time evaluating other avenues to sell Pasquale's products.

As the franchising was becoming more difficult, John presented an idea to sell Pasquale products through supermarkets. His plan was to sell Pasquale ingredients and furnish a pizza "make up unit" to each supermarket. In this plan, one of our field representatives spent time at each site. Before they left, they took the time to train the people operating the in-store delicatessen. Reluctantly, Neal and I accepted John's plan. The first test supermarket was in Louisville, Kentucky. At first, the test was dismal because the freight cost more than the product. Pasquale was giving the supermarket a make-up unit with equipment valued at five hundred dollars. Plus, we sent a field representative, which was also expensive. As the weeks passed by, our concern for this program became more pronounced.

We were at the point of discontinuing this program when John Sanford received a call from the Louisville Kroger division stating they wanted the program expanded to all supermarkets within the Louisville division. This was the best news we had heard in a long time. This meant we would be shipping full trailer loads of product to the Kroger division located in Louisville. The supermarkets would order the Pasquale products and equipment from the division warehouse.

Suddenly, we moved from a loss to a profit. After approximately two months, John received a call from another Kroger division wanting the Pasquale product in their division. We became concerned as to whether we could operationally handle the new business. As this was taking place, John received a call from the Kroger headquarters located in Cincinnati, Ohio wanting to put Pasquale product in all divisions as soon as possible. John was definitely the protagonist who saw an opportunity in the supermarket industry and who continued, against skepticism and criticism, to move the company's sales, profitability, and acquisitions to become an international entity. Supermarkets were selling pizzas as fast as they could be made.

Again, this posed a problem operationally, but a good one. Internally, we took the position that we could ship anything John could sell, which was a stretch. We needed addition cold storage place. This prompted us to store product at Finley Cold Storage, an outside storage facility. Every week John called in to the company and reported that a new company or division had signed up and wanted the program installed as soon as possible. This was wonderful news to all of us in management, but bad news for production and warehousing because they were producing and shipping all they thought they could.

After meeting with those in production and warehousing, the new orders were shipped on time to meet the required schedule the chain requested. Often one could hear Roy Laney and production personnel cursing about the situation, hoping not to be heard.

MAFIA

In the early days at Pasquale, one would occasionally hear someone ask if the executives of the company were affiliated with the Mafia. This assumption grew as the company grew from a regional, national, and international company. During this time, Pasquale was purchasing huge quantities of mozzarella cheese from all cheese producers in the United States, Canada, and England. It seemed companies that purchased substantial amounts of cheese were thought to be in the Mafia or connected to the Mafia. When Neal, John, or I was asked the question "Are you connected to the mafia?" We would always give the same answer: "We ask the questions!" This answer gave a mysterious twist to our modus operandi.

During this exciting time, I received a call from a board member with Day's Inn. The board member was very articulate in expressing the need for a new President and CEO to run the Day's Inn chain. He explained the requirements for the position in detail and expressed his feeling that I was the person to take that position. It may have been an unusual thing to do, but before going to Atlanta, I informed Neal about the initial call, the follow-up calls, and the planned meeting in Atlanta. I expressed to Neal that I was not thinking and had not thought about leaving Pasquale, but that I thought it would be good for me to at least meet with the board member, who had been a first-class gentleman. Neal reminded me that money was still very tight, and interest rates were generally too high for most companies to expand, especially companies like Day's Inn, which took a lot of capital to build new units.

After a couple of follow-up calls, I made arrangements to fly to the Day's Inn headquarters in Atlanta. I was met at the airport by the same board member with whom I had been conversing. I had already asked many questions about their operation. He had responded by supplying me answers to these questions along with the financial data concerning the company.

I spent spending approximately four hours with the members of the board. After meeting with them, I had enough information to see that the company was not expanding its units because the interest rates were nearly twenty percent in the mid-1970s. Gasoline had almost doubled in cost. The personnel of the company, as well as most others, had cut down on traveling. Fewer people traveled, thus causing occupancy in hotels and motels to decline drastically.

My meetings with the board of directors at the Day's Inn made me realize that a move to that company would not be wise. I am sure that they were searching for some "miracle worker" to straighten out an already dismal situation. I left for Birmingham with my mind made up.

I flew back to Birmingham the same day and arrived at the airport late in the evening. The first thing I did was to call Neal Andrews and relate what I had learned, which were almost the same things he had stated. I told him I was committed to Pasquale Food Company. It was an opportunity to thank him for the positive things he had done for me. I made a commitment that I would strive to perform in such a manner that Pasquale Food Company would meet its maximum potential. After this conversation, nothing was ever mentioned about Day's Inn.

Over the years Pasquale had evolved from an autocratic management style to one that was based on Management Based Objectives. Key personnel at Pasquale attended outstanding schools and seminars during this time, such as The President's Association and several others. It took time to teach personnel that planning starts from the bottom and moves up to the top.

As the planning transition was taking place, the climate or culture of Pasquale was also changing for the better. We made sure that each employee understood that the essence Management by Objectives (MBO) meant that there was participative goal setting. Standards were set and actual performance was measured by those standards. When I joined Pasquale, there was little planning, and all that was done, was done at the top of the company.

Now all planning started at the bottom of the company and moved through the various echelons to the top of the company, where it was scrutinized several times. It often happened that the plan was sent back to the bottom echelon if the numbers appeared to be wrong or if there was insufficient data to support the plan. We reached the point in planning that at the end of each month and at the end of each fiscal year, the plan and actual performance were very close. Any differences in the two had to be explained in detail. Each employee had to take ownership of his or her area of responsibility.

PASQUALE HUMOR

The following anecdotes reflect a sampling of the humor that permeated Pasquale Food Company for the seventeen years I was affiliated with the company.

In reading this humor, one must remember that I had spent fourteen years with Associated Grocers of Alabama, which a very conservative company. I knew that Pasquale was a very different company with an unknown culture. However, I did not realize it was going to be a shocking difference.

During my first week at Pasquale Food Company, Neal Andrews called a field representative meeting to be held in the conference room. At about 9:00 a. m. on Friday morning, the field representatives started arriving. I remember some of the names but not all: John Bonanto, Jim Hayes, and six or eight others. The meeting started at 10:00 a. m. Neal conducted the meeting. He made some visual observations without comment. All the field representatives were obese and wore suits that were too big for them, which made them look even larger. Neal stood on the stage of the room and looked at what I thought was an agenda.

At that time Neal was wearing a cream-colored suede suit. As he started talking, I will never forget his opening remarks.

He looked out at the field representatives, who appeared to have eaten all the pizzas the company had sold. After pausing for a few minutes, Neal said, "You goddamn overweight people, what in the hell are you doing out there in the field, other than satisfying your voracious appetites, and sitting on your very fat asses." Each individual looked as if the apocalypse was near. Neal left an impressionable impact on each of them. I knew that, compared to Associated Grocers of Alabama, I was entering the twilight zone. Once the meeting was over, Neal looked at me and said "Good meeting."

One of the young ladies who worked in our office sat on the copier without undergarments and made pictures of her. I will not name the young lady to protect the guilty. After that day, I don't remember anyone using that copier again. It was leased, and within days it was picked up by the leasing company while delivering a larger copier.

Most of the single men and several married men identified the young lady from the picture. The names of the single and married men will never be revealed, because even today it would cause too many problems. Neal Andrews was the adjudicator, but I don't think it was ever mentioned due to the sensitivity of the situation. No one would speak about it, but several said that Neal seemed to be thrilled.

The first telephone call I heard Neal take was transferred from the customer service department. Apparently, one of the franchisees had a problem with some product that was bad when he received it. Neal picked up the telephone without considering that the person on the telephone was a customer. Instantly, Neal said, "You son-of-a–bitch, why are you calling and giving my customer service department a hard time." I left the room in amazement at how anyone could talk to a customer in such a manner and retain their business, but we did. When Neal hung up the telephone, he said, "Sometimes you just have to be curt."

As most companies do, our stockholders meeting were staged. At one of our meetings Doug Owen, the purchasing director for the company and a stockholder, made a motion from the floor, requesting that the company make a contribution to Samford University to purchase instruments for the Universities a cappella choir. Doug pulled this stunt knowing that a cappella choir doesn't use instruments. At the same meeting, Neal Andrews requested that the company send him dividends and no one else. The stockholders rejected the request, but it took steel balls to ask the question.

Jim Hayes, a field representative, was called in from his territory to manage a pizza restaurant located in Forestdale, Alabama. His talent was needed to turn the restaurant around and have it become profitable. Jim was a large man, weighing approximately two hundred and seventy pounds, and he was six feet seven inches tall. One afternoon I received an urgent and alarming call from one of the restaurant employees. Jim was in the loft over the ladies' bathroom observing the ladies through a small hole he had pierced in the tile. While doing this, Jim fell through the fragile ceiling tile into the bathroom and partially landed on the lady who was using the bathroom. Neal, John and I, were on top of this situation with urgency. We were very concerned about the lady, but also about the legal ramifications that were possible because Jim was a fool. Once we arrived at the restaurant, Jim had departed, never to be found. Fortunately, the lady was not injured, but she was highly offended and a little embarrassed. We did not have any legal problems and made the situation right with the lady.

We often discussed this situation and tried to understand why a two hundred and seventy pound man would be stupid enough to crawl into the ceiling of the restaurant and look into the ladies' bathroom. The ceiling was hanging tile, and sometimes just fell out. We assumed he was trying to see something. It was a subject that was talked about for years as "Jim's view."

I remember as if it were yesterday, because the situation I am going to describe is true and is not something you hear every day. Doug Owen, Larry Traywick, and Bud Green were standing near Roy Laney's office. Roy was the warehouse manager and was usually early to work. This morning Roy had not arrived, so the three standing there speculated that he must be sick or have had an accident. In a few minutes, Roy drove into the parking lot. He got out of his car carefully and walked toward his office as if he had suffered an injury. Observing the discomfort on Roy's face, Doug asked Roy if he had a problem. The answer Roy gave was stunning as he said, "Boys, I think a broke my male organ." Doug, Larry, and Bud started moving away quickly, as Roy entered his office and moved into his chair.

I understand none of the three had the courtesy to ask Roy about the problem and whether there was anything they could do, or to offer to take a look at the problem and maybe drive him to the emergency room. This reflected poorly on Doug, Larry and Bud, because Bud was a nurse in the military while stationed in Japan. Doug and Larry were thought of as friends of Roy. I don't think Roy ever forgave them for turning their backs on his front in his time of need. Roy said their refusal to help him reflected the transparency of their true feelings toward him and mankind.

The companies I managed over the years had so much humor, such as the above, that I have started writing a book on odd, bizarre, obnoxious, and unusual humor.

HEINZ CORPORATION

In June, 1985, several executives from the Heinz Corporation visited Pasquale. We were sure they had intentions to purchase Pasquale. We were correct in our assumption. The senior spokesman stated that they had paid attention to all the publicity that the company had continued to receive, and they were there to discuss the possibility of purchasing Pasquale. Neal Andrews responded by stating that he had not given any thought to selling the company, and he said that he felt the company was on a very high growth track. Yet Neal said we were open for discussion and stated that everything was for sale at some price. I noticed that one of the Heinz representatives flinched when Neal said that.

Eventually, both parties became serious and started in-depth discussions about the possibility of selling Pasquale. However, Neal contended throughout the discussions that the company could not be purchased based on current sales and net profit. The company, with its growth rate and profitability, could possibly be sold on future sales and earnings. Pasquale had just ended its fiscal year on May 31, 1985, and reflected sales of eighty million dollars with a net profit of ten percent, or eight million dollars.

We spent the entire day discussing Pasquale. The Heinz representatives had many questions about the company included in a binder. These questions had been typed prior to the meeting. The day ended without discussing price. When the meeting concluded, their senior representative stated that they would return to Heinz, and present their recommendations to their superiors, and get back to us within one week.

They had rented a car and left for the airport near 4:00 p.m. Neal, John and I were worn out from being in the conference room all day. We decided to contemplate the conversation and get back together the following morning.

However, once I was back in my office for approximately one hour, I remembered that I had left my binder with their questions in the room where we had met all day. When I went into the conference room, I noticed a blue official-looking book placed in the seat of a chair, near where one of the Heinz representatives had been sitting. I walked around and picked the book up. I was awed when I opened. I found all the questions, answers, and notes left by Heinz in the book.

Once I perused the contents of the book, I met with Neal Andrews and John Sanford just "to do the right thing." In Pasquale lingo, this meant read and make copies. I think both knew I had already read the book. The answer was "yes." This gave me time to make copies of the total book. When I finished, I called Heinz headquarters. I could not reach any of the Heinz representatives who visited us that day. I left a message that we had found a book that belonged to one of them and it would be sent by Federal Express that day.

The next morning Neal, John, and I met to discuss the Heinz meeting. One thing we discussed was the price Heinz had placed on Pasquale. We agreed that we would not sell the company for the amount reflected in their book, but we agreed to wait for Heinz to reply. As they had said, we received a call, which was placed on speaker phone for both parties. At first, we let them do all the talking. Another executive had joined the conversation. He had additional questions for us to answer. Finally, the executive went through a fairly long discussion about Heinz, which we could not care less.

The Heinz representative finally got to the core of the conversation. He stated that he, along with their financial personnel, was willing to pay sixty-eight million dollars for the company. At that time, Neal discussed the current status of the company and the five-year plan for the future.

After some additional back and forth conversation, Neal, John, and I informed the Heinz representatives that we appreciated their interest in Pasquale, but that but we just could not sell the company at the price offered. We told them we were open to an additional discussion; however, we concluded that the company was more valuable than sixty-eight million dollars. Both parties thanked each other and hung up the telephone.

JOHN LABATT

In 1984, Pasquale acquired the Oscar Mayer building on Valleydale Road. The new facility was to become a pasta plant. We had hired Ron Cook, who had run a successful pasta company in New York, to run the business. We asked him to go to Italy to buy the latest and best equipment for the new plant. Ron lined up avenues of supply that met the pre-determined quality of product and supplies, and he hired the personnel needed. When this was completed, we were quickly in the pasta business.

In July 1985, Herb England with John Labatt, Ltd. visited Pasquale under the pretense of the possibility of co-packing pasta or perhaps selling John Labatt, Ltd. our newly acquired pasta company. When he came, the company was running well. Neal, John, and I took him to lunch at Highland's Bar and Grill. It became very obvious to us that Herb England was not there to discuss co-packing or buying the pasta company. He was there to evaluate the possibility of purchasing Pasquale Food Company, Inc. He inquired about the total operation, especially Pasquale Food Company. We had heard that John Labatt, Ltd. had purchased several companies in the United States and was in the process of buying other food companies.

We were correct in our assumption. Mr. England obviously had given Peter Widdrington, the President and CEO, and the board of directors a very positive report concerning the overall operation of Pasquale Food Company, Inc. Within a few days, Herb called us again and asked if he and a group of financial personnel could visit us. We told Herb that we approved of his request. We knew for sure that John Labatt, Ltd. was interested in purchasing Pasquale. Should this purchase come to pass, we were prepared to place tremendous emphasis on the potential of Pasquale Food Company, Inc. and the synergy possibilities if John Labatt purchased other companies in the United States.

Meanwhile, I found out a lot about John Labatt, Ltd. John Labatt was headed by a flamboyant President and CEO, who had spent some time in California and who had a flair for life in the United States. He also had a tremendous ambition to expand Labatt by purchasing companies in the United States. We kept this information in mind as we discussed the possibility of selling Pasquale.

We quickly realized that we would be interfacing with a large group of financial experts. Therefore, Neal, John and I, with the assistance of Mr. Tom Carruthers, a senior partner with Bradley, Arant, Rose and White, put a superb plan together if the purchase took place. Within a few months of negotiating, Pasquale was sold to John Labatt, Ltd. additionally; John Sanford and I sold our stock and stock options to Labatt at nineteen dollars per share. The final documents were signed and the money changed hands on December 9, 1986.

Neal decided to leave the company as soon as it was sold. Neal had two Brinks trucks come to the company to load the money he received from the sale of the company. The company personnel helped to speed up the loading process. John Sanford, Doug Owen, Virgil Stokes, and I pitched in and dragged the bags of money from Neal's office to the front door to make it easier on the Brinks personnel. It took over two hours to load the trucks. The money was then on its way to an unidentified bank. John Sanford strained his back while pulling the bags to the front door and today still suffers from that injury. Neal kept one large bag from being loaded on the Brinks trucks because he said he "needed some spending money." A little humor here!

We knew that once Neal left the building, he had no intention of coming back. I felt sad. Some of us knew that we would never work harder, make more money, receive more perks, or have as much fun as we did with Neal Leroy Andrews and Pasquale Food Company, Inc.

John C Sanford, Lester Nuby, Jr., and Neal Andrews, Jr.

Pasquale's Food Company's Big Three

CHAPTER TWENTY-EIGHT

PASQUALE SOLD TO JOHN LABATT

During the negotiations with Labatt, John Sanford and I realized that it was going to be necessary to continue with Pasquale for some period of time. Prior to concluding the negotiations, both of us signed long-term employment agreements and were guaranteed ample salaries and bonuses if we met the performance projections. Overall, it was a superior package, with perks of value. John and I knew we had a major task to accomplish.

After Labatt completed the purchase of Pasquale, John and I met with Peter Widdrington, President and CEO of John Labatt, and other Labatt executives. We were assured that there would be no changes in the operation of the company. However, John and I had been around too long to believe this would actually be the case. We knew that at some point Labatt would sink its claws into Pasquale.

During the first two years after Labatt purchased Pasquale, there was little involvement from Labatt in the company's operations. At the end of each month, our staff prepared an in–depth presentation for Labatt's Board of Directors meeting. I attended the board meetings and make the presentations in London, Ontario, Canada. Prior to making the presentation, I got with our sales personnel and operations personnel for a thorough update. I also met with each company or division manager in order to get information I would need to answer any potential questions I might be asked. Actually, I was presenting what our competent personnel had put together. Fortunately, I was able to answer the questions. All Labatt board meetings were held in London, Ontario, Canada. The presentations covered all financial information. Graphs, charts, financial ratios, and projections compared to actual. After each presentation, there were questions from board members and Labatt executives. The presentations went well because the Pasquale personnel did an excellent job putting the presentation together.

Beginning the third year of the acquisition, Labatt started becoming more and more involved in the everyday activities of Pasquale. There was no good reason for this to happen, because the company was running well, as indicated with checks and balances to measure the performance of the personnel. However, I, along with other top executives of the company, was required to attend seemingly useless seminars in Chicago or Canada. Of course, this tended to pull us away from what we needed to be doing at the company.

Gradually, the seminars began to involve staff and sales personnel. Historically, sales personnel were never pulled out of the field. The only exceptions were attending one corporate meeting per year, a brokers' convention, or hosting a food show at the McCormick Place in Chicago. We were well aware that the grassroots of our business revolved around sales. That involved working directly with supermarket headquarters, retail groups, and brokers. The idea, obviously, was to increase sales and profits. In helping the retailers gain sales and profits, we were accomplishing our corporate goals.

John Sanford and I often discussed why Labatt would pay one hundred and sixty-two million dollars for a company that was performing in an excellent manner and want to change anything. At the time when Labatt purchased Pasquale, the company had ended its fiscal year with sales in the amount of eighty million dollars, with a net profit of ten percent. The company had no debt and thirty-two million dollars in the bank. However, we both knew it was the "nature of the beast" that the parent company would become negatively involved. On most occasions, the individuals involved who had nothing to do with the purchase transaction and were not cognizant of the company's operation.

The involvement of Labatt continued to increase, especially in the area of centralizing computer systems. Their intention was to change the climate of the company to be more accordant with Labatt's operations. As Labatt became more involved, Pasquale was changing from a company in which everyone knew what their jobs were and what they had to do to accomplish the company's goals.

Labatt did not take into account that it takes five to seven years to change the climate or culture of a company. This is not an easy task. There was an obvious difference in the personnel employed in Birmingham, Alabama and the personnel in Canada and Europe, even though Pasquale was owned by Labatt. Their involvement became detrimental to sales and profits. The morale of the company's fourteen hundred personnel was at an all-time low.

By January 1, 1989, Pasquale was a very different company compared to the Pasquale that Labatt purchased on December 9, 1986. Obviously, Labatt purchased U. S. companies blindly and did not understand the U. S. market. To an outsider, Labatt was a great company with which to be affiliated. They employed thousands of personnel. However, there were three components missing as they acquired companies in the United States. They did not understand the market; there was no plan; and they had no sense of humor. In writing this book I tried to think of humorous things that happened during my tenure with Labatt. I could not think of one humorous thing that I could write about within the Labatt Company. The only humorous thing was the amount of money they paid for Pasquale Food Company.

In January of 1990, I was asked to attend a meeting at Labatt's headquarters in London, Ontario, Canada. The presidents of all Labatt companies were also in attendance. The purpose of the meeting was to receive an overview of John Labatt's overall operations, including sales, profits, and acquisitions which had been made over the past few years, mostly in the United States.

In approximately five years, Labatt had added, through acquisitions, more than three and half billion dollars in additional sales. After the acquisitions, Labatt had annual sales in the amount of six and half billion dollars. This was impressive, but in most cases they paid too much for each acquisition. These acquisitions added to Labatt's overall sales, but did not add profitability and cash flow that Labatt was accustomed to receiving. Top executives at Labatt did not understand that the gross profit and net profit for food-related companies in the United States was not as high as it was in Canada. Labatt owned a lot of companies, including a beer company that enjoyed forty-one percent of the beer market in Canada and reflected high sales and profits.

Unfortunately, Labatt did not have a professional plan to absorb the newly-acquired companies. For example, after Pasquale was acquired, months passed before I knew to whom I should report. I assumed I reported to Peter Widdrington, the President and CEO. However, during this time there was little reporting and little direction from Labatt. This was the case with most of the companies Labatt acquired in the United States. Companies never were able to meet their potentials because no plan was in place. The possible synergies were never capitalized.

After several months, I was informed that I was to report to Frank Elsner, the president of Chef Francisco, a soup manufacturing company, located in Eugene, Oregon. Frank was very busy running his company, which had annual sales in the amount of one hundred twenty million dollars. Yet he was asked to have all the companies in the United States to report to him. Frank was an excellent manager who did not interfere with the companies that reported to him. This approach has some good and bad aspects. It is nice to be left alone to run one's company, but it is important that the person one reports to is accessible.

The last segment of the meeting in London, Ontario was devoted to the decision that Labatt had decided to centralize the companies in the United States into Eugene, Oregon, and Canada. The date for this consolidation was scheduled for July 15, 1990. We were also informed that it was possible that Labatt would sell some of the companies prior to July 15, 1990. Most of us who were responsible for running these companies believed that the board of directors of Labatt wanted to divest itself from the U. S. companies, and return to the "Labatt" prior to these acquisitions. Others hypothesized that Labatt had acquired the companies hoping they would be purchased by one of the large beer companies.

We were asked if any or all presidents would like to relocate to Canada. I had been asked this question every year when evaluations were being completed. Each year, I stated that I was not willing to relocate to Canada. I do not think the Canadians actually believed I would not relocate because I would make a substantial amount of money because of moving allowances and salary adjustments.

At the end of this meeting, everyone was asked to keep the consolidation of the companies in the United States confidential until one month prior to relocating to Eugene, Oregon or Canada. I understood why Labatt did not want to make an announcement at least five months earlier. All persons employed by the companies in the United States would start seeking other jobs. This would place those companies in a crisis mode.

I had compassion for our employees and had to think this situation through and come up with a plan that was better. I decided to take a couple of weeks to evaluate and analyze the thirty–day notice Labatt wanted the U.S. presidents and CEOs to give their employees. I was searching for a plan that would meet the needs of both our employees and Labatt. Our situation in the Birmingham and Nashville companies was different from most of the other companies located in the United States. Our Birmingham facility and Nashville facility were unionized. Pasquale had a legal responsibility to give these employees a sixty-day notice. Additionally, it did not seem fair to inform fourteen hundred employees that the company headquarters and divisions would be relocating to Eugene, Oregon, and Canada with only a thirty-day notice.

I finally made the decision not to say anything about the Birmingham headquarters moving to Eugene, Oregon and Canada until April 15, 1990, which was sixty days earlier than Labatt wanted. I did this in order to give the union the required sixty-day notice in Birmingham and Nashville. I knew that announcing this was going to be devastating to most employees because they would not be able to get another job.

There were one hundred and sixty-five employees headquartered in Birmingham. Approximately twenty of the employees, who were field representatives and regional managers, would not be affected, at least in the short term.

I decided to call all division managers and vice presidents on April 15, 1990, and inform them of the decision Labatt had made, which would affect our companies in the United States as well as two in Canada and one in Manchester, England. I called John Sanford first, who was in England at that time, as well as each division manager. I scheduled a meeting with all our employees who worked at the Birmingham facility. I explained the rationale Labatt used in making the decision. The employees were shocked and had so many questions that I could not answer them all. Many employees were highly concerned about how they were going to make a living.

I discussed the changes that Labatt was going to make, which included relocating most of Pasquale's headquarters to Eugene, Oregon, and possibly some to Canada. As I attempted to relate the changes that were to take place on July 15, 1990, everyone was painfully quiet. I explained that I had known about this since January, but was asked not to announce it until June 15, 1990. I explained that I was probably going to have a difficult time with Labatt because I had not kept their decision and timing to relocate the company, but I was willing to suffer the consequences. I also informed them that many of them would have an option to relocate to Eugene, Oregon, and Canada as full-time employees. Another option, which some personnel could choose, would be to temporarily relocate to help out during the transition.

This was a sobering meeting for me and the employees. When the meeting ended, the employees talked to each other in small groups. Most employees were saddened, but for some unknown reason, Millard Deason, the company's financial officer, laughed out loud. Again, we had a company with a sense of humor.

On June 14, 1990, Frank Elsner flew to Birmingham to meet with me for most of the day to discuss the transition. He asked about how the news was accepted by the employees. He also wanted to know if there were any problems with the unions. There were problems, but the company had given the required sixty-day notice, which met the legal requirement. I informed Frank about the various divisions in the United States, Canada, and Manchester, England. We also discussed the military commissaries which represented approximately twenty million dollars of our sales. I expressed my desire to stay in Birmingham. After additional discussions, Frank said he would prepare a separation package for me. After a week, I received the package. I received full salary for two years, all benefits for two years, and the option to purchase my company car at book value. The package was very generous and more than I expected.

From April 15, 1990, to July 15, 1990, the company continued to operate as normally as possible while plans were being made to move to Eugene, Oregon or Canada. During this time, some employees found other jobs. A few weeks after July 15, 1990, everything remaining at the Birmingham headquarters was auctioned. The moving and auction were saddening, as this ended a company that had been headquartered in Birmingham since 1968.

The relocation affected many employees who lost their jobs and a working environment that was very unique. The personnel at Pasquale worked diligently despite any challenges. Moreover, the company was staffed with people that had very different personalities, which made it a fun place to work. In evaluating all the companies I have run, I have never experienced the fun, humor, and laughter that Pasquale had. It seemed that everything we did had an element of humor. Even though the move took place more than twenty years ago, many of the former employees see or talk to each other about the funny things that happened at Pasquale.

Looking back, it was awesome to get paid a lot of money, receive bonuses, have all medical expenses paid, and get travel allowances, clothing allowances, a company automobile, and other perks. Besides that, John Sanford and I owned stock in the company through stock options, along with direct stock purchases.

I will never forget how I reached this pinnacle. I remember every detail of what it took to reach this point compared to where I started in life. I was sure of one thing; generational poverty had been crushed in my life and would never appear again. There is a cadre of individuals, a staff of officers, and other key personnel who assisted me in reaching this apex. I have shown my appreciation to many, but there are thousands I have not been able to contact. If you are reading this book, you know who you are. I deeply appreciate your help in making my life wonderful.

Those in 1990 who did not believe Labatt was positioning itself to be purchased were wrong. In 1995, John Labatt Ltd. was purchased by a Belgian brewer; it is now part of Anheuser-Busch InBev. InBev is a multinational brewer, and is the world's market leader.

Neal Andrews, Jr. leaving his office the evening of
December 9, 1986, after John Labatt Ltd., purchased
the company for one hundred and sixty-two million dollars.
Someone asked Neal why he was carrying such a large bag
of money. His response was, "This is only pocket change."

149

Neal's departing words, as he could speak several languages:

Adiós, Au revoir, Arrivederci, Shalom, Ciao,

Auf Wiedersehen, khodaa haafez, and Goodbye!

CHAPTER TWENTY-NINE

PERRY COUNTY FOODS

After Labatt purchased Pasquale Food Company, I was burned out. I decided not to pursue any additional opportunities for nine months. All I did was spend time with my family and play tennis twice a day. My family and I spent time at our lake house in Alexander City, Alabama. I spent a lot of time sitting on the deck looking out at the beautiful lake, and I often watched the sun go down or come up. I loved to ride the jet skis with my son, Les. I wanted time to think about my life, how it had initially begun in the clasps of poverty and come to where I was today. I evaluated each phase of my life, which included the good, the bad, and ugly. I was healing from years of not taking a vacation, not spending enough quality time with my family, and thinking about the relatives and friends I left behind. I asked myself if the success I had reached and enjoyed was worth the price I paid. I concluded that there was not a clear-cut answer to my question. However, I concluded that due to my success I was fortunate to offer my family and some friends a better life. As I overcame the burnout, I knew I would do the same thing again.

After I began to digest what had happened in the years with Associated Grocers of Alabama, Pasquale Food Company, and John Labatt, I realized that I could not be idle. I had to find something else to do to keep my "brain greased." I gave some thought to getting away from the food industry completely. I evaluated other companies that were for sale. However, after evaluating several companies, it was apparent that I should continue in the industry I knew best.

During those months, John Sanford and I continued to talk frequently. He had come across a company, Perry County Foods in Perry County, Ohio, which was similar to the Pasquale divisions. In February, 1993, we decided to look into the prospects of buying this company. It was a small manufacturing facility that produced pizza crusts, par-baked baked pizzas, and pizza components, and it had a small division that was in the fund-raising business. It had all the necessary equipment including a large freezer and ample cooler space.

The company was owned by three individuals, Ken Edelbrock and the Chaffee brothers, who lived in Indianapolis, Indiana. They were absentee owners who visited the company a couple of times each year. They funded the company through debt and some personal funds. They owned the facility, equipment, furniture, and fixtures, plus freezers and coolers. It was the perfect facility to do the things that we had done at Pasquale. In addition, it had a fund-raising division and several options upon which we could build.

John and I requested data such as an income statement, balance sheet, cash flow statement, list and value of inventory, accounts payable, current and long term debt, equipment, and other assets and liabilities for review. In approximately one week, the company's financial officer Harold Rosenfield had put together thoroughly the information we requested. At that point we began to analyze the data. We conducted a due diligence process as thorough as possible without bringing in a certified public accountant. We later found this decision to be a mistake. There is no way to gather the information about a company without a thorough analysis of the company.

Once we decided to purchase the company, we met with Jim Rotch, a Birmingham–based attorney with Bradley, Arrant, Rose, and White. Jim had worked with us on all acquisitions at Pasquale and was deeply involved when Pasquale was sold to John Labatt, Ltd. Once all documents were prepared, Jim met John and me in Indianapolis,

Indiana, to conclude the purchase with Ken Edlebrock and the Chaffee brothers. After several hours of negotiating several unresolved issues, all parties signed the documents. At that moment, John Sanford and I owned Perry County Foods, Inc. The next morning John and I drove to Perry County Foods and started our involvement in the company.

We believed that we could purchase the company and run it from a small office in Birmingham, which proved to be erroneous. Once we finalized the purchase, we went to the plant to evaluate the management, personnel, facility, products, and customers. We quickly determined that one of us would need to spend ample time at the facility to reorganize the company, policy, rules, purchasing, and other needed changes. The company was sold to us with documentation that annual sales were approximately six million dollars.

John was the partner in sales and the person who would increase the sales at Perry County Foods. This meant that I would be spending a lot of time at the facility, which concerned me. The company was six hundred miles from Birmingham. It was too far to drive, and flying could become expensive. Once we took over the ownership of the company, I spent ten days living at the Fairfield Inn, located in Zanesville, Ohio, which was fifteen miles from the facility. During the ten days, reality smacked me in the face, and the reality was that I was going to have to spend a considerable amount of time deeply involved in the running of this company.

During the first three months, I negotiated a monthly rate at the Fairfield Inn located in Zanesville, Ohio, and I ate dinner at the Red Lobster next door. However, I quickly became tired of the same food every night. Sometimes I drove into Zanesville, which was a few miles away, to eat at a different restaurant, and then walk in the mall. After a while, this routine became redundant. I started purchasing easy-to-prepare food at the grocery store and eating in the room. After three months, I negotiated a six-month rate at the Fairfield Inn. I fell into a routine of getting to work at seven a.m., leaving work at six p.m., and driving the fifteen miles to the Fairfield Inn, where I cooked a frozen dinner in the microwave. Then, I usually did some work, called home, read the newspaper, and watched television until I went to sleep.

After being away from home almost every week for months, I leased a condo for six months, and I rented furniture to make the condo livable. I was flying or driving home every ten to fourteen days. Being away from home was beginning to take a toll on me emotionally, but I could not find a solution to the problem. The company was difficult to run because the product was received during the day, and most of the production and packaging of pizzas was competed on the night shift.

We also had a core of great employees that were the anchor of the company. They could be depended on day and night to operate the company. However, Perry County was the poorest county in the state of Ohio, and the pool of employees was not good. A large number of people in the area were on welfare or some other government program and did not want to work. The company had approximately thirty extra employees on "stand-by" to make sure there were enough workers for a full shift on the day shift and night shift. It was not uncommon to hire a person who never showed up. Others would take off a day or two just because they wanted to take off.

The night shift had the most employees and precipitated multiple problems. Married men and women were "crossing the pizza" line as we called it. One night I was called by the police to come to the plant because a jealous husband was there with a shotgun threatening to kill the man who was allegedly involved with his wife. This type of problem seemed to be ongoing. Most of the infidelity was conducted outside the company, although it originated on the company premises. There were many employees on the night shift who consumed alcohol or used drugs.

One day John Largent, the operations manager, found a man and young lady making out in the freezer. John came to me and asked what we should do about this situation. My first response to John was, "Anyone who can make out in a freezer that is ten degrees below zero deserves a medal or a bonus." After some discussion, John met with the two and explained that not only was their act against company policy, but also that it was highly dangerous for them to be in the freezer when no other employee was aware of where they were. John told them that some of time the emergency lever did not work, and if they were locked in the freezer they could be frozen to death quickly. He also told them how embarrassing it would be for their family to find them frozen together. I don't think anyone was in the freezer again under those circumstances. However, what they did not know was that the temperature in the cooler was only thirty-five to thirty-eight degrees. Perry County Foods also had a sense of humor!

It soon became apparent to John and me that the previous owners had intentionally falsified the annual sales. Therefore, John and I put an extensive report together and drove to Indianapolis, Indiana, where the owners lived. We presented the evidence that indicated that we had been misled or lied to during the due diligence process. The previous owners had stated that the company had annual sales of six million dollars. Once we had purchased the company and begun operation, Harold Rosenfield, our financial officer, informed us that the company had annual sales in the amount of three and half million dollars. Harold was now on our team and he openly enlightened us to the deception. After Ken Edelbrock and the Chaffee brothers reviewed the evidence we presented, they agreed to pay the company five hundred thousand dollars for the deception, but they wanted five percent of the company's stock. John and I took the offer and purchased a small pizza facility in Altoona, Pennsylvania, in order to give us additional production capacity. During this time Kane Kulas, an excellent salesman who had previously worked for Pasquale Food Company, was employed to sell the company's products to new accounts and service the existing accounts. A few months later Louis Mango, who had been a salesman at Pasquale Food Company, was also employed as a sales representative to further expand the company's business.

One afternoon John Sanford, Kane Kulas, John Largent, and I were driving to Altoona, Pennsylvania to spend a couple of days at the plant. As we entered the city limits of Altoona, we found that every hotel or motel was fully occupied. Finally, Kane asked one of the service desk personnel what was going on in Altoona. She told him there was a Shriners International Convention in town. This was not news we wanted to hear. She said that there was a motel approximately eight to ten miles down the road that could possibly have vacancies.

By that time, it was almost 11:30 p.m. Out of desperation; we started driving toward the motel, using the instructions given to us by the desk clerk. It seemed as if we had driven thirty miles, but at last we were on the road which should lead us to the motel. All of us were ready to sleep. As we drove into the hotel gravel parking lot, we all said at the same time, "We are at the Bates Motel!" (the movie depicted in the Alford Hitchcock movie *Psycho*). It was as close to replicating the Bates Motel as anything I could imagine. We were desperate! We stopped! The sign was not lighted; no one was in the "so-called" front office. After knocking on the front door for a while, a little old man opened the door. We told him we needed rooms for four. He said that he only had two rooms left. He went on to say that the rooms were twenty dollars per room. This told us something, but it was almost 1:00 a. m. and we were ready for any place to sleep. John asked if the rooms had telephones and the little old man replied, "No." He pointed to an outside telephone booth.

Considering that there were only two rooms available, we had to pair up. My "luck of the draw" was that John Largent and I would be sharing a room. The old man indicated where our rooms were and handed us a key. When we opened the door to our room, it was extremely old. The shower was so small that a man the size of John Largent, at two hundred and forty pounds, could not get into it. There were small green lizards running across the floor. There were roaches, dead and alive. The room only had one double bed, which posed a problem. John was a very large man who would easily take up two thirds of the bed. We were so tired that we fell into the bed and were sleeping within minutes. I was thankful to lie down anywhere, even in a room like this.

All was well for about forty five minutes. I thought a herd of hogs had been let loose in our room. John was snoring louder than anyone I had ever heard. I was desperate to sleep, so I woke him up, and told him I could not sleep because of his snoring. He turned over; the snoring stopped. I went back to sleep, but it was only a short time until the hogs were back. I got up and tried to find any area in the small room to sleep so that I could get away from John. There was no place, so I was back beside John, who continued to snore like a hog. I decided this was not going to stop, even with a pillow over his head, and one over my head. I must admit, as tired as I was, I had an evil thought; pressing the pillow closer to John's head. Just a thought!

156

I finally gave up, deciding he could not help it, and there was nothing I could do but endure it and try to sleep. I kept thinking if I had a pint of Canadian Club, a bottle of cheap wine, or a bottle of sleeping pills, I would consume them all just to get some sleep. I suffered through the night, realizing the next day I was going to feel and look like a zombie, and I did. I took a shower with the water as hot as I could stand. The bugs, lizards, and other insects seemed to enjoy that night a lot more than I did. I wondered if they had possibly "sung and danced a jig" while scampering around the room during the night.

As we drove out of the parking lot of the motel, I was bemoaning the terrible night I had endured. When we got on the highway, I looked back at the motel. A very old house sat on the hill above the motel. Scenes from *Psycho* blurred my vision for a moment. I felt sure Alfred Hitchcock was smiling from his grave. I never looked back.

Kane Kulas, John Sanford, and John Largent must have slept better, because they did not complain. The only comments they made concerned the condition of the rooms. I felt a tinge of resentment because they felt good and said they slept well.

We were hoping for a place to eat and drink a lot of coffee. Near Altoona, we found a restaurant and had breakfast and a lot of coffee. We went to our facility without enthusiasm, and left early to drive all the way back to Zanesville. We had no desire to spend another night in that "Godforsaken" area. There would be no other night at the "Bates Motel."

I had been away from home nearly one and half years and I was mentally and emotionally exhausted. I flew or drove home every ten to fourteen days, but it was not a good way to live. Being alone over an extended period of time is very difficult, but something I recommend to everyone. It is a good time for self-examination. I experienced this, and I had a lot of time to review my life. I learned more than I can describe when I started looking inward rather than outward. I started looking in the mirror and taking a close look at me. The more I looked, the more I realized that I did not like the person I saw. My emotions, feelings, heart, and soul opened up, and I saw myself for the first time, maybe as others had always seen me. It was not a pretty picture, but rather one that was embarrassing and hurtful, and one that I did not want to frame and display.

I realized that God had placed me in this situation in order to get my attention, to see myself as He saw me, hopefully to change my life to one in which I could look in the mirror with happiness. I fell on my knees by my bed and confessed to Jesus Christ everything that had to be flushed out of my heart. I confessed things that I had forgotten. I cried until I could not shed another tear, and finally I went to sleep. Each night I continued to dissect every phase or passage of my life, because I wanted to understand how I had reached this point. This internal evaluation helped, but I had not turned my life over to Christ. I really wanted to, but I thought I would be giving up something. "Alone we find solitude, together we find love." These words are from the book, *Love is an Attitude,* written by Walter Render.

CHAPTER THIRTY

THE A. & M. PARTNERS

In the fall of 1994, John Sanford and I were approached by an ex-broker who had represented Pasquale and John Labatt. He told John Sanford and me about a "so-called" financial wizard he knew who worked as a liaison between buyers and sellers of companies. He also "supposedly" had the ability to find quality investors who would be interested in our company.

After several discussions, John and I decided it would be to our advantage to bring in additional investors in order for the company to continue to grow. We could also pay off some of the debt we had incurred when we purchased the company. We decided that for a two million dollar investment, we would give up forty-nine percent of the company stock.

At that time we were not aware of whom the investors were, but as we continued to discuss the deal, the investors surfaced. They were known as the A. & M. Partners.

John and I met with the Partners at their office in Washington, D. C. There was not much discussion because our ex-broker and financial wizard had already informed the partners about Perry County Foods.

The partners agreed to purchasing forty-nine percent of the Perry County Foods stock. After additional discussions, we agreed to accept two million dollars and give up forty-nine percent of the ownership of the company. We learned later that the finder was going to receive a fee for his services and ex-broker assumed that he was going to play a role in the operations of Perry County Foods.

The new stockholders encouraged us to move the corporate offices from Perry County, Ohio to the Ash Building in Birmingham, apparently not realizing the additional cost to the company. In addition, they were in favor of building a testing laboratory in the Birmingham office. This was a large additional cost compared to the size of the company. The Board of Directors was comprised of John Sanford, the two new partners, and me. In January of 1995, we relocated the corporate offices from Perry County, Ohio, to the Ash building in Birmingham, Alabama.

Once we moved the offices to Birmingham, we hired a financial officer. He was hired through an employment agency, had worked as a financial officer for one of the large banks, and had outstanding credentials. He had been evaluated by an industrial psychologist and had received an excellent review. He was qualified to perform the job, but his attitude and the way he treated the personnel reporting to him was deplorable. After a few months he was terminated.

During this time Leslie, my daughter, continued to suffer from a severe case of anorexia. She had reached the point that she had to have immediate medical attention. Jackie and I, through a local doctor, located the best eating disorder treatment centers in the world. The one we chose was located in Topeka, Kansas. We decided that we would do everything necessary to save the life of our daughter. This included selling our houses and everything we owned. With the situation being as it was with Leslie, I felt it was time to be with Jackie and the rest of my family in an attempt to save Leslie's life.

On October 19, 1995, I resigned from Perry County Foods, Inc. I continued to own stock in the company and thought it would eventually increase in value. Once I was back in Birmingham, we made a reservation for Leslie to enter the Menninger Clinic, located in Topeka, Kansas, on

November 15, 1995. I flew out the day before Jackie and Leslie to make arrangements to have Leslie checked into the clinic.

Leslie did not want to go, and Jackie had a terrible time getting her to the airport in Birmingham and to Topeka, Kansas. However, they arrived the next day, and Leslie checked into the clinic the next morning. The facility looked like a small college campus, which we found unusual. Jackie and I had a very uneasy feeling because Leslie did not want to stay there and did not want us to leave. We flew back to Birmingham with very heavy hearts and hoped and prayed that we had made the correct decision.

After Leslie had been there for approximately one week, she started writing us letters that reflected improvement. We talked with her by telephone, and it seemed that she had adjusted to the clinic and program and was improving every day. It was important for her to get out of the clinic and come home before Christmas in 1995. Jackie and I flew to Topeka, Kansas, and spent the night. We checked Leslie out the next morning. This took more time than we wanted, but she had dramatically improved in every way. After checking out, we flew back to Birmingham with an optimistic outlook because our sweet, wonderful baby girl had greatly improved and was coming home for Christmas. She wrote some wonderful letters. I still have all of them in the Menninger file. Occasionally, I pull out that file and read the letters again.

The new investors were involved in the business both directly and indirectly. They immediately closed the one Division and demanded that certain personnel be terminated. They placed greater emphasis on the cookie business, which gave the company increased sales, but with little or no profit. Salaries were cut and benefits terminated, and the company was in turmoil. Personnel such as Kane Kula's and Louis Mango, who were the sales force, left the company and took other jobs. I learned that the new Partners intentions were to outsource the products to other countries to cut down on costs. This was the thought pattern President George H. Bush pushed and George W. Bush would follow after being elected president. Today the country is suffering from those flawed decisions.

LAWSUIT

At the time I resigned from the company, the inventory was one million, five hundred thousand dollars. The accounts receivable was one million, two hundred thousand. However, the new partners did not want me to receive any information pertaining to the company's status or performance after I left. They had a financial scheme in the works. They instructed Harold Rosenfield, John Largent, and other key employees to discontinue all communications with me. I heard from insiders at Perry County Foods that I could be dangerous and a determent to the new partners plan. However, after I left the company, I continued to be informed by two employees who knew what was going on and what was happening to the company. The new partners had a plan when they purchased stock in Perry County Foods to push me and others out of the company. They had a longer term plan that will manifest itself near the end of this chapter.

As early as July, 1995, I was beginning to put together an outline of the ploy that these new partners were organizing. After they owned forty-nine percent of the Company's stock, they highly encouraged the company to move its offices to Birmingham. John Sanford and I reluctantly conceded. When John and I asked about or discussed the move to Birmingham, their answers were ambiguous. This move took place in order to keep John and me away from Perry County Foods.

This was the beginning of a longer term plan that they had put in place. Their plan was partially working, because after the move to Birmingham, I spent less time in Perry County Foods than I had previously spent. At the same time, the new partners were developing a dialogue with the previous owners who continued to hold the lease on the facility. This was the beginning of the end for Perry County Foods, Inc.

It was unfortunate, but we had a Judas in the company who became part of the plan to take over the company. No one in the company knew about this person other than me. I concluded early in life that a Judas was a person who was devoid of loyalty. Loyalty is one of the most cherished of human virtues. Philosophers have reflected on the importance of loyalty in all human relationships. Loyalty is faithfulness or devotion to a person, country, group, or cause. Ethicists have pronounced loyalty to be one of the goods of life. A traitor casts a feeling to the recipient that is most difficult and most confusing and inflicts hurt that is far beyond description, bordering on surrealism. After a considerable amount of reading, studying, and making various comparisons, I came to the following conclusion. A Judas is a person who is comparable to a child molester–they cannot be rehabilitated or cured. It is impossible for me to describe the feeling inflicted by a Judas. "Judas" was not fully aware that his involvement in the company would come to an abrupt conclusion, and that the new partners, would kick him out of their bailiwick as soon as they achieved their plan.

I hired a private investigator to scrutinize everyone inside and outside of the company that had anything to do with the company. This included the new partners. The investigation was expensive, but it was worth the cost. The total investigation cost me approximately forty thousand dollars. It proved to be the best investment I had made in a long time. It is unreal to find out what people are really thinking and doing. It is difficult to imagine that anyone would do anything to be classified a "Judas." The information received through the in-depth investigation at first made me nauseous and cast a shadow on mankind for a while. It is very difficult to think that anyone could betray another person. As I was thinking this, I suddenly remembered that one of the disciples betrayed Christ with a kiss. His name was Judas.

Dorothy Ann Willis Richards, the forty-fifth governor of the State of Texas, coined the fitting phrase, "Poor George, he can't help it; he was born with a silver foot in his mouth." She was referring to George W. Bush. I changed the phrase to silver boot because it seemed to be more becoming

When a person is elected President by the people, why aren't the most qualified people selected to participate to lead our country? It is neither the President, his cabinet, congress, lobbyists, nor big business that is slowly killing our country; it is cronyism and nepotism. Review the effect that cronyism had on New Orleans, in 2005, after the hurricane Katrina disaster. Consider the suffering and the many that died because President George W. Bush selected a totally unqualified individual to head up FEMA. The Director of FEMA, Michael D.

Brown, was criticized so severely that he resigned. Why? He was one of the Bush administration's cronies. This is only one of the hundreds of examples.

I understand that while the United States was really at war with Iraq, the people who lived in Kuwait were going out of their country until the war was over. Or maybe a better way of stating it: the people who lived in Kuwait took a vacation.

When John Sanford and I purchased the company in April of 1993, we arranged a one million, two hundred thousand dollar line of credit. The company pledged its inventory and receivables as collateral. Approximately five months after I left the company, the new partners, and AmSouth Bank placed a one million, two hundred and fifty thousand dollar law suit against me. This was the amount Perry County Foods owed AmSouth for the line of credit that had been used. Once I received the lawsuit from the new partners along with AmSouth, I hired Tom Harris, an attorney I knew from the past when he was with Sirote, Permute, Friend, and Friedman. I spend several hours giving Tom an overview on Perry County Foods, the new partners, and AmSouth Bank Tom took my case, and started preparing my defense against the people and entities listed above. I liked Tom Harris because he would take a case against the big banks, big business, or any other entity. He was a shrewd ass-kicking attorney, when ass-kicking was necessary. My case was going to force Tom to purchase new shoes once the case was over.

We assumed that the bank in Indianapolis, Indiana, would send the bank records pertaining Perry County Foods when subpoenaed, but they did not cooperate, and we could not get them. We knew the previous owners had a strong relationship with the bank.

The day I arrived to be deposed, I sat on one side of a long table beside my attorney, Tom Harris. We looked into the eyes of the partners, and twelve individuals who were mostly lawyers. The new partners had three attorneys from Washington D.C. In addition, AmSouth had four or five attorneys. John Campbell, the loan officer, and another AmSouth representative were also there It was overwhelming to see so many people on the opposite side of the table. Tom whispered that we were well prepared and for me not to be concerned with the number of people across the table. He assured me (and I needed it) that the strength of this case was not in the number of attorneys and other associated personnel, but in the case.

The opposing attorneys stated over and over what they had calculated as the value of Perry County Foods, which was worthless per their analysis. However, Tom had told me that we had the advantage because we had a "bomb" to drop on them at the appropriate time. At that time, I did not know what Tom was talking about, because he had not informed me about a bomb, or where it was coming from. He had not told me because he wanted to make sure he had the document in his hands before discussing it. Plus, he would not find out if he could get the document until after the first day or second day of my deposition.

After the first day of being deposed, I did know how many days the case would continue. I thought it was going to last four or five days. When Tom Harris and I arrived the first day, one of the attorneys representing the new partners was the first to start deposing me. Depositions are not a lot of fun. I had to be constantly alert to answer the never-ending questions. One thing the opposition did not know was that this was not my "first rodeo."

I reverted to my personal formula that had catapulted me to the top of Associated Grocers of Alabama, Pasquale Food Company, John Labatt, Ltd., and through the ranks in the military. Over the years, I had been deposed many times and had learned how to size up the attorney, how to answer questions, how to not answer questions, and how to frustrate the deposing attorney. My attitude was to ignore all procedures and professionalism and go for the kill.

In this lawsuit, I think I had spent more time with Tom Harris, preparing our defense, than the opposing side had spent. It took me about two hours to get into the rhythm of the deposition. At that time, my demeanor changed to a tactic of intimidation in every way possible. I gave a louder response, would not answer the questions, used the old phrase, "I don't remember; I don't recall." I was as indignant as possible. I often reversed the question to the deposing attorney, which was unacceptable. I continued my pace which was manifested through arrogance, intimidation, and blaring responses to questions. I denigrated the new partners every time there was an opportunity.

Around 3:00 p.m. on the first day of being deposed, the deposition was stopped while a judge was called to come over or give a ruling by telephone because we had reached an impasse. I refused to answer the questions. The day ended and I was completely wiped out mentally, emotionally, and physically. As I reflected on the end of the first day, I remembered that I had been deposed many times, sometimes in trials before juries, and sometimes with only a judge. I had never lost a case.

Before I went home at the end of the first day, Tom Harris, my attorney gave me a copy of the "bomb." He had a courier pick it up in Atlanta and deliver it to him at the end of the day on Monday, my first day of being deposed. Then, I went by Tom's office where he made copies of the prospectus. We spent time reviewing the document and planned our strategy for the next day. After the meeting at Tom's office, I took a copy of the prospectus home to study and dissect it. As I read the fraudulent prospectus put together by the new partners, or their attorney's. I was confident that I was going to win this case. My adrenaline was flowing and I did not want the movie to end.

The next day was going to be "Bomb Day." These men had never endured pauperism as I had, and they lacked the character it builds and the mental toughness I had gained. I considered myself a specialist in handling people who had grown up in a soft, plush environment.

Before the law suit was filed against me, I heard, through certain Perry County personnel, that there was some concern or fear that I possibly had documentation that would be detrimental to their fraudulent suit. I believe when one is a fraud it is easy to file a fraudulent law suit. The two new partners, along with the other intellectuals present, fell into this category.

Months after I resigned, I learned through key personnel at Perry County Foods that the company's inventory and accounts receivable were vanishing without the company receiving the money for these two assets, which totaled approximately two and one half million dollars.

This was more than enough to liquate the debt should the stockholders make that decision.

I arrived at the deposition with Tom Harris' son, who was also an attorney, on the second day. He had actually spent more time on the case than his father. All the other stooges arrived and sat on the other side of the table as they had on the previous day, displaying their pious faces. Tom joined the deposition at 10:00 a. m. He had prepared notes for us to discuss at the lunch break.

The word was leaked, intentionally, from the opposition that they had a document that was going to bury me. This concerned me, but I knew there was not a document of any magnitude that I could not handle. As a matter of fact, as the second day began, I was actually looking forward to the day because I had reached deep down in my heart, mind, and soul, and was going to use every ounce of intellect, energy, intimidation, arrogance, and controlled anger that I could.

One of the attorneys read a letter that was signed by the finder, outlining the current status of the company. Once he finished reading the letter, in a voice as loud as I could respond, I said, emphatically, that this person did not know a damn thing about the company and did not write that letter. I stated the letter was written by the ex-broker who was trying to get into the business because he had lost his brokerage firm.

All of this was exactly what I wanted; the deposition was going the way we planned it. Once the judge talked by telephone with one of their attorneys and Tom, my attorney, we reverted back to a normal deposition for a short time. Tom asked me to hold it down a little bit. But, at that point, I was not willing to listen to him because I was convinced that I was going to easily win the case. I had already made it known that I was never going to pay one cent. I was in the rhythm that I enjoyed, and felt as if I were in a movie being watched by millions.

It is unusual how Tom Harris was able to get the "bomb" document. Several days before the deposition started, Tom Harris was in a car with three other attorneys, driving to Atlanta to attend a seminar. While driving, there was obviously some conversation among them, and the name, Pasquale Food Company, came up. Pasquale was well known and many people made a lot of money when the company was sold to John Labatt. Tom was fully aware of Pasquale, and one of the other attorneys had owned stock in Pasquale, and knew Neal Andrews, John Sanford and me.

In the course of the conversation, one of the attorneys dropped a bombshell. He mentioned he had a prospectus on a company that was registered in Washington, and somehow my name was associated with Perry County Foods. Perry County Foods was listed in the prospectus, along with several companies, in order to form a fairly large company that was going public or to do an initial public offering.

On Tuesday morning, we decided to drop the "bomb" on the opposition at the end of the day. I prepared charts, graphs, and spreadsheets, comparing the value of Perry County Foods in the prospectus, to the value of what Perry County Foods was worth according to the new partners. The deposition dragged on as I continued to give my deposing attorney "hell."

As the day moved on, I became more adamant because I knew we were getting close to the time to drop the bomb. As I glanced at my analysis of the fraudulent prospectus I could hardly wait to present it to the stooges. I knew I would win, embarrassing the twelve on the opposite side of the table, especially their attorneys. I was confident that new partners had not informed their attorneys about the fraud they had planned. Still, I continued to contain myself without getting into the prospectus.

The value of Perry County Foods was brought up again by the opposing two attorneys, and I could hardly contain my excitement, and I looked at them through fixed eye contact that did not move for as long as I could keep from blinking. As the two attorneys went over the value of Perry County Foods with their superior tone of voice, I was spreading out before me the "bomb" data that was going to change the tempo of this deposition quickly. Once they completed highlighting the company's value at no value, I slowly started my controlled response.

I stated that I would like for their attorneys to go over again how they were able to calculate the value of Perry County Foods, Inc., at a zero value. They seemed eager to slowly explain how they concluded the value of the company at zero. I assumed from their response that they felt that it was necessary to more slowly this time, and in more detail, because they were explaining it to someone from Alabama, and they were elitists from Washington. This just delayed the "bomb" that was about to blow their asses off. These intellectual, Ivy League pinheads and attorneys, with zero scars, mentally or physically, did not have any idea what was about to happen. I listened with serious concern on my face as they slowly outlined the zero value of the company again. Once they had finished, I politely thanked them for going over the facts again. Then, with a very concerned look on my face, as if I were going to agree with their analysis, I slowly and methodically placed documents in front of me that covered approximately four feet of my side of the table. As I glanced at them, I could see the wonder and concern in each of the twelve faces across the table from me. Then I started slowly, and continued to talk in a professional manner, respecting those on the other side of the table for the first time.

I said in a firm voice, "Gentlemen, I am holding in my hands several documents, spreadsheets, and analyses of the true facts of this case, backed by indefensible evidence." I went on to say that I was going to slowly go over the data with them, with the understanding that they would be able to comprehend it. I told them that as I went over the documents, to feel free to stop me should they not understand. The first document I went over was a prospectus listing several companies that the new stockholders purported to own, including Perry County Foods, Inc. I had made copies of the prospectus for each person in attendance. First, I refuted the analysis that they had presented, placing no value on Perry County Foods Inc. I told them to read the section of the prospectus noting the value of Perry County Foods, Inc. as ten million, two hundred thousand dollars, based on the new partner's analysis. The owners listed in this prospectus were both of the new partners. I told them to note that Perry County Foods, Inc. was listed along with numerous other companies in the prospectus to form a fairly large company. The intention of this prospectus was to do an initial public offering or an IPO in the State of Virginia.

Based on the attorney's stunned look, it was apparent that the A. &. M. Partner's had failed to inform their attorneys about the prospectus. Tom Harris and I were about to wet our pants as they were reading a copy of the prospectus. It was as if they were viewing an unbelievable document or a miracle. I offered to explain the spreadsheets and analyses if they would like. The attorneys declined my offer. I watched the two new partners as their attorney's whispered questions. As no surprise to me, they asked for a fifteen-minute break. When we were back in the room, the opposition seemed to be much more subdued than the first day.

After a short time, the meeting was adjourned; there would not be a third day of my deposition. The opposing group, including the attorneys, looked like scolded children walking out of the room flaunting their Brooks Brothers attire. This made Tom Harris and me extremely happy. It was very difficult to realize that the partners, along with their cronies, had attempted to pull off a major fraud. In my mind, it is criminal to not inform one's attorney or attorneys of everything. I believe the new partners did not tell their attorneys the total truth about the case. If so, what they did was a disservice to their attorneys by not telling them the truth and placing them in an embarrassing situation.

The lawsuit was filed because the new partners believed that, because of whom they were, I would be intimidated and settle quickly rather than go through the ordeal. This was a mistake because I did not care who they were, and I relished the satisfaction to beat the hell out of them and their high-powered attorneys. I don't think they had encountered anyone before who was looking forward to an attack on them and their attorneys, with no respect for any of them. I made an overkill effort to denigrate them and their attorneys every time there was an opportunity. These two individuals were the epitome of the people I enjoyed humiliating. I do not think they had the opportunity to grow up in the environment that I did. I have never regretted growing up in poverty because it gave me a dimension that few human beings have and, in this case, I capitalized on it.

Tom Harris told me that we needed to schedule some time to start preparing for a counter suit. He intended for the opposing attorneys to hear the statement, and they did. I was extremely happy that I had selected Tom Harris because he would take on banks, corporations, individuals, legal firms, or any entity, because he did not have ties to anyone or any company. I was also happy that he was willing to take my case, and I will always owe him a debt of gratitude because he was able to get a copy of the prospectus. This document won the case. I can honestly state that this suit was one of the hardest ordeals I ever faced. I had assets that were of value, such as our home located on Cherokee Road, a house on Lake Martin, two other houses, mutual funds, money market accounts, and other assets that could have jeopardized my family, should I have lost the case.

Because of my makeup, I made a decision up front, and let the opposition know, that they were in for a fight that they would lose. If I lost, I would appeal the case until I had spent every cent I owned. The debt owed to AmSouth would be paid by anyone but not me. One of these individuals called my home and spoke with my wife several times. Each time he talked with her he regurgitated disturbing news. Fortunately, my wife did not inform me of these calls until long after the lawsuit was concluded. This individual should be thankful that she did not tell me. If I had known, I would have been on a plane to pay him an unpleasant visit.

After the deposition was concluded, Tom Harris received a call stating that the opposing party would settle the suit if I would pay $1,090.000 rather than $1.250.000. Our answer to this offer was played back to them as a bad joke. During the next few days, Tom notified them that I was considering a counter suit for ten million dollars, and we were meeting to prepare the suit. Then, within days the amount they wanted me to pay AmSouth dropped to $750,000. We replied, "Are you kidding?"

A few days went by; one of the attorneys called Tom Harris and stated that I did not list the houses I owned in Gardendale and Cahaba Heights as assets. My response was, "I did not list the houses and I am not going to list the houses." These houses were bought for my mother and stepfather and for my wife's parents to live in the rest of their lives. I asked Tom to tell them to do whatever they wanted to do, but the two houses would not be listed as assets. I assured them that I had other assets that were not listed and would never be listed. We never heard these houses mentioned again. My short answer to them was "Go to hell."

In a short time, Tom called me and asked me to come over to his office. I quickly went. He said, "I think I have some good news, but before I tell you what it is, I am advising you not to take the offer." Then, he said they had dropped the amount from the original one million, two hundred fifty thousand dollars to one hundred sixty-five thousand dollars. Then Tom said, "I know you want to get past this situation, but if you pay one cent, you will hate yourself the rest of your life." I had previously told the goons that I was never going to pay one cent. I already explained to the opponents and others that, should I lose the case, I would appeal until I did not have a dime left. I took Tom's advice, and he relayed the news to the other attorneys that I was not willing to ever pay one cent. Tom and I assumed that the last offer was the amount they owed their attorneys and that they were attempting to get enough money to pay them.

The next week, one of the attorneys called Tom and wanted to draw up documentation that would bring the lawsuit to an end. However, they wanted mutual releases to keep me from filing a suit against them. I really wanted to file a suit against them, but I was drained mentally and burned out on this case. So we signed mutual releases and concluded this law suit.

I regret not filing a suit against these individuals and feel certain I would have won. These two were guilty of several infractions not outlined in this book. These two individuals used the word "disingenuous" often when talking about other people. After the lawsuit was concluded, I believed they were using the word referring to themselves. .

I write this with tremendous pride: "I won." I can proudly say that the formula that had always worked for me was outstanding in confronting these pinheads. Sometimes I think I would like to do it again. I often think of Tom Harris and appreciate that he took my case; he was a unique attorney who guided me through this painful ordeal.

Perry County Foods continues to operate under new ownership. Occasionally I call and talk to John Largent, who has continued to manage the company through very difficult changes. His motto is, "Owners change, products change, people come and leave, but John Largent stays." Many of the same personnel continue to work for the company and survived the many changes of ownership.

Once the lawsuit was over, a prominent Birmingham attorney, thoroughly connected to the Democratic hierarchy, called me. He asked me to come down to his office when I had an hour or so to discuss something that he thought was important, and maybe I would agree. In a couple of days, I went down to his office and met with him and a man who was with very prominent in the "DNC," or Democratic National Committee.

The reason they wanted to talk with me was because they had knowledge of the lawsuit and that I had won the case. They wanted to talk about the case in light of using the data, along with my involvement, to open the perceived wrongdoing by the Republican administration. The temptation was there, and after I left the attorney's office, I gave some deep thought to their proposal. However, at that point, I didn't want to get my family involved with this matter. To do so would almost certainly put their privacy and lives at risk. After a few days, I reluctantly called the attorney and told him I was not willing to divulge any information. Later, I received another call from a powerful Democrat who tried to get me involved. He explained to me how detrimental it would be to the country if another republican were elected.

In retrospect, he was correct. The deficit reached an all-time high; we entered the war with Iraq, which was not justified, causing thousands of men and women to lose their lives, and those who returned home had missing limbs, various life restricting-wounds, and mental trauma. All of us must ask, "Why, why, why?" I do not intend to outline the Bush administration's mistakes, but I do wish I had followed the format of what the unnamed attorney and the Democratic Party Representative wanted me to do. Looking back, and knowing what I know today, I should have worked with them, and maybe Al Gore would have been president. If I had worked with the DNC, I don't think I would have to refer to George W. Bush as a "hanging Chad."

You may ask; what was in this legal entanglement that would cause the DNC to want to talk with me. I would love to write a chapter to answer the question, but I am legally prohibited. At some point I will write a book on this matter that will be shocking.

I put the lawsuit, the depositions, and all the stooges behind me. I now reflect on this and the experience as something that I am happy about. I gained a lot of additional insight into people who will never get that silver spoon, foot, or boot, out of their mouths.

I can honestly state, without hesitation, that I would like a replay of this case. I would bring new meaning to being difficult. I know how to win and they don't. "Fellows, it's a formula that I used to win. I have at least one ingredient that you don't have, and you will never have. Furthermore, I doubt if you know, or will ever know, anyone who has that ingredient. This is information and terminology that you will never understand." Those born with the silver boot, silver spoon, or have everything given to them directly or indirectly will never win against those of us who came from hard backgrounds. I wholeheartedly contend. Attention: A. & M. Partner's: it may appear to be boastful, but if I had been on your side of the table with a dozen attorneys, I would have won the case you lost.

As I reflect on this case I always remember the last two words, from the last episode of one season of the television program *Breaking Bad*. I Won!

CHAPTER THIRTY-ONE

MY FORMULA FOR SUCCESS

I want to emphasize that my formula for success was cultivated and molded from the time I was approximately seven years old through age twenty-four. I became keenly aware of what it was going to take to be financially successful. I continued to refine my formula as I matured and gained additional experience. The point I want to make clear is that my formula is for me and not for anyone else. I would suggest that anyone at any age find the formula that works for them. Everyone who chooses to make financial success their goal should evaluate the goal carefully. It should be discussed with people who have gained financial success, who started at the poverty level or near the poverty level. I state this because, after seeking wisdom from a broad selection of people who are trustworthy, one may discover that this is not the goal or goals one wants to seek. Making a lot of money comes with a personal price for the whole family.

Beginning at approximately seven years of age, I began to notice the differences in people, how they talked, how they dressed, their attitude, motivation, and passion. Doing this prompted me to realize that I was different and did not fit in with my immediate and extended family. I did not talk much, but I listened more than a seven year old should. I became keenly aware of facial expressions, tone of voice, body language, and eye movement. I put these together with what was being said or talked about. I continued to hone my ability to read situations based on these observations, during the first grade, high school, three years working for Associated Grocers of Alabama, two years in the Army, and three years in the Army Reserve. These experiences plus working in the Judge Advocate General's office gave me additional knowledge. Working at Associated Grocers of Alabama at the lowest level, and spending two years in the Army starting at the lowest grade level was very good for me. This experience gave me the education which I needed to complete my formula on how to move from the bottom of a company to the top. Just working hard is not the answer. There are millions of people who work extremely hard but never reach financial success.

As noted in other chapters in this book, I was different from my family. I was always concerned that I did not fit in with them. I was aware of this and so was my family, to the point that I became a loner, which bothered me very much. I watched as my stepfather and my brother, Donald, prepared to go hunting and fishing. I did not like to do these things and refused to participate. I was silently critical of decisions made by my mama and stepfather and knew that long term, the decisions were going to produce negative results. As I was silently evaluating, analyzing, and criticizing, I felt guilty, because it felt wrong. I did not have the appreciation for them that I wanted to have. They took care of me and provided for me the best they could afford to under the circumstances.

I did then, and today, appreciate everything they did for me because I knew how hard my stepfather worked, and how difficult it was for him to manage. I think seeing how difficult life was, financially, for my parents caused me to make a pledge to myself that I was never going to endure the things my mother and stepfather endured. Poverty is denigrating, causes a loss of self-esteem, deflated pride and ego, and an unworthy feeling, and it puts one in a caste system. I was motivated to break the cycle of poverty at any personal cost. My mother and step father were suffering from generational poverty, and they did not think it was possible to change. I knew in my heart that I was not going to perpetuate another generation of poverty. I concluded early that I was going to have everything I needed and wanted, see the world, and make a better life for those around. In doing so I knew the price, the sacrifice, and all the things spelled out in my formula to achieve this.

I was interested in playing football and baseball; my favorite sport was baseball at Falkville High School. It was a wonderful feeling to wear the "Blue Devils" jacket which, by the numbers of letters, reflected how many years one had played football and lettered. Baseball was my game, because I grew up playing the game every day that it was not raining, sleeting, or snowing. The mountain boys, as we were sometimes called, had an advantage, and it reflected in playing high school baseball.

I played in a rock and roll band, and sang in a quartet that won second place in the State finals. I had a lead role in our senior play, which took a lot of practice because I was afraid that I might forget my lines. I did not understand and do not understand today why I was active in sports, plays, music, and never had one relative come to anything in which I was involved. Not in at high school or grammar school. I noticed other parents were always at the football games, baseball games, plays, and other activities in which their sons or daughters were involved. I am not writing this because I feel sorry for myself, but because I just never understood! No one in my immediate or extended family ever asked about the things I loved. I expected someone to ask who won the game, what songs did your quartet sing to do so well, who is in your string band, or how are you doing in school. I am not casting blame or aspersions upon anyone in my immediate family or extended family. I concluded there was something wrong with me, which gave me assiduous vibes. I felt I had been, and was continuing, to face irrefutable headwinds that were anonymous. As I grew older I realized that my family was preoccupied with the never ending economic conditions, the war, and the residuum of the great depression which caused them to have little involvement in their children's lives.

The time I worked at Associated Grocers of Alabama, plus the two years in the Army, and three years in the Judge Advocate General's office, in The Army Reserves, gave me the ability to turn what I had considered negatives into positives. I accepted the difference I felt. I realized it was me; I was going to turn everything about me into a positive. I worked on this every day and night until I reached the time when I had achieved this goal. Until this time I had several people telling me how I should be, which was completely wrong. A quote listed in another part of this book, written by Harvey Fierstein states: "Never be bullied into silence. Never allow yourself to be a victim; accept no one's definition of your life; define yourself."

Accepting who I was became the first step in defining, honing, and putting into practice a formula that I knew was going to work for me . This was going to move me up the ladder at Associated Grocers of Alabama.

My formula worked because it was designed or custom made for me, but it is not recommended for anyone else. This is not a book to teach anyone how to achieve his goals. There are thousands of books one can purchase that provide thousands of systems or methods to reach success or to get rich overnight. There is no book written to date that will lead a person to success unless he extrapolates parts of the books and tailors a formula for himself. Most books are written for the writer to make a lot of money, not to impart knowledge that is factual. It is just to give the reader a motivational hype that will last for a few days. In my obsession with success, I tried to interposition myself with poverty on one side and my hopes, dreams, and plans to become successful on the other side.

As you read the formula that worked for me, please keep in mind that I grew up in generational poverty. This is a very hard environment. I decided early that I was going to be harder than the circumstances that surrounded me. I adopted the following formula based on two things: genetics and environment.

After many years I worked out my formula.

- **Motivation** – This is the driving force of desire behind all deliberate actions of all human beings. Motivation is based on emotion– specifically, on the search for satisfaction.

- **Mystique** – due to my personality it was normal for me to possess this trait. I did not allow anyone to really know me outside of my immediate family. I did not talk about anything personal or comment on anything that would open the door for anyone to see in or develop a view of my life. My personal life was unknown, and I kept it that way.

- **Aspiration**- hitching one's wagon to a star, reaching high; "the desire of the moth for the star." [Shelley]

- **Perspiration** – Doing whatever it takes to accomplish the task, if it means having to be drenched with sweat.

- **Ability to read people** – I had studied, analyzed, and evaluated body-language every day all my life. In making body movement a lifetime study, the one most powerful part is the eyes. It is said that the "eyes are the windows of the soul." I don't know if this is true or not, but I do know that by looking into the eyes of a person one can gain a tremendous amount of insight. ("Trust your instincts. Intuition doesn't lie." Oprah Winfrey, "*O*" magazine, November 2008.)

- **Working** –I decided to work harder and produce more than other personnel.

- **Intelligence**–A very general capability that, among other things, involves the ability to reason, plan, solve problems, think abstractly, comprehend complex ideas, learn quickly, and learn from experience. It is not merely book-learning, a narrow academic skill, or test-taking smarts. Rather, it reflects a broader and deeper capacity for comprehending one's surroundings – "catching on,"- "making sense" of things, or "figuring out" what to do. (Article from Mainstream Science on intelligence–1994.) I knew that to be financially successful it was going to take a balance of sagacity, common sense, and humility. Humility was going to be the most difficult for me, but it was often necessary. Mark Twain once said, "Don't let schooling interfere with your education."

- **Available** – I made it a priority to always be available for overtime, weekends, and nights, and for any job that needed to be done.

- **Nonconformist** – I rarely agreed with the people with whom I worked.

- **Temperamental** – The personnel throughout the company knew that I had a reputation of not taking any verbal abuse from anyone. Once in a while I would intentionally exert the fear factor. If provoked, I would take physical action. I was not willing to accept a nickname, be picked on, or even be looked at with the wrong expression.

- **Prepared** – I made it a priority to be prepared for work, meetings, discussions, or whatever the subject matter. Once I found out the subject matter to be discussed I would, if necessary, spent all weekend learning more than I expected other people to know.

- **Passion** – I knew early in life that if I were passionate about what I was doing, I would reach the assignment, schedule, or goal, or even exceed it.

- **Determination** – I was willing to move around, over, under, or step on anything in my way to reach the top.

- **Handle difficulty** – I would handle difficult things that almost all other personnel did not want to do or just could not handle: situations such as terminating personnel, meeting with people that were "so- called" educated or experts in their field. I prepared and took them on anyway-doing whatever it took to win. I liked negotiating prices when it was assumed the best price had been reached. When the best price possible was said to be reached, I considered that as my starting point.

- **Fear factor** – When everything else failed, I used the fear factor which will work, it is not recommended. At times I exerted a boisterous and belligerent attitude.

- **Intimidation** - Most people are easily intimidated if one reflects a certain persona and asks difficult questions coupled with mystique and a tough approach.

- **Willing to pay the price** – All of the above were the components that worked for me. However, I was willing to pay the price for what I wanted or the goal I wanted to reach. That was the most important factor of all. If and when there was competition, I sized the person or persons up and learned as much as possible about them, their family, friends, and the things that were important to them. Once I found this out, I could usually determine what price the competitor was willing to pay. I knew I was going to win because I was willing to pay the price regardless of the price. I learned early in life that I could circumvent ninety-five percent of the people, but there were about five percent who wanted, in the military, and at Associated Grocers, the same thing I wanted, and that was to move up the ladder. The five percent were my competitors, but I never found anyone in the military, Associated Grocers, or other companies that were willing to pay the price. I never had to use the price I was willing to pay compared to others and to date have not divulged that price. This paragraph is not recommended for anyone else because there is danger in this approach to winning. The price may come too high. I am not willing to list the price I would have paid if necessary. I did what I had to do to move out of poverty. In taking this approach a person will have, as I do, a long list of regrets.

My definition of a formula: It is the fuel that allows common people to attain uncommon results.

IT'S ALL IN YOUR MIND

Whatever you hold in your mind will tend to occur in your life.

If you continue to believe as you have always believed, you will continue

to act as you have always acted. If you continue to act as you have

have always acted, you will continue to get what you have

always gotten. If you want different results in your life or your work, all

you have to do is change your mind.

Anonymous

Through using the above approach and my formula, I was fortunate to move from a private to a staff sergeant in less than two years while in the Army. It usually takes at least five years in the army to be promoted to this level. I am certain my last promotions were enticements to re-enlist. As stated earlier, I was drafted into the army and thought it was the worst thing that had ever happened to me, but after two years I was "brainwashed" and gave some thought to re-enlisting. If I had chosen to do so, I would have gone through military school, graduated as a Second Lieutenant, and quickly been promoted to a First Lieutenant. After that I would have had an opportunity to become a Captain, Major, Lieutenant Colonel, and other possibilities beyond that. I learned in the two years spent in the military that to become a Brigadier General one must have achieved at a very high level of performance. One must also become recognized within the Army hierarchy. As I listed earlier in this book, I was drafted into the army and it felt like I was on a trip to hell. However, looking back, after spending two years in the United States Army as a staff sergeant with one of the top divisions-The Second Armored Division, "Hell on Wheels," I feel honored to have served my country.

CHAPTER THIRTY-TWO

REGRETS

Often, people are asked, "As you look back over your life, do you have any regrets?" This question is usually asked to elderly people, but sometimes asked to people that are younger. Unfortunately, for most people most of time, the answer is, "I have no regrets," and "If I had my life to live over, I would not change anything." When I hear this answer, I believe the person is either not being truthful, has not analyzed every minute, phase, or passage of his or her life, or just can't remember. I believe it is impossible to have no regrets and not be remorseful, regretful, or unhappy about things one has said, done, or thought. I think those people who are asked that question are giving a quick, thoughtless answer. In some cases they want to present a life that was lived near perfection, to impress everyone, or to reflect a sanctimonious persona or false piety. Some people make the old statement, "I have no regrets in my life; I think everything happens for a reason." In my opinion it is an impossibility to live life from childhood through adulthood, and never do anything deserving regret. This could be called the big lie!

I have a lot of regrets that I am going to list in this chapter.

My definition of regret is pain of mind because of something done or experienced in the past, with a wish that it had been different; a looking back with dissatisfaction or with longing; grief; sorrow; especially, a mourning due to the loss of some joy, advantage or satisfaction; to feel troubled or remorseful over something that one has done or left undone.

I regret that I did not have a better understanding of my wife, Jackie, in the early years of our marriage, and realize that she was and is very different from me. I had a short temper, did not listen to her carefully, and brought my work and problems home, dumping my frustration on her. The attitude that everything was going to be done my way was truly wrong. I regret making decisions without thoroughly discussing them with her. If we had made decisions together, we would have made better and more beneficial decisions. I regret not understanding that Jackie could not handle conflict and would not and could not participate in it. I regret that I did not have a better understanding of the responsibility she had in caring for three children less than four years of age. I truly regret that I had a very strong opinion about everything and expressed those opinions frequently and harshly if necessary. I regret being away from home as my position in various companies became more demanding. I regret that I was not able to participate in Kim's, Leslie's and Les' activities at school and outside school. And I regret not spending more quality time just with my wife. Because my wife has been my life!

I regret not understanding my daughter Leslie's illness for a very long time, and this still hurts me today. But I finally understood. She knows that I love her with all my heart. She knows that I now understand and will help her in every possible way.

I regret making harsh remarks to my daughter Kim when she was enduring some difficulties. She was our first baby. Now that she is an adult, I often remember the thrill of her when she was born. I love her very much. Sometimes, it is easy to over-speak and regret it later. I have. Now we have a wonderful relationship that makes me very happy. She is happily married to her husband Scott Reynolds. He is a person so much like her; they are perfectly suited to be together.

I regret the harshness I exercised in the early days at Associated Grocers of Alabama, especially the fights when individuals were physically injured, and my unusual attitude which was, "I am not willing to take anything from anybody, verbal or physical, at any time." I learned early to, in a fight, hit first and hard, because I believed I had to in order to win. Many times I was hurt but never let anyone know.

If someone looked at me in a manner I did not like, or said something that really had little meaning, I was in their face and in most cases there was a fight, with that person injured. I was born with an unusual outlook and a different attitude than my family. I regret acting out these attitudes.

Even as a child I was not willing to take anything from anybody. I regret this more than I can describe. Some things are not worth the fight. In many of these misunderstandings I was also physically hurt.

While our house was being remodeled in early 1989, we made a deal with a doctor that we would sell him our house. His request for us to move out of the house within thirty days posed a dilemma. However, he had the answer to the problem, and that was for us to move to the seventh floor of a hotel which he owned at a nominal charge. We took his offer and put all our furniture in storage because the remodeling was going to take approximately six months.

We moved into the hotel, which was fine other than trying to find things that we should have kept out of storage. Approximately six weeks after we moved into the hotel, I woke one morning to get my car and go to work. At that time we had our three children whose cars were also parked under the secured deck at the hotel. There was a guard posted on the floor where we had eight automobiles parked. As I walked up to open my car I noticed someone had used something like a crow bar to pry open the door. Then I noticed my daughter Kim's convertible BMW had the top cut off, and my convertible Corvette had the top cut off. Our Aerostar Ford van was stolen and later found in another state. The other cars and truck were not damaged. I called the police and talked rather harshly to the security guard. I was quick to see that no one was going to talk because they all were part of the theft and destroying of three cars with one vehicle stolen. The police wrote up a report, but I knew they were not going to do an investigation.

Once the Aerostar Van was repaired, it was returned to me. Everything had been repaired inside and out including repainting it, because it appeared that one of the last things done to the Aerostar was to toss a can of red paint that hit the front of the hood and covered the van with red paint from front to back. Once the van was back in Birmingham, I took control of it knowing that I did not want to keep it because it was tainted. As I looked at the van, I felt the boiling rage inside me, and thought how much I wanted to find the people who stole the van and vandalized several of my cars.

During the short time I had the van, before trading it for another vehicle, I decided to do what the police probably did not do, and that was to go through the van with a very fine-toothed comb. I started inside and placed my hand down between the back and the seat. I was very surprised to find something in there, and pulled it out, and it was the driver license of a twenty-five year old young lady who lived in the area. I did the same thing in the next seat and pulled out a pay check stub from a company in a nearby city with a young man's name on it. The front seat yielded the pay check stub of another young man who lived in Birmingham. I went down to the police station near the hotel and made the evidence available to the officers on duty. After talking about the theft and the destruction of my vehicles, I could sense that they were not interested and were not going to do anything. I went home very distraught about this situation. I became convinced that these people should pay for their crime.

After thinking about it for several days, I decided that I would apply the punishment to each one of the three. The vandalizing of my cars and stealing my van made me feel like I had been personally violated. It was a feeling that I can't put into words. Maybe rage comes closest to how I felt. My intensity was immense, and I was going to find out who did this dastardly destruction and have the police and legal system handle it, or I would take matters in my hands.

Sometimes we become ensnared and intoxicated by the idea of power; we believe that if we can attain a certain level of power, we will be free of tyranny. The vandalizing and stealing of one of my vehicles seemed to give me additional power and rage. However, power for its own sake brings no relief, no solace, and no happiness. It is the way in which we use our power that can make us content, but few of us intend to use it, because we are too focused on the attaining it for the sake of having it. This is a mistake that I think most people make without truly recognizing it. I regret falling into this crevice.

I called the young lady and confronted her with her driver's license. She gave me a story that she had lost her purse on the city. She said probably someone took it, and that was the person who stole my van. I left and drove sixty miles and confronted the young man that had left his pay check stub in the van. I told him the other two individuals had identified him as the thief who also damaged my van and did tremendous damage to my cars. I put him under so much pressure that he thought I was going to kill him. I did not kill him, but I took my police baton and broke four of his fingers on his right hand. I left and gave him my name and told him if I ever heard anything about the fingers being broken, I would be back with punishment ten times as severe as broken fingers. He confessed that the other young man and young lady were in on vandalizing my cars and stealing my van.

I drove back to Birmingham and located the other young man. I asked him if he were part of the threesome who vandalized my vehicles and stole my van, and drove it to out of state. At first, he assumed I was affiliated with the police. I informed him I was not affiliated with the police, but was there to discuss the vandalizing of my cars and the stealing of my van. I asked why they further vandalized my van by throwing a red can of paint that hit the hood and splattered over the top and sides of the van. The more I thought about it, my rage ticked up a notch or two. I was in a destructive mindset and very close to an insane state of mind. It is impossible to explain to someone who has never hit someone in anger or who has never been hit, and realizes that the hitting would not end, could not end, until the opponent was hurt really badly. My rage overcame everything in one violent, terrifying moment, and I took my police baton and broke four of his fingers on his left hand, just as I had done to the young man sixty miles away.

I then drove to the nearby city where the young lady lived and informed her that both the other young men had stated that she was part of vandalizing my cars and the leader in stealing my van. I called her and she agreed to meet me at 4:00 p.m. in the parking lot of a fast food restaurant. It was wintertime, and it was almost dark. I told her that what she had done along with the other two young men was unforgiveable and that I wanted to talk to her in person before going to the police. Surprisingly, she met me in the designated parking lot. She admitted she was involved in everything. She said they drove the stolen van out of state with drugs in the van. She admitted the drugs were used by the three of them and they also took drugs there to sell. I had never hit or harmed a woman before, and I thought about not hurting her. But I was really upset about what had happened and the time it took to get my cars to the shop, the cost to repair them, and the cost of the rental cars until my cars were repaired.

I looked at her and told her the two thug friends of hers had had four of their fingers broken. At that point she became a smartass with me, and I took my fist and broke off her upper front teeth. I asked her if she would like to go to the police department and I would go with her. She said no and got in her car and left. I have never heard anything from these three thugs since the winter of 1989. They deserved to go to prison for several years.

I went down to the hotel and confronted the guard, who denied that he knew anything about the vandalism and stealing the van. I had not told him anything, so I asked him how he knew about the vandalism and that the van was stolen. He knew that I knew he was part of the plot as I replayed the events that took place that night. I explained my relationship with the owner of the hotel and that I could have his job eliminated. After that comment I took my police baton, and without notice I struck him across the nose with the night stick, which I am sure broke his nose. I asked him if he wanted to call the owner of the hotel and discuss the events, and he said no. I asked him if he wanted to call the police, and he said no. I regret the action I took with these four people more than anything I have ever done. Vengeance was not mine to take. Vengeance is destructive, for it simply perpetuates and accelerates the breakdown between persons. Revenge invites its own retaliation. Punishment may be appropriate when it is so designed that it enables persons to learn appropriate behavior in dealing with others. However, punishment without forgiveness becomes vindictive. I suffered with a feeling of ambivalence for a very long time after these events. Two young men had broken fingers, the guard had a broken nose, and the girl had two broken teeth. Was it worth it for me? No!

After these traumatic events I went through a quiet time, contemplating, reflecting, remorseful, cooling down, regretful, hurting inside. Quiet often brings a peace of its own—a time to reflect, to strengthen, and to forgive. I continue to have the personality that prompted me to take the brutal action listed above, but would I do that today? No!

I regret not spending more time with Jackie's mother and dad. They were gracious to me from the first time I met them until they passed away. I will never forget the manner in which they treated me. The years being with them went by too fast. They were wonderful people.

I regret not understanding my stepfather or showing more concern, care, and love for him. He treated me as a very special person, and never said an unkind word to me throughout my life. I often think he treated me better than his own children. He was one of the best men I have ever known. I often miss him and remember how hard he worked to provide for his family. He said to me many times, "I am proud of you."

I regret being over the top egotistically, narcissistic, prideful, vain, and other adjectives that could be added. It took too long for me to see me.

I regret terminating personnel harshly when it could have been handled professionally.

I regret not being closer to my extended family, but time always ran out before I could do all I wanted to do and should have done. It hurts to realize I was different, and I regret the harm this may have caused.

I regret not having more in common with my mother, my stepfather, my two brothers, and my sister as we grew up. Rick probably does not fall into this category because I was nineteen years of age when he was born. I was the black sheep of our family, not because I chose to be, but because I was just different.

One question I have had for many years is this: "Why is it that everyone who does anything wrong has a disease?" I have had many run-ins and many problems with people who are classified as having a disease when there was not a damn thing wrong with them other than not being a man. A person has the free will to do or not to do. These people whom I punched in the mouth chose to get punched in the mouth. I do wish I had walked away. Back to my question, and I hope there is an answer. Slowly but surely, are we going to reach a point when people are not responsible or accountable for anything they do? Will our society reach a time when responsibility and accountability are not expected? The following is advice for everyone who falls in the category of: when feeling depressed, lonely, rejected, terminated, and hurting mentally or physically. Do what the rest of us do; suffer through the ordeal. Suffering is good for the soul. You will feel better about yourself and will not have to deal with the aftermath that sometimes cannot be undone. Those who ease their pain with drugs, alcohol, pills, and other ingested pain relievers are very selfish people, who are more interested in themselves than they are those they pretend to love. I regret that people are becoming more fragile and tender and unable to tolerate pain. Learn to be tough rather that a whining weakling. Obviously, this excludes all people who have physical or mental challenges.

Even though I was not part of the situation, I regret the manner in which the Board of Directors at Associated Grocers of Alabama treated Mr. R.C Riley after I resigned from the company. Due to the shabby treatment he received, I hired him as a buyer for Pasquale Food Company.

I regret the situation that happened at Associated Grocers of Alabama that destroyed my friendship with Philip Watts. This situation is too complicated to explain, but it was the result of small people with smaller minds jockeying for position, infighting, and politics.

I regret that John Campbell, a loan officer with AmSouth, was caught up in the law suit which involved The A. & M. Partners and AmSouth Bank. John was a professional who did not deserve the involvement, which I am sure, affected him adversely.

I regret not keeping in contact with the three military men in my unit while at Fort Hood, Texas: Warren Officer W.I. Robinson, Master Sergeant Vevercia, and Staff Sergeant Morgan. These three men helped me in every way possible, and their support and advice helped me to formulate a style that helped me quickly move through the various echelons in the Army and at Associated Grocers of Alabama. "Hell on Wheels," Second Armored Division, I shall never forget, and I am very proud to have served in this great Division and the Army.

I regret believing there was not anything I couldn't do better than anyone else. Everyone has the ability and talent to do some things, but not everything. Everyone has limitations on what they can do. The "Peter Principal" will kick in at some point. "The Peter Principle" is the principle that "in a hierarchy" every employee tends to rise to their level of incompetence.

Some may adhere to The Red Queen's Hypothesis or principle that states: for an evolutionary system, continuing development is needed just in order to maintain its fitness relative to the systems it is co-evolving with. The term is taken from the Red Queen's race in Lewis Carroll's *Through the Looking-Glass.*

"I did it My Way," is the title of a popular song. Doing everything one's way spawns many regrets. I paid a very high price for many things when I did it my way. I regret doing too many things my way for a long time.

I regret waking up at 2:00 a.m. and getting out my 38 Smith & Wesson pistol and driving to a man's house to confront him about some things he had said about me which were lies. I had suffered with anger and rage all day and most of the night, and I could not control my emotions any longer. So, at approximately 2:45 a.m. on a Tuesday morning, I knocked on the man's door until he finally opened it. As he opened the door I placed my pistol barrel under his chin. He was shocked, stunned, and was not able to speak for a few minutes. After he was able to speak, he apologized, and said he would undo any harm his words may have caused me. It is sad to say, but there was a second or two that I almost pulled the trigger. I regret this and thank God I did not pull the trigger. My parting words to him were, "Don't let me ever see you again," and I haven't. My advice today to everyone is never to have a weapon in your hand when you are angry, upset, or overcome with rage.

I regret that my relationship with George Little ended with some bitter feelings. George did many good things for me and I will forever be thankful for his support. If he had lived, our relationship would have been restored.

I regret shooting at a man as he drove his car past mine. I am thankful that I did not hit him. Otherwise, I would be wearing an orange suit. I had some problems with this gentleman, but this was not the ideal manner in which to resolve the situation. I regret doing this.

I regret not being closer to Ralph, my uncle, over the years. As long as I can remember, he was my playmate, best friend, and my relative. We grew up together and had many years of wonderful times. Once I graduated from high school, I went into the business world, got married, and spent two years in the United States Army. Ralph continued to live and work in the Cullman, Alabama area and, due to our very different lives, we did not see each other often. Again, I wanted to see him more often and continue to fumble around with music as we did when we were teenagers, but I was stretched to the breaking point; what I "wanted" to do never happened. This has always tugged at my heart. Prior to his death, we discussed Jesus Christ. From those conversations, I knew he had accepted Christ as his Lord and Savior, and I knew he was saved. Knowing this warms my heart and gives me peace of mind that one day I will see him again. We may be playing country music in heaven. He died on April 25, 2010. Ralph was the relative that was closest to me other than my immediate family. We grew up together and enjoyed many days of fun. I think of him often and miss him very much.

I regret the outcome of my relationship with Wyndall Causey, a financial officer, at Pasquale Food Company. He resigned from the company to join another company. On his way out of the building he stated to several people that I was the most egotistical S.O.B. he had ever met. At the time he was right. I regret placing myself in this category and to be referred to in this unforgettable manner. Wyndall, I truly regret whatever I did to cause you to feel this way, but I am sure you were correct in your feelings. Forgive me.

I could write additional pages on regrets regarding my wife and children. I make no excuses for the things I regret, because the dedication to my company brought on most of them, so I can only blame myself. Through my wife's help and understanding, I have overcome most of my regrets listed above. My wife and children helped me see me. Additionally, my wife helped me to eventually understand that Jesus Christ died for my sins, past, present, and future. I appreciate her never giving up on me. Once I accepted Jesus Christ as my Lord and Savior, my wife and children saw a new and different man.

My biggest regret is not accepting Christ at an early age. If I had done this, I truly believe I would have been more successful in the business world. If I had had Christ in my heart, I would have been highly successful even if I had made what is called a "living."

It is my hope and prayer that our children have Christ first in their lives. I know my wife and children would have had an easier and more enjoyable life if Christ had truly been guiding me through the years. Many people think wealth, houses, cars, etc., are a prerequisite to happiness. This is a misconception that is not true and is usually believed by people who have not had wealth. Wealth does not add to happiness, but too often, makes one's life worse and unhappy. This statement is not intended to dampen the spirit, ambition, goals, and so forth, to do better economically or to have a reasonable life. If a person has that, and his family, and Christ in his life, he or she will be happy.

This regrets list gives the reader an insight to the life I have led. Nevertheless, one thing I have done over the past few years was to call, email, see, or write to those people that I knew in my heart I treated unfairly. Once contact was made, I reminded each person of the time, place and occasion, and I expressed to each one that I was sorry for the various incidents, and asked each one for forgiveness.

Some people did not remember the situation which I described; others said it had been too long ago to think about, but they forgave me, while others just laughed about it and wanted to reminisce about what they referred to as "the good old days." Some people said that I had a very tough job and they understood some of the stances I took. Making these contacts did more for me than it did for those I contacted.

Hopefully, by listing my regrets openly, the reader of this book will give some thought to this subject, and come to grips with his or her regrets. In addition to the forgiveness of Jesus Christ, expressing one's regrets to those people harmed may clear his or her conscience and bring closure to the people harmed. One feels a certain relief and most likely will be happy about what one did. I want to make it clear, if one has accepted Jesus Christ as your Savior, it is not mandatory or necessary, since Jesus Christ has forgiven our sins. However, I knew if I contacted each person I had harmed or treated unfairly, I would feel better, and I do.

I only have one person left on my regrets list to reach, but I will continue to look for him and have the same conversation as I did with others I felt I had wronged in the past. This last contact will be the hardest of all, but I am trying to locate him at this time. This one is a person I terminated on Christmas Eve. Looking back, this was insane, because I should have been sensitive enough to realize that it was the wrong time to do something like this. I could have postponed it until after January 1st.

I am sure that I have left out some regrets, but these are all I can remember. I am certain that I offended, hurt, and treated some people unfairly without knowing it.

I often wish my life was a hand-written story, using a pencil, so I could go back and erase the mistakes. Most of us make mistakes that are chiseled in granite and cannot be erased. I regret that it took me too long to discover that some fights are not worth it, even if one wins. I also discovered that some fights are fights are worth fighting, even if one loses.

Have you ever dreamed of a distant time, when you made a wrong decision? Would you go back, and change your mind, and consider making a revision? (By: Lance–Show poetry)

"There is so much good in the worst of us, and so much bad in the best of us, that it hardly behooves any of us to talk about the rest of us."
- Edward Wallis Hoch.

CHAPTER THIRTY-THREE

ONE DREAM MY SON FULFILLED

I did not realize that my son Les, who was eighteen years from being born, would fulfill most of my dreams and ambition in the music arena. When my son Les was approximately six years old, I purchased him a very good Kay guitar. During the first year, he did not seem to be interested. But when he was approximately seven years old, the music bug bit him. He started showing real interest in the guitar, so we let him take lessons with the best guitar teachers in Birmingham. The lessons were very helpful, but it was obvious that he was naturally very talented.

He had a band in both junior high and high School that was excellent. Once he enrolled at Birmingham Southern College, he kept the music going and developed gigs in all types of venues. After that, he and his band, Verbena, were on the road playing across the United States and Europe. He played with many of the older established bands. He and his band were guests on the Dave Letterman Show, the Conan O'Brian Show, and, the Ellen DeGeneres show. He played the drums on many tours and shows, but I believe the guitar is his favorite instrument. He learned to play all instruments and was a studio musician with Sony in Los Angeles, California for several years.

Additionally, Les writes, records, and publishes for him and other musicians, both locally and nationally. Currently, he lives in Birmingham with his wife, Roni, and three beautiful girls, Ella, age five, Edie, age three and a baby granddaughter, Fiona Wren Nuby born on March 12, 2012. They are beautiful. He performs his musical work in a recording studio in Homewood, Alabama, a suburb of Birmingham, Alabama.

Even though I tried to talk him into a secondary occupation, he followed his dream, and in doing so fulfilled a large part of my dream, through him. I love him and have admiration for following his dream. Our house is filled with acoustic guitars, electric guitars, one classical guitar, a baby grand piano, a banjo, and various amplifiers. These instruments are in addition to the ones he keeps at his studio. There is rarely a day that I don't pick up one of the instruments and play a few chords. Music is therapy for me, and I think most musicians will confirm this statement. When my son, Les, is around I never pick up an instrument, because he is so good, I feel embarrassed for him to hear me.

Music was my first dream, but once I knew it was not possible, I took my second dream, which was business, and I reached or exceeded every goal that I formulized in my early years. I still have that first dream and a burning desire for music, and it's not over until it's over, and even then, it's still not over!

CHAPTER THIRTY-FOUR

THINGS I LOVED
CHEROKEE ROAD HOUSE

In 1960, when Jackie and I moved to Birmingham, we often drove around to view various areas of the city. One area which was striking at that time was Norwood. It had beautiful large houses with landscaped laws. We admired another lovely area, Mountain Brook. We dreamed of living in an area like those, but we knew that houses were much more expensive than we could afford. I wondered what it would have been like to grow up an environment like those. It was certainly a "far cry" from Bell Springs Mountain.

Our favorite road was Cherokee Road in Mountain Brook. There was one house that always caught my eye. I made it a point to drive by this house often. As I admired the house, I made a pledge to myself that someday it was going to be ours. When I was thinking this, Jackie and I were living in a basement apartment across the street from Birmingham-Southern, where Jackie was attending college. At the time, it seemed like a dream that could not come true. Jackie would have thought I was joking or had become senile at an early age if I had mentioned this to her.

Mountain Brook was originally developed in 1929 by a local developer, Robert Jemison, as an exclusive subdivision, and it was incorporated on May 24, 1942. The plans, by Boston-based landscape architect Warren H. Manning, called for estate-sized lots, along with winding scenic roads, and denser commercial development centering around three "villages" known as English Village, Mountain Brook Village, and Crestline Village. Nature preserves on the adjacent slopes protected the area from urban encroachment, and bridle paths created a recreational network within the development. The house that I dreamed about, very early in life, that would someday be mine, had all the above characteristics.

In 1979, our family moved from Vestavia Hills to Sherwood Road in Mountain Brook. I drove by the house on Cherokee Road every morning on the way to work and back at night for ten years, when I was not traveling. This house was built in 1953 and was known as the Woods' house. It had a large front yard with St. Augustine grass, the roof was Mexican tile, and the house was made of brick and painted white, with a long winding driveway and tall white columns. The house also had housekeeper's quarters, which was a small apartment.

After living in Mountain Brook for almost ten years and driving by the house almost every day, I was beginning to wonder if the house would ever be for sale. However, after thinking this, within a month, I drove by the house and did a double take! There was a For Sale sign in the yard near Cherokee Road!

I called the real estate agent and confirmed that the house was for sale. Mrs. Woods had continued to live there, but due to her age and health, her son wanted her to move into an assisted-living home. Jackie and I looked at the house and discovered it looked very different from Cherokee Road than it did up close. The house needed a tremendous amount of repair, maintenance, and remodeling. It was obvious that there had been little or no upkeep on the house for years. I was interested, but very disappointed at the condition of the house and grounds.

I wanted the house, but the price was very high, and it was going to take a lot of money to remodel it to the point where we would be happy. The price of the house, plus the remodeling cost, was overwhelming.

We were having a very hard time deciding whether to buy or back off. One contractor estimated the repairs; bringing the house up to code and the remodeling we wanted would cost approximately $300,000. During this time, a second person stepped up to purchase the house and had made an offer which I found to be high. The offer on the table, with earnest money in the hands of the real estate broker, put additional pressure on my wife and me to make a decision. Years later, I learned that the other potential buyer was Ed Hardin, a prominent Birmingham attorney. Some years later, I told Ed I had often wished he had increased his offer and purchased the house instead of me. I made this statement because the remodeling and repair costs were stunningly more than projected.

After contemplating this major decision for several days, we had to make a counter offer or forget it. I called the broker and made an offer above the offer on the table and tripled the earnest money. After a few days, we received affirmation that we had just purchased the house. It was a feeling of ambivalence; I did not know if I should laugh or cry. I wanted to purchase the house but did not pick up on the fact that my wife did not want to purchase the house. I had wanted this house for twenty-nine years and kept waiting for the house to be placed on the market. I had developed an emotional attachment to it in order to fulfill a dream developed in 1960. One of the reasons Jackie did not want to purchase the house was that the house we lived in on Sherwood Road had just been remodeled to reflect everything we wanted in a house. Other factors were the cost of the house, the cost of remodeling, and the displacement of our family for at least six months.

We put our house on Sherwood Road up for sale. Once it was on the market, Dr. Donald Kahn and his future wife, Shirley Sallaway, looked at our house carefully and left without comment. I had no idea what our house was worth. But, as potential buyers looked at it, I realized from the broker that it was worth much more than I had thought. I was really surprised to find out the amount our house would bring, and in the numerous potential buyers who were interested. One component that made the house more valuable was that it was on approximately three acres of land. Even in 1979, land in Mountain Brook was valuable. Plus, the house had been completely remodeled, including finishing the basement. Additionally, we had put in a wonderful in-ground pool that added to the value of the house for some potential buyers.

After several more visits by Dr. Kahn and Shirley, they purchased the house at what I considered a good price. In doing so, he had one condition: that we would move out of the house within thirty days from the day the transaction was closed. We agreed to his condition, which put us in a very difficult situation. After some conversation with Dr. Kahn, we concluded a deal. We would place all our furniture in storage and move into the Pickwick Hotel, which he owned. We would take the seventh floor and pay a nominal amount per month until our house was ready to be occupied.

The difficulty in getting everything packed and designated for storage was overwhelming. We had to keep clothing and other needed items out of storage and move them to the Pickwick Hotel. Even though we had enough space at the hotel, it was not like living in our house where we could find the things needed. But somehow it all came together, and we lived on the seventh floor of the Pickwick Hotel.

The remodeling of the Cherokee Road house started the first week in February of 1989 and was finished on July 28, 1989. Two weeks prior to July 28, we moved all our furniture out of storage and into the house. Jim Mezrano, a design professional, had been involved with us on this project and helped select colors and some additional furniture. Jim and others assisted us in getting into the remodeled house. The past six months of living in hotels and the remodeling had worn everyone out. It was a joy to move out of hotel rooms and get back to normal.

During this time, Kim and Leslie were enrolled at Birmingham-Southern. In 1992, Les also enrolled at Birmingham-Southern. Jackie enrolled at the University of Alabama in Tuscaloosa to earn a doctorate. We had three attending Birmingham-Southern at the same time, which was a noticeable cost. But Jackie and I thought the greatest thing we could give our children was as much education as they wanted. Kim, Leslie, and Les graduated from Birmingham-Southern. Kim moved to Tuscaloosa and attended the University of Alabama. Kim just needs to complete her dissertation to earn her doctorate. She majored in

Romance Languages and Literatures and speaks Spanish and French fluently.

One day Jackie and I realized that our children were all gone—either married or in school—and would not be coming back home. Jackie commuted to the University of Alabama for four years. I was in Perry County, Ohio, seven to ten days at a time before returning home. After analyzing the situation, we concluded that we were paying for lawn maintenance and maid service, but were at home very little. Plus, we did not need a six-thousand square foot house. Once we were through sorting the overall situation, we concluded that we should sell the Cherokee Road house and move into a smaller house. It was a difficult decision for me, but, right or wrong, I had fulfilled a dream that I had when Jackie and I were living on the edge of poverty. And that is being kind to the word poverty.

We placed the house on the market, reluctantly, and in a short time we had a buyer. We intended to move out of Mountain Brook, but in looking for houses, the one we wanted was in Mountain Brook and met our expectations. We purchased the house from a doctor who was relocating his practice to Alexander City, Alabama. On March 1, 1996, we moved from Cherokee Road, to our current house, and continue to live there. It is also a wonderful house, but not quite up to the house on Cherokee Road.

In 1987, Jackie and I decided to ask our parents to move from North Alabama and relocate to Birmingham so we could be near them as they were growing older. We furnished a house for each at no cost to them as long as they lived. Unfortunately, in December of 1997, Jackie's mother had a stroke and was rushed to St. Vincent's Hospital. She never returned home. Jackie's father passed away approximately four years later. We miss them very much and often.

Leslie is a professional artist with paintings throughout Alabama and the United States. Her talent sets her apart from the majority of artists. I admire her for believing in her style of art and not being willing to change just for money.

Les was devoted to music and was traveling around the country with his band, *Verbena*. They were enjoying some success as well as doing what young men and women want to do-to be free to travel and see the United States, and sometimes the world. I wanted Les to continue in school and carve out a profession, but at the same time, I understood, because when I was his age I had the desire to do the same things he was doing.

WILLOW POINT, ALEXANDER CITY, AL

In 1986 my wife and I purchased a condominium on Lake Martin a few miles west of Alexander City, Alabama. The condo was just perfect for our family. It was in excellent condition and was as close to the water one would want. We loved the house and the wonderful environment. I was influenced by Neal Andrews, who had purchased a house on one of the points near the Willow Point Country Club. Russell Lands developed the area, and it was known as the nicest and cleanest lake in Alabama.

Our children were at the prime age to enjoy the condo and the environment it offered. After purchasing the condo, we purchased the necessities to enjoy our first weekend. First, we purchased a pontoon boat, two wave runners, a speedboat, and a fishing boat, plus the accessories that we needed to enjoy life on the large beautiful lake. The first day that Jackie, Kim, Leslie, and Les went to the condo, Leslie was taken to the hospital because of an accident on a motor scooter. She was not hurt badly, but bruised and a little skin scraped.

After a while, we settled down and became accustomed to the condo, various water vehicles, and the lake. On Fridays, my wife and children went to Lake Martin. I would go down after work, and get there around 7:30 p.m. It was an awesome sight to wake up in the mornings and look out across the beautiful lake.

During this time we joined the Willow Point Country Club, which had an excellent golf course and a great place to eat, as well as other activities. The country club was located adjacent to the lake and was picturesque. It was also in walking distance from our condo.

There was a marina where we stored our pontoon boat and other water vehicles when we were not there. The wave runners were usually pulled out of the water and placed adjacent to the condo, or affixed to the floating dock. My only regret is that we should have purchased a condo or house on the lake three or four years earlier, so our children could have enjoyed the lake longer before entering college.

In 1988, we decided to sell the condo and we purchased a house that was barely under construction. Bruce McCleary was the builder of our house; he had built most of the houses in the general area. Our house was on one of the points next to Neal Andrews' house and Bruce McCleary's house was on the opposite point. The house was approximately 3,600 square feet, and was two stories, with most of the bottom floor very open, with windows that allowed a wonderful view of the lake from every room. The house was elevated above the lake, making steps and platforms part of the beauty of the house. The steps, several platforms, and additional steps led down to the floating dock.

Les and Jimmy, Kim's high school boyfriend and later husband, loved to ride the wave runners. One day they were "goofing off" and ran into each other, causing damage to one of the wave runners, which had to be sent away for repair. Everyone in our family enjoyed skiing, motor boating, or using the pontoon boat to move along slowly or lie out in the sun. The fishing boat was rarely used, so I gave it to my brother, Donald. One year one of our wave runners was missing for approximately six months, and then one day it was back, tied to our dock. Prior to its return, I had contacted the marine police in Alexander City and run notices in the available newspapers. It was a mystery that we never solved.

The summer months were the prime time to enjoy the lake, but it was also beautiful in the winter months. When it snowed, the area was just beautiful, with the snow in the trees and covering some of the open areas. I have pictures of the lake house covered with snow, which created an unusual scene.

One of the negatives in owning the condo and house was that it took a lot of cleaning and maintenance. It was not unusual for Jackie to spend a lot of her time at the lake cleaning, for others to enjoy. It was also expensive to maintain and to pay for the utilities, taxes, insurance, and a pro-rata share of the general area upkeep.

Each Fourth of July, the lake was filled with pontoon boats, wave runners, and other water vehicles. The lake was so congested with various water vehicles that it was sometimes dangerous. At nine o'clock on the night of July fourth, there were spectacular fireworks similar to the ones on Red Mountain in Birmingham. There was a tremendous amount of celebration, coupled with lots of alcohol, and possibly other mind-altering substances. Fortunately, I don't remember anyone getting hurt during this time.

As our children got older and enrolled at Birmingham-Southern College, the frequency of our visits to the lake house became less every year. When Kim graduated from Birmingham-Southern, she and Jimmy moved to Tuscaloosa so that she could work on her doctorate and Jimmy could go to law school. Leslie and Les were continuing at Birmingham Southern, with Les focusing on music with all the free time he could spare. During this time, Leslie attended Sarah Lawrence College in Brookline, New York for one year.

As the children grew older, they spent less and less time at the lake house. When Jackie and I went by ourselves, it was never the same as when our children were there. Eventually, we were going less than ever before. The last two years we owned the house we rarely went, and in 1994, we decided to sell the house. However, we did give serious consideration to selling our house in Mountain Brook and moving to the lake house as a permanent residence. All our connections were in Birmingham, and it was a one-hundred sixty-mile round trip from Birmingham to the lake house. After careful evaluation, we decided that the distance from Birmingham was too far from our families and from where our children would possibly live. We loved Birmingham, too, and had developed a comfortable feeling in Birmingham.

We placed the lake house on the market. It was purchased within a couple of weeks at a price almost twice the amount we had paid for it six years earlier. We had a house of furniture to place in storage and water vehicles to sell or give away. The pontoon boat, speed boat, and wave runners sold quickly, but getting the furniture to a reliable storage facility took a little time.

However, if we had known that on December 17, 1997, we were going to have a granddaughter, Sarah Kirstin Witcher, we would have kept the lake house for her to enjoy. I know she would have wanted to go there every weekend and spend a lot of time there in the summer months. She is now fourteen, and it would have been a wonderful place for her and friends to have fun along with adult supervision.

Lake Martin was a wonderful experience for our family and fulfilled one of the dreams I had when I was a small boy. I will always have fond memories of the condo, the wonderful house, the beautiful lake, and the well-positioned country club. Our house, the houses in our area, the country club, and the lake were a picturesque scene.

DOGS

I grew up on a farm in the rural North Alabama, and I was expected to have a love for animals. At the time I was growing up, I did like the pigs. There were a lot of other animals, horses, mules, pigs, chickens, dogs, cats, horses, goats and wild animals. It was like growing up in an animal kingdom. When I was approximately twelve years old, our family had a horse that I loved to ride. Later the horse got out of the fence, fell into a deep crevice, and died before anyone could find him. This touched my heart for a long time.

Jackie had grown up differently. She only had one pet, a dog called "Midnight," a mixed Labrador and Cocker Spaniel. Midnight was treated as a family member. Jackie loved Midnight and was really hurt when he died. He passed away when we were in Texas. Her parents did not tell her until we came home to visit after a year. She was crushed. One of the first things she asked was, "Where is Midnight?" She often mentions his name with fond memories.

Jackie and I had never wanted to have a pet, especially in the house. This was about to change. In 1993, my daughter was sick and had been in and out of hospitals and clinics for several years. One day, while I was in Zanesville, Ohio, Jackie called and asked what I thought about purchasing a pet for Leslie. I was not opposed because I had always heard that an animal or pet had a therapeutic effect on people that were sick, confined, or alone.

When I arrived home on Friday night, I walked into our kitchen, looked down, and saw an animal that was about five weeks old, weighing about five to six pounds, with very large bulging eyes. It was a pug. This little dog was the cutest little animal I had ever seen. I picked her up and looked into those big eyes and felt the thick, soft fur that reminded me of a soft stuffed toy.

I fell in love that moment. Her name was Ling Ling, and she was just a fur ball with large eyes. Leslie lived in an apartment in Mountain Brook and was enrolled at Birmingham-Southern College. After a few weeks, Leslie discovered she could not adequately take care of Ling Ling, so we took her. For the first time in my life, I really loved an animal. She continued to grow and reached approximately eighteen pounds, which is average for a female pug. This little dog added a dimension to my life that I had never felt before. It was almost like having a new baby. I had two bulldogs prior to Ling Ling, but did not know how to properly take care of them. Both died prematurely. The bull dogs' names were Pudgie and Beau. I will always regret not knowing how to take care of them. I should have realized that I was at work or traveling too much to have animals at that time.

Several months after Ling Ling came to live inside the house with Jackie and I, before I knew what was happening, Jackie went out to purchase an additional pug for my birthday. In the process, she purchased Ping Pong and, while there, could not bear to leave his sister Olivia. Now we had three pugs, which all slept in a baby crib.

A little later the wife of a man who lived in Atlanta passed away. He was in a wheelchair but owned a seven or eight month old male pug. After his wife's death, he contacted a veterinarian clinic to keep the pug until a suitable owner could be located. He wanted to give the pug, Buster, to someone who would take care of him. A partner of mine, Richard Gotlieb, had a daughter who lived in Atlanta and heard about the pug. She mentioned it to Richard, who in turn mentioned it to me. I had a telephone conversation with the owner and a spokesman at the veterinarian clinic. In approximately one week, Richard's daughter came to Birmingham and brought Buster with her. I drove to Richard's house, and he had Buster in his car garage. When I opened the door, Buster ran and jumped into my arms; it is unusual for a pug to jump like that. He was so beautiful and wanted full-time attention, which he received.

Once I brought him home, we believed that he had been accustomed to sleeping beside his owner. During the first two weeks, he slept beside me every night. After two weeks, I felt a responsibility to call the previous owner and give him an update on Buster. During the conversation with the gentleman, we learned that Buster had slept beside him in a chair adjacent to his bed, but not in the bed. Jackie and I had planted a new thought in Buster's mind, and it was one that he did not easily relinquish.

One of my son's friends worked at an animal clinic in Vestavia. An elderly lady purchased a pug and was told it would only grow to a maximum weight of nine pounds. Even though he was extremely thin, the pug already weighed more than nine pounds. The lady purchased him believing he would be a small dog that she could easily pick up and handle. She asked the clinic to house him until an owner could be found who would take good care of him.

Then another pug came along. One afternoon my son, Les, and his friend brought him home for us to keep. His name was Pug Bug. He was so emaciated that it hurt to look at him. He had already received all the necessary shots, so we started feeding him alone in order for him to eat all he could, hoping he would quickly gain weight. It took a while before he started gaining weight and began to look like a pug. Today he is still with us and is overweight, with the personality of a puppy. I love him very much!

A few months after Pug Bug was given to us, the animal clinic on Rocky Ridge Road was holding a pug that was lost, without identification, in Homewood. Whoever found him took him to the clinic to hold until the owner could be located. The clinic ran ads and did other things trying to find the owner. I think that after thirty days, the clinic is free to sell the dog, give the dog away, or continue to try to find the owner. More than thirty days had passed and no one claimed ownership. Jackie called and met with the veterinarian who owned the animal clinic on Rocky Ridge Road and discussed paying the boarding fees and other charges if we could have the pug. A deal was made, and Jackie brought him home. His color was fawn with black typical markings, but at that time he did not have a name or we didn't know his name. Leslie named him Rupert. Rupert is still with us, overweight, with the best disposition and personality a dog could have. He is lovable.

In the mix of all the above, I often drove to the Galleria and walked through a couple of times. I always stopped at the pet shop or area where fish, turtles, snakes, and other animals were for sale. In visiting the shop, I noticed a pug which I had not seen before other than in pictures. He was jet black. I could hear people in the store asking, "What kind of a dog is this black one?"

I went into the pet shop for five weeks without missing a week. Each time, I would look at the black pug, and I was beginning to believe he was growing up inside a cage. The first time I saw him, I asked one of the workers the price of the black pug. She said the price was one thousand dollars, but also stated that most people did not know what breed he was. The fourth week, I asked the manager how much it would take to purchase the black pug. She said one thousand dollars, but today she would sell him for seven hundred fifty dollars. The fifth week, I drove from my office to the Galleria with the thought that if he was not sold, I was going to purchase him and take him home with me. I walked into the shop and the first animal I saw was the black pug. I got with the manager and said to her, "The black pug is growing up in that cage." Then I said, "It is cruel for an animal to be caged like that for an extended period of time. I am going to make you an offer to purchase him today, and I hope you take it." She asked, "What is your offer? I said, "Six hundred sixty dollars, and that is a final offer." She said "You have just purchased yourself a pug." I paid her in cash, got all the documents, put him in my arms, and walked to the car.

He sat on my left arm as we drove home. Once at our house, he was free at last, and was one of the most loving, beautiful dogs I have ever been around. Leslie named him Oliver. I felt they were all favorites, but Oliver was special. Unfortunately, Oliver is not with us now, and I miss him often.

One day my wife called me from the University of Montevallo and said someone had found a puppy under an old truck. I had the feeling that we were going to the dogs, but I drove down to Montevallo and picked up the female dog. She had a blue tongue, which indicated she was part Chow and part Collie. When we picked her up, she was like a fur ball, with feet that were as large as my fist. She is a reddish golden color with golden-colored eyes. My granddaughter, Sarah Kirstin, named her Molly. Today Molly weighs approximately sixty pounds and is another beautiful, sweet dog that I love. When our granddaughter was five or six years old, she would ride Molly-fun for both! Molly is overweight too, but she is a big, lovable animal.

We recently inherited a dachshund that one of my wife's students owned. Her student was concerned because there were three small children at her house that were "a little rough" on the dog. She wanted Jackie to have him because she knew we would take good care of him. He is, again, one of the most wonderful animals I have ever seen and is very jealous of other dogs getting any attention. His name is Duke and he has been one of our greatest joys.

I only have one thing to ask, from everyone, "Please don't offer us another dog!" We have "truly gone to the dogs" and have more than we can handle. All right—maybe one more!

CHAPTER THIRTY-FIVE

THE TURNING OF MY
HEART A NEW LIFE

As long as I can remember, I attended church with my mother and Grandma Millican, who made sure we were all present. The little church I best remember was a Free Will Baptist church located on Bell Springs Mountain. The church was a small wooden church with hard wooden benches to sit on and a pulpit, with no rooms for different classes. Sunday school classrooms were divided much like a hospital room, with cloth affixed to a wire at the top which could be pulled to close off a small area. Because of this arrangement, the class next door could be heard as well as the one you were in.

There was an old upright piano and worn-out songbooks. I can close my eyes and see and hear Mrs. James playing the old standard gospel songs, as people sang as loudly as they could. Everyone sang, regardless of whether they could carry a tune or not. I continue to love gospel music and sing when I am sure no one can hear me. In front of the church was a very large oak tree that had been there as long as anyone could remember. In the summer it was beautiful, with limbs that covered a large area of the front of the church. Sometime the "Decoration Day" lunch and dinners were under this tree on long wood tables. The shade from the enormous tree helped keep the area cooler and the food out of the sun.

In the area where we lived, there were three churches: a Free Will Baptist church, a Methodist Church, and a Church of God. The people who lived in our area attended all three churches, depending upon what activity was being conducted. In the summer months the Church of God would start a revival. It would last through August. Sometimes, usually adjacent to the church, the members would build a bush harbor, which was a structure built by using leafy tree limbs and other bushes that would form a semi-covered place to hold the revival services outside.

It was always hot during the revivals, even at night, but it was also hot inside the church building. At that time, all rural churchgoers used hand-held fans to move the air in front of their faces. I enjoyed going to the Church of God because it was different. The music was played using a piano, guitars, and other stringed instruments. Sometimes the whole congregation sang; other times one or two people. Occasionally, a quartet sang.

Those who attended this Church of God expressed their emotions more than people did at the Methodist Church, or at our Church, the Free Will Baptist. I always questioned why there were differences in these three churches. Someone told me they were different dominations, something I did not understand. The reason we went to the three churches was because there were no other places to go for entertainment or recreation. These three churches filled a void in the peoples' lives. They were place of worship, but also a place of recreation.

One of the most enjoyable events I can remember at Bell Springs Free Will Baptist Church was "Vacation Bible School." This school only lasted a short time, maybe a week or two, but the people who taught the school were very good and interesting. They imparted Biblical knowledge and taught us how to make various things and carve interesting things such as frogs from a soap bar. The only thing wrong with "Vacation Bible School" was that it did not last long enough.

Every year, the fourth Sunday in May was designated as "Decoration Day." This was a day when relatives and friends of those buried in the cemetery brought flowers or other appropriate items to place on the grave sites. It was a day to remember and honor those who had passed. In those days it was an all-day activity that involved the normal Sunday services, guest singers, quartets, and other musical groups. At approximately 1:00 p.m., everyone went outside the church to where food was served on long tables. It was always an overwhelming amount of food. There was enough food that some people would eat again prior to leaving for home at the end of the day. The day was often referred "as all day singing, with dinner on the ground."

Most years it was very hot in the church. Almost all ladies brought hand fans which they moved back and forth in front of their face to cool them. Some churches furnished fans that had advertisements printed on both sides of the fan. The advertiser was usually a funeral home or a florist.

Once people joined our church, the Free Will Baptist church, there was a date scheduled during the warmer months for them to be baptized. In those days, churches did not have accommodations for baptisms within the church facility. The baptisms for our church and many other churches in the area were performed at Flint Creek, near Lacon, Alabama. The church members, along with other people, would flock to the area of Flint Creek to observe the baptism.

Prior to the baptism, the boys my age would tell the younger boys and girls that were going to be baptized that we had seen a lot of snakes in the water where they were going to be "dunked." Occasionally, one or two would refuse baptism because of the bogus comments we made about snakes.

The pastor of the church would lead those to be baptized, one at a time, into water that was approximately up to the pastor's waist. Once he had secured the correct area, he would take the person's hand and place his other hand on their back and dunk them quickly under the water, and then pull them upright. It seemed that each person had a different reaction to their baptism. Some were startled and very quiet, while other would shout and sing praises to God. It was an experience that I will never forget.

After being scolded for asking, I was told the water washed away the person's sins and that it was necessary to be baptized in order to go to heaven. In most church denominations, baptism or "immersing" was and is a ritual that gives the rite of admission into the church. Some churches believe and refer to baptism as a sacrament and an ordinance of Jesus Christ. In some cultures, the baptism is also called christening. However, that usually meant the baptism of infants. Where I grew up, it was called dunking the person under water and quickly out. Occasionally, I heard someone say the preacher or minister held a person under water longer because they had more sins to wash away. Some people said if this were true, many dunked would drown.

After Jackie and I were married, we went to church on a regular basis. When I went into the army, we attended a small Baptist church in Belton, Texas, near where we lived. Jackie quickly became aware that the young lady who played the piano was going "all out" to develop a relationship with me. I think the reason it took me longer to see what Jackie was seeing was because she was a woman. I had never had a woman conduct herself in such a bold manner. Once the situation was obvious, we discontinued going to that church and did not see that young lady again.

Once I was discharged from the Army and after Jackie graduated from Birmingham Southern College, we moved to Birchwood Street in Center Point, Alabama. We lived there for approximately one year before purchasing our first home in the Bridlewood Estates development in Center Point. We lived there for approximately two years. During the time we lived in Center Point, we went to several Baptist churches. Then we moved to Vestavia in 1969.

We lived on Tyler Road, in Vestavia, Alabama, from 1969 to 1979. We attended Vestavia Hills Baptist Church. This was the church that our three children attended. I remember vividly the time, effort, and energy Jackie had to expend getting the children dressed. Usually, we stopped at the House of Pancakes for breakfast, which was another trying time for Jackie and me to get seated, order, and have the children eat without dumping a pancake on someone. Sometimes they were unruly, but we got through breakfast and went on to church.

We became members of Vestavia Hills Baptist and attended on a regular basis. It was a nice church, with good people and wonderful music, and at that time in my life, it felt good to have our family attending church. I thought that by attending church, I was fulfilling my obligation to God. I did not realize it then, but at that time I had not accepted Christ as my Lord and Savior.

In 1979 we purchased a house in Mountain Brook because we believed the school system was better. Kim attended the first grade at Vestavia grammar school and then enrolled at Mountain Brook Elementary to begin the second grade. Kim, Leslie, and Les all attended the Mountain Brook school system and graduated from high school. Jackie was involved in every phase of their school activities and was the shuttle driver that made sure each child reached their destination. We purchased a house from Grady Barnett, who had been in franchise sales at Pasquale Food Company. Grady was very intelligent and an unusual man. He had been married several times. His current marriage seemed to be working fine. He married a lady much younger and told everyone how happy they were and how much he loved his wife. Approximately six months prior to selling his house to us, he was telling some of us that late at night, around midnight or after, he would quietly move out of the bed without waking his wife, get dressed, and go out for three hours or more, and quietly return and get back in bed with his wife. After hearing this, which was true, all of us that knew Grady speculated that the marriage would not last another three months. We were correct.

Shortly after moving to Mountain Brook, we started attending Mountain Brook Baptist Church along with our children. While we were attending this church, Jackie, my wife, started attending, a Bible study that was being conducted by Martha Sue Sanford, the wife of John Sanford, who headed sales at Pasquale Food Company and worked for Associated Grocers of Alabama during the same time I was working there.

I noticed Jackie had underlined many passages in red. Many verses were highlighted in yellow and she had written notes in the margins of her Bible. This caused me concern because the Bible was a book that you did not write or underline in or use colored markers to highlight. As Jackie became more involved, she attempted to enlighten me about the Bible study and a preacher/teacher who lived in Pensacola, Florida. She said it was a Berean Bible or Grace Church that was very different from the traditional churches.

At some point, Jackie started taking our three children to the Bible studies which were held in the daytime for those who could not attend on the scheduled night. It was also held on Monday night at seven o'clock at John and Martha Sue Sanford's house. Once Jackie started taking our children, my anger level started rising. I informed her that if she chose to attend that was fine, but she could not subject our children to this unorthodox, unknown religion. I could see the disappointment on Jackie's face when I took a hard and harsh approach on this subject.

Months after Jackie started attending the Bible study, an unusual thing happened. Neal Andrews came into my office and said that I should attend the Bible study that Jackie and Carol, Neal's wife, attended. Neal said, "I don't think you realize how much that would mean to Jackie." The next Monday night, our family went to the Sanford's house at seven o'clock. For the first time, I was introduced to Brother E.C. Moore, who was the preacher/teacher of the study group, known as the Berean Bible Church. He taught in Birmingham and held Bible studies elsewhere every night of the week. I was surprised that there were twenty or more people attending.

At exactly 7:00 p.m. Brother E.C. Moore opened the Bible study with a prayer. He asked everyone to open their Bibles to certain books and verses that were going to relate to the message he was going to deliver. I had not brought a Bible, but John Sanford handed me one of theirs. I fumbled around trying to find the books and verses. It was difficult, but I eventually found the correct passages, but only after it was too late to read with the rest of the group. After I had been in the Bible study for thirty to forty-five minutes, I knew there was something different and wonderful there; even though I did not know what is was at that time. After that meeting, I gave a lot of thought to it, but I did not really know what the first Bible study I attended was about.

The next Monday night, I went again with my wife and children. This time I took a notebook to write down as much as I could so I could compare my notes to the Bible verses. After a few weeks, I asked Brother

E.C. Moore to order a Bible for me just like the one he had. It was a King James Version. Within a couple of weeks I received my Bible.

I was beginning to understand and accept that I had been going to Church most of my life, but knew very little. This troubled me more than anything had in a very long time. I started analyzing why I did not know anything of significance about the Bible. As I continued to attend the Bible studies, I found I was having a very difficult time absorbing what was being taught, but I was not willing to give up. I knew in my heart there was something different and wonderful in these studies; I could feel it. It was one of the times in my life that I felt stupid, but I was not willing to give up.

It took months to reach a conclusion why I knew little about the Bible. Once I reached that conclusion, it was sobering to face the truth. I concluded and believed with all my heart that the ministers, preachers, or teachers in the traditional churches did not really teach much. I started thinking as far back as I could remember. What did I hear in the traditional churches? I went to Sunday school, yet most of the time, there was no person knowledgeable enough to teach others. The time was spent talking about an Alabama or Auburn football game or some other news story. Then the class was over. Next, I went to the eleven o'clock service. The first forty minutes was spent singing, taking up an offering, and hearing announcements. Then, the minister would take approximately twenty minutes to deliver his message. Sometimes, little stories were told that took up some of the time. Then, a call to the altar song was sung, followed by a prayer, and church was over. I left the church feeling that I had fulfilled my duty, and I subdued my guilt by attending church.

I accepted that I did not know anything about the Bible other than what I heard over and over from the books of Matthew, Mark, Luke, John, and a little about Acts. Then I discovered the real reason I knew so little about the Bible. The Old Testament and New Testament were presented as a continuous book without understanding the need to "rightly divide" the Bible. I was beginning to see the things that Brother Moore was teaching. The entire Bible is *for us*, but only a certain segment of the Bible is *to* us. This idea was new to me, but it was becoming easier to understand.

The Old Testament through Acts and Hebrews through Revelations are "for us," but Romans through Philemon is "to us." These books of the Bible present the Mystery to us, the Gentiles, and they open our eyes to the fact that we are saved by grace. Eventually I was grasping what Brother Moore was teaching and rightly dividing the Bible. I wanted to accept Jesus Christ as my savior and allow him to guide my life until I died. But I could not humble myself and place my hand in his hands for the rest of my life. I kept thinking that I would turn my life over to Christ next week or next month, but I kept pushing the date into the future. I thought I would have to give up something. I continued attending the weekly Bible study and learned a little more each week, not realizing I would never truly understand the Bible until I was saved. Brother Moore taught that to truly understand the Bible you must be saved.

During the time that Jackie was attending the Bible studies, we continued to attend Mountain Brook Baptist Church. As I accepted the Bible study and was beginning to understand the Bible for the first time, Jackie, our children and I continued attending church on a regular schedule. Jackie and I were in the same Sunday school class. Gradually, Jackie started participating in the class discussions. When the Sunday school teacher read verses from the Bible and started giving an explanation of the verses, Jackie gave input which was in conflict to what the teacher was teaching. This went on for several weeks until one Sunday we were asked where we were getting all this information that they had never heard. As Jackie attempted to answer their questions, the look on their faces reflected shock, confusion, and anger. After that day, we knew that we had to leave the church or we would eventually be asked to leave. We decided to depart from Mountain Brook Baptist Church, and we never returned.

I will never forget the night I turned my life over to Jesus Christ. As stated earlier in this book, I always believed there was a God, but I could not reach the point where I was willing to turn my life over to Him. After accepting Christ, I could understand the Bible, and Brother Moore's messages were easier to understand.

The turning of my heart and following Jesus Christ does not mean that I will not continue to commit sins. I am still a carnal human being with ongoing temptations to sin. But once I accepted Jesus Christ as my Lord and Savior, I have a compass, a barometer, and the touch of his hand to guide me, to keep me away from sin. My conscience is my guide, and when I am tempted to do anything that would not be pleasing to Jesus Christ, my conscience lets me know. Often times, because I am still carnal I may let my temptations, desires, or what I want to do overpower what Christ would have me do.

According to the King James Bible, man was born with a sinful nature. Sin is by nature and sins are an action. Jesus Christ, God's only Son, came to this earth and spent thirty-three years of his life as God and man before being put to a cruel and grotesque death for past, present and future sins. In order to be saved, all one has to do is accept Jesus Christ as Lord and Savior. One can become a Christian and a child of God by accepting Jesus Christ. You will move from the old man to a new man, and you will not give up anything. Rather, you will have gained everything. Everyone is, or was a sinner; if saved, it was by grace.

After I accepted Jesus Christ as my Lord and Savior, my eyes were opened for the first time. My outlook on life changed. I felt happiness that I had never felt before. I did not worry about death and going to hell as I often had. I stopped worrying about getting older and concluded that age should be embraced. I appreciate every day because I gain love, experience, and wisdom. Once I felt Jesus Christ in my life, I started talking to others who would listen. I often talk about my journey in reaching Christ.

I stated in an earlier chapter that while spending almost full time in Zanesville, Ohio, I reached the point that I felt God had placed me in the situation to humble me and get my attention. During that aloneness, I had time to evaluate my life and look to inward rather than outward. I did not accept Christ at that time, but the stage was set.

Today, if I knew I were dying, I could face it, knowing that I was on a journey to be with Christ in Heaven. The reason I want to live is to be with my wife, children, granddaughters Sarah Kirstin, Ella, Edie and Fiona Wren. I want to live to help, protect, take care of, and love them.

I often thank God that my salvation came by hearing the word of God from Brother E.C. Moore. My wife never gave up until I attended Bible study. I am thankful that my wife took our children Kim, Leslie, and Les to the Bible studies. I know that each one of them knows the truth. I also thank John and Martha Sue Sanford for holding many of the Bible studies at their home.

Most of all, I thank Brother E. C. Moore for devoting his life to teaching the word of God. His devotion led him to travel wherever a group of people wanted to hear the word of God. Brother Moore was the only minister, teacher, or, preacher I ever met who taught the truth and was not concerned if the message hit someone between the eyes. He taught the truth without reservation because he did not want anything from anyone. It was refreshing and wonderful to be in the presence of Brother E. C. Moore; he had everything to give and nothing to gain other than teaching the truth which might bring a sinner to Christ. This was his earthly reward!

One of the greatest things that Brother E. C. Moore did was to bring Brother Nolan Butler and others into teaching the Bible study classes. Brother Moore is no longer with us, but he prepared Brother Nolan Butler and many others to continue the Bible studies and bring the word of God to people who may turn their hearts and lives over to Christ. I often thank God for Brother Nolan Butler continuing the Grace Bible study at a tremendous sacrifice to himself and his family.

CHAPTER THIRTY-SIX

LOOKING BACK
WHAT I BELIEVE

When I look back over the years, God has blessed me beyond description. I have been blessed with a wonderful wife, three children, four granddaughters, two sons-in laws, Scott Reynolds and Mike Charito, one daughter in-law, Roni Nuby, and an extended family. Additionally, we have been blessed to have as many as eight wonderful dogs. How can one be unhappy with that many animals who want to sit in your lap? I have been extremely fortunate to have enjoyed the things on this earth that interested me and have the things I wanted.

As mentioned several times in this book, I have had a wonderful time almost every day at work, while getting paid. One of the most gratifying accomplishments in my life has been following my formula that I spent years perfecting. This formula guided me to reach and exceed my goals, including breaking the yoke of generational poverty. I would not change growing up in poverty, but I have thought about what it would be like to have inherited a large trust fund.

Generational poverty is thought by many to have long-term effects on one's life. Regrettably, the poverty gap is getting wider in the United States and around the world. Most of the time we build a mental block or wall between us and the devastating poverty that is taking lives every day. The "have nots" population is getting larger, with our government officials sleeping or concerning themselves with being re-elected. I wrote this book because I grew up in poverty; I lived it. I know the effects of poverty. In writing this book, I hoped that it would inspire readers to become keenly aware of the poverty in their families, city, state, and nation. Let's not ignore poverty in third world countries. Let's not hide from reality. Let's all do everything we can to become knowledgeable about poverty and do something to ease the suffering.

I am remorseful that following my formula adversely affected some people. I have listed many regrets in chapter thirty-two. I have communicated with the people that were harmed or treated unfairly and expressed my remorse and asked their forgiveness. I did not have to do this, because Jesus Christ had already forgiven my sins, past, present, and future. However, communicating with these people was very good for my conscience, and hopefully it had a positive effect on their lives. I feel the touch of his hand to guide me through each day. I regret not giving my life to Christ at an earlier age. I did not. Now all I can do is try to please him.

My first and greatest challenge was to find a way out of poverty. I thank God for giving me the ability to accomplish this and allowing me to help others in my family and outside my family. I often thank God for what we have, and I often thank him for what we don't have. As the saying goes, "Be careful what you ask for; you might get it."

Jackie and I discovered that even when we were in poverty, we were givers, not takers. I think this attitude came from my background in poverty and Jackie just being a giving person. We think it is a natural thing to give to others rather than take from others. We enticed our parents to sell their houses in North Alabama and move to Birmingham, where we could be close to them as they aged. It took a while to convince them, but eventually they sold their houses and put the proceeds from the sales in the bank for them to use later. Jackie and I only had one stipulation, and that was we would purchase a house of their choice. They would live in the houses as long as they lived, without any expense. In 1987, our parents moved to Birmingham within a few miles from us. My parents selected a house in Gardendale, Alabama, near my sister, and Jackie's parents selected a house in Cahaba Heights, Alabama, only a few minutes from us. Jackie's parents have passed. My stepfather has also passed. My mother, at ninety-two years of age, continues to live in the Gardendale house alone. Making these houses available to our parents was one of the greatest moments in our lives.

We made our home on Cherokee Road available for many organizations such as the Heart Guild, The Humane Society, and The Museum of Art, to have banquets and hold meetings. In many cases we not only furnished our home, but also the food and drinks that made the functions successful.

We were fortunate to not only educate our children to the highest level they desired, but were also fortunate to help several other people gain an education. We have paid for funerals and cremations, and purchased cars for some people. The true blessing comes when one helps someone in need and no one, except the donor and the recipient, ever knows. Gifts given for recognition are hypocritical and self-serving. The experience of helping our fellow man generates an internal sensation that warms our hearts and those of the people we help. In today's economy, many people are suffering and in desperate need. Reach out to them! There is no better feeling than to drive someone to a clothing store to purchase clothes which they need desperately. There is an inexplicable reward in those deeds.

Even though Jackie and I have always been givers, my feeling was truly enhanced when I turned my life over to Jesus Christ. One should not forget that "**God gave his Son for all of us.**"

The following words and music were written by Mosie Lister. This song was performed by many artists, but Elvis Presley, in my opinion, had the best version.

HIS HAND IN MINE

You may ask me how I know my Lord is real

You may doubt the things I say and doubt the way I feel

But I know he's real today he'll always be

I can feel his hand in mine and that's enough for me....

WHAT I BELIEVE:

God IS:

I believe that there is one, and only one, true living God. He is an infinite, all-knowing spirit, in three Persons—the Father, the Son, and the Holy Spirit—each equally deserving of man's worship and obedience.

THE BIBLE IS GOD'S WORD:

I believe that the King James Bible is God's revelation to people, divinely given through human authors who were inspired by the Holy Spirit. Therefore, it is truth without error. God is the Bible's author. The Bible is totally sufficient and completely authoritative on matters of life and death. **Timothy 2:15**: "Study to shew thyself approved unto God, a workman that needeth not to be ashamed, rightly dividing the word of truth."

I believe that people are God's special treasure, fashioned by Him in His own image as the crowning work of his creation. All human beings are born with a sin nature. Only by the grace of God through Jesus Christ can they experience salvation. **Hebrews 9:22**: "And almost all things are by the law purged with blood: and without shedding of blood is no remission of sins." **Titus 3:5**: "Not by works of righteousness which we have done, but according to his mercy he saved us, by the washing of regeneration, and renewing of the Holy Ghost."

I believe in the deity of our Lord Jesus Christ, in His virgin birth, and in His sinless life. As God's Son on earth, He was both fully God and fully human. I also believe in His miracles and His substitutionary and atoning death on the cross. Christ arose from the dead, ascended to the right hand of the Father, and will return in power and glory, hopefully, soon.

THE HOLY SPIRIT IS GOD

I believe the Holy Spirit is supernatural and sovereign, spiritually baptizing all believers into the Body of Christ. The Holy Spirit "uses God's Word to mature believers into the knowledge of Christ." Ephesians 1-17 and Colossians 4:13.

SALVATION IS BY FAITH ALONE:

All human beings are born with a sin nature, separated from God, and are in need of a savior. That salvation comes by faith in Jesus Christ. This salvation is wholly based on God's grace on the basis of the redeeming blood of Jesus Christ at Calvary. Because of his shed blood, we have faith that, by grace we are saved. We are not saved by works. The entire redeemed are secure in Christ forever because our sins were paid for at the cross. It's a done deal! **Ephesians 1:7:** "In whom we have redemption through his blood, the forgiveness of sins, according to the riches of his grace." **Ephesians 4:32:** "And be ye kind one to another, tenderhearted, forgiving one another, even as God for Christ's sake hath forgiven you." **Colossians 1:14:** "In whom we have redemption through his blood, even the forgiveness of sins." **Colossians 2:13: Colossians 3:13:** "Forbearing one another, and forgiving one another, if any man have a quarrel against any: even as Christ forgave you, so also do ye."

GOD'S PLAN:

I believe that all people who put their faith in Jesus Christ are immediately placed by the Holy Spirit into one united spiritual body, the body of Christ. **I Corinthians 12:13:** "For by one Spirit are we all baptized into one body, whether we be Jews or Gentiles, whether we be bond or free: and have been all made to drink into one Spirit."

GOD HOLDS THE FUTURE:

I believe that God will bring the world to its appropriate end after Christ rules on the earth for one thousand years. Before that time, Christ will appear in the clouds, and the dead in Christ will rise. Those living in Christ will rise next and appear in the clouds with Jesus Christ.

CHAPTER THIRTY-SEVEN

MY BIOLOGICAL FATHER MURDER MYSTERY

As stated in the beginning of this book, once I reached the age of approximately four, I wondered where my father was, and I asked a few questions. The only answer I received from my mother and family was that he was gone. I picked up bits and pieces from my uncles or strangers. As I became older, as a teenager and then an adult, I was never told anything. I had too much pride to ask. I had never seen a picture of him. I only conjured up thoughts of what he would be and act like. I was twelve years old when I learned that my father's name was Lester Lee Nuby.

When I was twelve my uncle Albert said to me, "I have something to tell you, but you can't let anyone know about this conversation." Uncle Albert told me that my father was murdered. He also said no one ever knew who did it. Obviously, I had never known my father, but this revelation brought tears to my eyes, and I felt alone and empty. I thought about this for a long time. I did not see a picture of my father until a few years ago. I never revealed the things my uncle told me until now. I blocked this out of my mind and never asked questions until I had almost finished writing this book. However, I always thought it was strange to never receive an explanation, especially after I became an adult. His name was never mentioned. It was as if he never lived. Sometimes people would ask me what happened to my father. I eventually learned to give the standard answer "I'd rather not talk about it."

After becoming an adult, I drove to the cemetery located in Leesdale, Alabama, near Hartselle. Once I arrived at the cemetery I did not know in which area to look, but I walked past gravestones until I saw one that had the name, "Lester Lee Nuby," November 24, 1913–November 23, 1937. Seeing this gave me the strangest feeling I have ever had. I have been back several times and each time, I have an unusual feeling seeing my name on the gravestone.

I had almost finished writing this book when I decided that I was going to find out the truth, regardless of the toll it might take. I concluded that after almost a life time of not knowing, it was past time to find out. My brother Donald and my sister Wilma met with my mother and me.

I had written a list of questions, including the facts about my father's murder. This meeting took place in April of 2011. After discussing and getting answers to many of the less difficult questions, which I needed in order to complete the writing of this chapter, I asked my mother to tell me about my father: what was he like, where did he work, and how was he murdered. These questions caused a momentary pause, as her face reflected a look of reminiscence and sadness. Her expressions turned to one of deepening concern and seriousness. Her demeanor and tone of voice reflected an event that touched her heart and one that caused deep emotional pain for her.

Donald and Wilma recognized the momentary situation and injected themselves into the conversation in order for my mother to have time to gain her composure. My conversation with her took into consideration the difficulties she had endured over her lifetime. Recognizing that she was ninety-two years old, I tried to make the conversation as simple and easy as possible. Because of this, I probably did not get all the pertinent information surrounding the murderer of my father. After a few minutes, she started relating the mysterious information I had wanted to know since I was approximately four years old.

She said he was a handsome man with an outgoing personality. She said he played baseball, was well liked, and would do anything for anybody. She commented on their personal relationship and how much they loved each other, and how good he was to her. She said he was very happy that they were going to have a child. He was hoping for a boy. She said my father spent one year in the Civilian Conservation Corps, better known as the "CCC," in 1936, because it was impossible for anyone to find a job. The CCC Camps provided relief and employment for millions of young men. My mother and father were married on May 5, 1937. Because of the economic circumstances brought on by generational poverty, the Great Depression, and World War II looming on the horizon, they lived with my father's parents in Lacon, Alabama.

My father and grandfather worked for a man whose name was J.B. Patterson. Mr. Patterson owned much of the land, a retail food store, and a company which crushed limestone rock into smaller pieces which were used to build highways. She explained that the work was very hard, even for a young man. However, people would take any job to support their families. The place my father and grandfather worked was referred to as the "rock crusher" or "spirit crusher." Mr. J. B. Patterson had the reputation of being a very difficult, hard, and unfair man. Those who worked for him were paid in tokens which could only be spent at the grocery store he owned.

She said that the night my father was murdered, they attended a box supper at Bell Springs Baptist Church. When the box supper was over and they started to leave the church, it was beginning to rain. My father did not want his wife to walk in the rain from Bell Springs Church to Lacon, which was approximately four miles, because my mother was pregnant with me. In those days it was not uncommon for people to walk where they wanted to go, because few people had automobiles. He asked my mother to spend the night with her parents, Ethel and Charlie Millican, who were also at the box supper. He would escort them home and then walk to Lacon in the rain. My mother said he felt it was necessary to walk home that night because he had to be at work at 7:00 a.m. the next morning. He was afraid of losing his job should he not report at the scheduled time. She spent the night with her parents, and he started walking home.

He had walked half of the way home and was continuing on Highway 31 North. He had walked down Lacon Mountain and was approximately three hundred yards south of Flint Creek when someone either attacked him from the side of the road or moved up behind him. The person who murdered him used a bat, club, or some other object, and knocked his brains out of his head. The best my mother remembers, he was found on the left side of Highway 31 North, where a car almost ran over him. Whoever the driver of the car was either confirmed the death to my mother or called the authorities, who informed her of the brutal murder. A few people believed the killer followed him from the church to my grandfather's house and knew he would be walking home alone.

He was murdered on November 23, 1937. Had he lived, he would have been twenty four years old the next day. I was born on April 30, 1938, approximately five months after my father was murdered. It is overwhelming to think about the agony my mother must have endured, being pregnant, and knowing her husband was murdered. Only God knows how she managed to handle the tragic situation.

In looking into this as deeply as I could, I found there was never an investigation because in those days rural areas and small towns did not have law enforcement personnel qualified to find out what happened. I understand some people speculated about who the murderer was, but no one ever came forward, naming the person. I have talked to a cousin, who knew very little about the murder. I am certain there is additional information pertaining to my father's murder which I will probably never know. At my death I hope to be buried beside him. This will be the closest I will ever be to him on this earth.

When I was approximately twenty-five years old, a man put the barrel end of a rifle in his mouth and pulled the trigger with his thumb, therefore blowing his brains out. He was at home alone when he took his life. I understand he left a note stating that he killed my father and could not live with himself any longer. I have not been able to confirm this event. If true, I understand that this man and my father were best friends. No one ever knew what the conflict was to prompt such a dastardly act. It is a sad and strange situation, and no one really knows the facts.

Some of the unknown information was my fault because I reached a time, early in my life, when I blocked this event out of my mind. In writing this book, all mind-blocks have been unlocked for the first time because some of them hurt too much to open earlier. Now that I know more, I will never understand why the information surrounding my father's death was not revealed to me in stages as I was growing up.

The only good thing that came out of this horrendous situation was that God gave me a stepfather who, in my opinion, treated me as good as or better than my biological father could have. He treated me as a very special child, adolescent, and adult. He gave me and our family everything he had to give. He passed away a few years ago with my brother, Rick, and me holding his hands. Again, he was one of a few people who said, "I am proud of you." These words meant more to me than anyone will ever know. He and I knew where I started in life, and he understood the seeming impossibility to move from generational poverty to the lofty positions I achieved. He was a person who would have been proud of me if I had not accomplished anything. I have never met another person who reflected the goodness in humanity as he did.

The information given by my mother, who is ninety-two years old, I believe to be true. However, it has been such a long time since my father's murder, in 1937 that many facts and details may have been left out, due to the lapse of time, and the lack of investigative abilities by the legal authorities.

Has it hurt me not growing up with a biological father? The truth is I have no idea. It's hard to miss someone you never knew. Was his absence the cause of my desire to break from generational poverty at any cost? Was his absence the cause of a mind set to achieve at any cost to me or others? I don't know.

CHAPTER THIRTY-EIGHT

"YESTERDAY WHEN I WAS YOUNG"

I conclude that most of us reflect on their teenage years, high school, college, and dating, as some of the best times of their lives. During those years, the majority of us didn't understand our parents and wanted to spend little time with them and all our time with our friends. Most of us assumed our parents were not too smart. It is only now that we understand our parents. As we reached the age of twenty, some older and some younger, we began to understand how very smart our parents were. Those years went by too fast; often we failed to enjoy the moment.

This book reflects a transformation of my life from poverty to success. The tone and fast pace I set in life to achieve financial success was without consideration of the more important rewards and pleasures in life. I achieved all my goals, plus many that were not in my plan. In doing so, I paid a heavy price and missed some of the simple, but important pleasures in life.

The following song recorded by artist Julio Iglesias has always struck a chord in my heart and sometimes surfaces a tinge of pain.

Artist: **Julio Iglesias**

Song: "Yesterday When I was Young"

The taste of life was sweet as rain upon my tongue

I played at life as if it were a foolish game

The way the evening breeze plays with a candle flame...

The above song, performed so well by Julio Iglesias, reflects sadness, regret, and happiness, but the song is true for almost everyone. Everyone would agree that growing up was a magical time to live. What could be more wonderful than youth, dating, and few things to worry about? There were only a few infinitesimal detours that caused a few distractions.

I have had a wonderful, beautiful and fulfilled life, that I thank God for every day. It was enhanced when I saw my wife-to-be when she was in the seventh grade and I was a senior. I was six years older than she was, but I knew she would grow up and I would be back at Falkville High School when she was a senior; then I would approach her.

After ten years of marriage, we were blessed with three children within four years: Kimberly Jacqueline, Leslie Paige, and Lester III. We now have a fourteen-year-old granddaughter, Sarah Kirstin Witcher, a five-year-old granddaughter Ella Raine Mahon, a three-year-old granddaughter, Edie Sophia Mahon. As I was initially writing this chapter, we are expecting an additional granddaughter in March of 2012. Fortunately, in holding the manuscript a few days to correct a few errors, I am thrilled to say that she was born on March 12, 2012. Her name is Fiona Wren Nuby and she is beautiful.

Additionally, we have a variety of beautiful dogs that are close to our hearts. Mordecai Siega wrote, "Acquiring a dog may be the only opportunity a human ever has to choose a relative." Anyone who adopts an animal is doing one of the most rewarding things in his or her life. The love and attention will be returned many times over.

Regardless of how we arrived at where we are today, let us be reminded not to take life for granted. Live each moment of life to the fullest, and remember that our own small lives form a part of a greater whole.

Those who have not endured the denigrating effects of poverty should not be too quick to judge or condemn. In most cases, poverty is not a choice, but a circumstance. Some people are able to break the chains of poverty, while most cannot. However, affluence or acquisitiveness can have a dehumanizing effect, though in a different manner.

The core of this book is about overcoming poverty. It is urgent to support those in poverty and do the things one can to assist them in breaking this worldwide depravity. Many of us only see poverty on television from the comfort of our homes and are quick to change the channel.

FROM THE GLOBAL TO THE LOCAL SCALE, PUBLIC

AND PRIVATE INSTITUTIONS HAVE TRIED

COUNTLESS INITIATIVES TO TRY AND REDUCE

POVERTY. TRUE DEVELOPMENT DOES NOT SIMPLY

PROVIDE FOR THE NEEDY BUT ENABLES THEM TO

PROVIDE FOR THEMSELVES.

Patterns of Wealth and Poverty by Chris Lauren

I ran so fast that time and youth at last ran out.

<u>"Yesterday when I was young!"</u>

FIRST WAS WRITTEN FOR:

Those who remember the past, looking

to tomorrow, but live today

Those who desire to move forward, and accept

what it takes to get there

Those who strive for monetary success, and are willing to pay the
price

to achieve it

Those who take little credit when things go right but, take most

of the credit when things go wrong

Those who understand that they determine who comes into their lives

Those who are brave enough to turn back the pages

and look at the passages of their lives

Those who have given their time and money without recognition

Those who think they have not done anything that needs

recognition, but everyone else disagrees

Those who understand that God gave his Son to die on a cross for

Our past, present and future sins, understanding that we are saved by

Grace, simply by accepting Christ as our Savior

FAVORITE QUOTES

Correct me if I'm wrong, but hasn't the fine
line between sanity and madness gotten finer?
George Price

Degradation: The continued poverty of the
majority of the planet's inhabitants
and the excessive consumption by
the well-off minority.

September 1999
United Nations-reported by
Dr. Klaus Topfer

I want you to have everything you want,
but not more than me.
Anonymous

We know in one part of our brain

that we are going to die, but on some level

we don't quite believe it.

Maybe, that is the rationale

That keeps us motivated and looking into the future.

Unknown

Life consists of what a man is thinking all day.

Zig Zigler

During a carnival, men put masks over their masks.

Xavier Forneret

You cannot consistently perform in

A manner which is inconsistent with

the way you see yourself.

Anonymous

It's all in your mind.

Whatever you hold in your mind will tend to

occur in your life. If you continue to believe

as you have always believed, you will continue to act as

as you have always acted, and you will continue to get what

you have always gotten.

If you want different results in your life or your work,

all you have to do is change your mind.

Anonymous

Will friends turn on each other, given enough time?

Lester Nuby, Jr.

Death is not the worst thing that can happen

to you, if you are saved by Jesus Christ.

Not living your life is the worst thing

that can happen to you.

Lester Nuby, Jr.

We are all mirrors unto one another.

Look into me, and you will find something of

yourself, as I will of you.

Walter Render

"Failure is not a crime, but aiming low is."

"If you don't have the guts to fail, you can't be a leader."

Dr. David G Bronner

CEO of Retirement Systems of Alabama (2009)

Live for today! Yesterday is a cashed check and cannot be negotiated. Tomorrow is a promissory note and cannot be utilized today. Today is cash in hand. Spend it wisely.

Minister John Edmund Haggai

"How to Win Over Worry"

May 1959